OXFORD LATIN COURSE

PART I

£4-

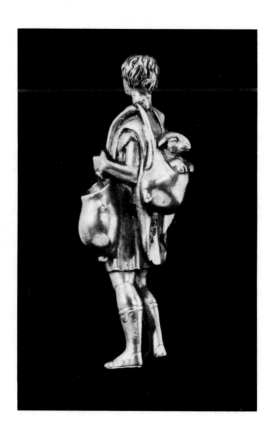

MAURICE BALME AND **JAMES MORWOOD**

Oxford University Press

Oxford University Press, Walton Street, Oxford OX2 6DP

Oxford New York Toronto
Delhi Bombay Calcutta Madras Karachi
Petaling Jaya Singapore Hong Kong Tokyo
Nairobi Dar es Salaam Cape Town
Melbourne Auckland

and associated companies in
Berlin Ibadan

Oxford is a trade mark of Oxford University Press

© *Oxford University Press 1987*
First published 1987
Reprinted 1987, 1988, 1989 with corrections, 1990
ISBN 0 19 912083 8

Acknowledgements

The illustrations are by **Cathy Balme.**

The cover lettering is by Tony Forster.

The publishers would like to thank the following for permission to reproduce photographic material:

Bardo Museum, Tunis p. 70 (bottom); Bildarchiv Foto Marburg p. 34; British Museum p. 1, p. 12; p. 28, p. 70 (top), p. 155, p. 164; Werner Forman Archive p. 29, p. 148; Fototeca Unione for the American Academy, Rome p. 121 (top); German Archaeological Institute, Rome p. 11, Athens p. 51; Giraudon p. 46, p. 79, p. 96/7; Robert Harding Picture Library p. 59; Michael Holford p. 43, p. 52, p. 63, p. 116, p. 175; C. Hülsen/Weidenfeld and Nicolson p. 126; Kunsthistorisches Museum, Vienna p. 55; Mansell Collection p. 22, p. 37, p. 42, p. 48 (left), p. 87 (bottom), p. 121 (bottom), p. 143, p. 153, p. 169; James Morwood p. 87; Musée Calvet, Avignon p. 21; Nelson Bunker Hunt Collection, Fort Worth p. 64; Grazia Neri/Mairani p. 30; Ny Carlsberg Glyptotek, Copenhagen p. 143; Octopus Publishing Group p. 66; Phaidon Archive p. 105; Scala p. 89, p. 123, p. 140; Ronald Sheridan p. 17, p. 48, p. 125, p. 164; Edwin Smith p. 154; Somerset County Museums p. 75; Jeffrey Tabberner p. 174.

Cover photo: Scala

The authors express their gratitude to all who have advised and helped with this course. They have special pleasure in acknowledging their debt to George Littlejohn of Smithycroft Secondary School and Keith Maclennan of Rugby School for their invaluable commentaries on the material, and to Robert Bass of Stoke Brunswick School for testing it.

Set by Tradespools Ltd., Frome, Somerset
Printed and bound in Great Britain by
Butler & Tanner Ltd, Frome and London

CONTENTS

INTRODUCTION

This course tells the story of the life of the Roman poet known to us as Horace. His full name was Quintus Horatius Flaccus, but we call him simply *Quintus*. Part 1 tells the story of his childhood and schooling, first in his home town of Venusia in south-east Italy, and then in Rome. At the end of Part 1 he is leaving Rome for university in Greece.

We have chosen the life of Horace as the subject of the book because he was an interesting person who tells us a lot about himself in his poetry. He rose from humble origins to become one of the leading poets of his time and a friend of the Emperor. He also lived through one of the most exciting and interesting periods of Roman history.

The story is told in Latin, the language spoken by the Romans. This is one of a large family of languages to which English and nearly all other European languages belong, as well as Indian and Persian. All are descended from a parent language, which is lost. A simplified family tree of these languages looks like this:

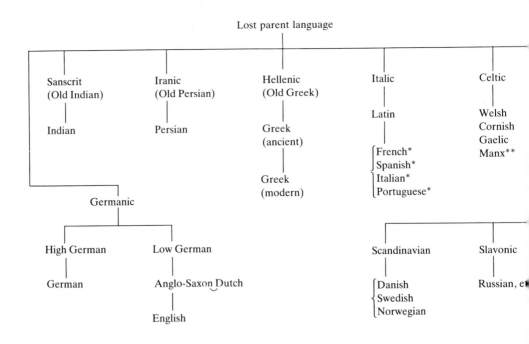

*These four languages, descended directly from Latin, are called Romance languages, i.e. languages descended from the language of the Romans.
**Manx, the native language of the Isle of Man.

Anglo-Saxon, from which English is directly descended, is only distantly related to Latin and is not much like it. But about one third of the words in modern English are not Anglo-Saxon in origin, but

orrowed straight from Latin at various stages of our history. Some
an only be fully understood if you have a knowledge of Latin. You
'ill find that you can understand and spell English better if you know
ome Latin. Equally, when you are reading Latin, the meaning of
1any Latin words is immediately obvious since the English words are
erived from Latin; for instance (Latin) **parēns** = (English) parent;
Latin) **accūsō** = (English) I accuse. This will be a great help in the
arly stages and you should always make full use of it.

You will not get far in Latin without some knowledge of
rammar, the names of the parts of speech and how they work. You
robably know about this, but, in case you do not, here is a short
1troduction.

A *sentence* is a group of words making complete sense; for instance
'John came'.
Every sentence must include a *verb*, a word which expresses the
action of the sentence, and a *noun* or *pronoun*. A *noun* is the name
of a person or thing; a *pronoun* is a word taking the place of a noun.
So, in the sentence 'John came', the verb is 'came' (this says what
John did); the noun is 'John'. Instead of 'John came', you could say
'he came'; 'he' is a pronoun taking the place of the noun 'John'.
You might want to say 'The boy came'; 'boy' is another noun.

Sentence analysis

'The boy came.' This is an example of the smallest possible
sentence; it consists of a verb and a *subject*. The subject of a
sentence is the noun or pronoun which performs the action of the
verb.
'The boy kicks the ball.' 'Kicks' describes the action of the
sentence. 'The boy' tells us who performs the action (subject). In
this sentence there is another noun, 'the ball', which is at the
receiving end of the action. This is called the *object*.
Who kicks the ball? The boy (subject).
What does he kick? The ball (object).

In the following sentences say which word is the subject and which
the object:
The cat caught a mouse.   The girl called the dog.   The cat dropped the mouse.
The dog chased the cat.   The dog bit the cat.

In English the answer is obvious, since we use a fixed word order:
ubject, verb, object. So 'the cat caught a mouse' means something
lifferent from 'a mouse caught the cat'. But Latin shows which word
s subject and which is object by changing the noun endings:

English: The dog bites the girl.
_atin: **canis** (subject) **puellam** (object) **mordet** (verb).
Latin usually puts verbs at the end of the sentence.)

English: The girl bites the dog.
Latin: **puella** (subject) **canem** (object) **mordet** (verb).

Notice that **puell-a** is used for subject, **puell-am** for object.

English also once changed some word endings to show the difference between subject and object, but only a few such changes survive, for instance:

I went; my mother sent me. I is used for subject, me for object; you cannot say: Me went; my mother sent I.

So also, 'Who did that?' 'Whom did you see?' Who is the subject, whom is the object.

The changes which take place in Latin nouns to show which noun is subject and which is object are called *cases*. The cases have names; the subject case is called *nominative*, the object case is called *accusative*.

So: The girl prepares supper   **puella cēnam parat**.
puella is subject and so in the nominative case; **cēnam** is object and is in the accusative case.

This may sound rather complicated, but it will become clearer as soon as you start to read Latin. The first stories are very simple and you should have no difficulty in understanding them. Every chapter begins with pictures, under which are captions in Latin. The meaning of these captions is obvious from the pictures, and you will be able to understand them even though not everything is at first explained.

Finally, you may ask 'What is the point of learning Latin?' We have already seen that all European languages are related to Latin and some directly descended from it (Italian, French, Spanish, Portuguese). A knowledge of Latin will make it easier to learn these languages and to understand our own language more clearly. Secondly, the history and writings of the Romans are interesting in themselves and still important to us. Our civilization is descended directly from theirs, and we can see their influence at many points both in our literature and in our lives today. You may be surprised to find that, in spite of the great differences between their way of life and ours, there are many likenesses; we probably have more in common with a Roman of Horace's day than with an Englishman of the Middle Ages. Lastly, to read and understand Latin, you must think straight; this is a skill which is most valuable in all school subjects and, indeed, in the whole of life. It would be wrong to pretend that Latin is easy but we hope that our course will make the process of learning it enjoyable.

G = grammar

V = vocabulary

? = background questions

CHAPTER I

hic puer est Quīntus. Quīntus est puer Rōmānus.

Quīntus in Apūliā habitat. Apūlia est in Italiā.

haec fēmina est Scintilla. Scintilla māter est.

Scintilla in casā labōrat. ecce! in hāc pictūrā Scintilla in culīnā est; cēnam parat.

haec puella est Horātia. Horātia fīlia est.

Horātia in culīnā est. ecce! in hāc pictūrā Scintillam iuvat.

Many English words are derived from Latin words, and so, if you know the English words, you will soon grasp the meaning of the Latin words. For instance

labōrat labour   **habitat** habitation, inhabit   **pictūra** picture

QUINTUS IS HUNGRY

Scintilla in culīnā labōrat; cēnam parat. Scintilla fessa est; ad iānuam it et Horātiam vocat. puella culīnam intrat et Scintillam salūtat; Scintillam iuvat. Quīntus culīnam intrat. nōn labōrat sed lūdit. puer ēsurit; cēnam videt. Scintilla in hortum exit et Horātiam vocat. Quīntus cēnam rapit et exit. Scintilla in culīnam redit; cēnam nōn videt; Quīntum vocat, sed puer nōn respondet. Scintilla īrāta est; aliam cēnam parat.

fessa tired
it she goes

lūdit he is playing; **ēsurit** is hungry
videt he sees; **in hortum** into the garden; **exit** goes out
rapit seizes; **redit** returns
respondet replies
īrāta angry; **aliam** another

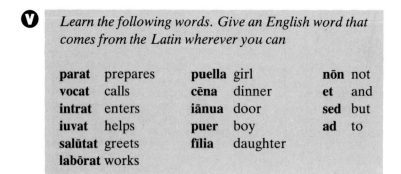

V *Learn the following words. Give an English word that comes from the Latin wherever you can*

parat	prepares	**puella**	girl	**nōn**	not
vocat	calls	**cēna**	dinner	**et**	and
intrat	enters	**iānua**	door	**sed**	but
iuvat	helps	**puer**	boy	**ad**	to
salūtat	greets	**fīlia**	daughter		
labōrat	works				

G **Subject, object, verb**

Sentences tend to be of the form

s	*v*		*s*	*v*
(Someone)	(is-doing-something)			
Quintus	is helping		**Quīntus**	**iuvat.**
Scintilla	is working		**Scintilla**	**labōrat.**

Column *s* gives the answer to the question
<u>Who</u> is doing something?
We call this the *subject*.
Column *v* gives the answer to the question
<u>What</u> is *s* doing?
We call this the *verb*.

Note: **Scintilla in casā labōrat; Horātiam vocat.**
Scintilla is working in the house; she calls Horatia.
labōrat = either 'she works' or 'she is working' (English has two
forms of the verb, Latin only one).
Very often there is no separate word for the subject in a Latin
sentence: **labōrat** he/she works. Column *s* and column *v* come
together here: *s+v*, e.g.

s	*v*	*s+v*
Scintilla	labōrat;	cēnam parat.

Many sentences have a column *o*.

s	*v*	*o*	*s*	*o*	*v*
Scintilla	is calling	Quintus	**Scintilla**	**Quīntum**	**vocat.**
Scintilla	is preparing	dinner	**Scintilla**	**cēnam**	**parat.**

Column *o* gives the answer to the question
<u>What</u> is Scintilla calling/preparing?
We call this the *object*.

Notice that in Latin the noun endings change:

s	*o*	*v*
Scintill<u>a</u>	cē<u>nam</u>	parat.

These changes in noun endings are called *cases* and have names.
The subject case is called *nominative*.
The object case is called *accusative*.

In the example above
Scintill<u>a</u> (subject) ends **-a** (*nominative* case).
cē<u>nam</u> (object) ends **-am** (*accusative* case).
So **puell<u>a</u>** is *nominative* (subject); **puell<u>am</u>** is *accusative* (object).

In what case are the following nouns?
iānuam, fīlia, cēna, puellam, Horātia

Exercise 1.1

*Copy out the Latin of each of the
following sentences and mark 's' over the
subject, 'o' over the object, and 'v' over
the verb. We call this to 'analyse' the
sentences. Then translate them*
1 Scintilla cēnam parat.
2 Scintilla fīliam vocat.
3 puella casam intrat.
4 Horātia Scintillam salūtat.
5 puella Scintillam iuvat.

Exercise 1.2

*Copy out the following sentences in
Latin. Fill in the blanks with the correct
endings and translate*
1 Horāti– in culīnā labōrat.
2 puella Scintill– vocat.
3 Scintill– culīn– intrat.
4 Scintilla puell– salūtat.
5 Scintill– fīliam iuvat.

Exercise 1.3

Translate into Latin

1 Horatia helps Scintilla.
2 Scintilla greets Horatia.
3 The girl calls Scintilla.
4 Julia enters the house; she closes the door.

she closes **claudit**

Exercise 1.4

Analyse and translate

If the subject is 'in the verb', i.e. not expressed, your analysis will be

$$o \qquad s+v$$

cēnam   parat   She is preparing dinner.

1 Scintilla labōrat; cēnam parat.
2 Horātia culīnam intrat; Scintillam iuvat.
3 Quīntus casam intrat, sed nōn labōrat.
4 Quīntus culīnam intrat; puellam vocat.

SLAVES AND FREEDMEN

The Latin poet Quintus Horatius Flaccus was born in Venusia, a large town in Apulia in south-east Italy, on 8 December 65 BC. In his poetry he tells us a great deal about himself and this book gives the story of his life. From now on we shall call him by the English version of his name, Horace. He came from a very humble background, though he was later to know the Roman Emperor and other great men. We know nothing about his mother and have invented the name of Scintilla for her, but Horace tells us much about his father, whom he loved and admired. He was an auctioneer who owned a small farm. He was also a freedman.

A freedman was somebody who had been a slave and then been given his freedom. The ancient Roman world depended heavily on slave labour. Men and women became slaves by being captured in war or by pirates. There was a flourishing slave-trade and it is said that at one of its main centres, the Greek island of Delos, 20,000 slaves changed hands in a day.

Once a master had bought his slaves, any children of the slaves became his property as well. Slaves performed household tasks or worked in agriculture or industry. If a slave had to row in the galleys or work in the mines, his life was very unpleasant indeed.

However, many masters realized that the best way to persuade their slaves to work hard and be loyal was to show them kindness. Everything a slave owned really belonged to his or her master, but many Romans encouraged their slaves by letting them keep any money they saved. Thus it was often possible for slaves to build up enough money to buy their freedom from their masters. In addition, masters could reward excellent service from slaves by giving them their freedom even without payment, either while the masters were still alive or in their wills. In fact almost all slaves who had a reasonably close relationship with their master could expect to be set free quite soon.

Though slaves won Roman citizenship with their freedom, they were expected to show obedience and loyalty to their former owner, who became their 'patron' instead of their 'master'. Most freedmen lived humble lives but some gained considerable money, power, and influence.

Horace himself, the son of a freedman, was never allowed to forget that his father had been a slave. There were always people about who would look down on somebody with his background, even though he was a Roman citizen and was accepted at the Emperor's court.

A Roman nobleman carrying busts of his ancestors

The following inscriptions were found on the tombstones (a) of a slave (b) of a freedman:

(a) Vitalis, the slave of Gaius Lavius Faustus and also his (adopted) son, born in his home, lies here. He lived for sixteen years. He was keeper of the Aprian shop, loved by the people, but snatched away by the gods. I beg you, passers by, if I gave you short measure to add to my father's fortune, forgive me. I beg you, by the gods above and the gods below, to look after my father and mother. Farewell.

Two freedmen, one of them a blacksmith, the other a carpenter. You can see the tools of their trade at the top and on the right.

(b) I, Gaius Julius Mygdonius, lie here, a Parthian by nationality, born free but captured in my youth and sold into Roman lands. When, with the help of fate, I became a Roman citizen, I gathered a nest-egg for the day I should be fifty. Ever since my youth it had been my aim to reach old age. Now, tomb, receive me gladly; with you I shall be free from care.

Write a short life of one of these two, using your imagination but basing your answer on the information given in the inscription.

CHAPTER II

hic vir est Flaccus. Flaccus pater est.

ecce! in hāc pictūrā Flaccus in agrō labōrat; agrum arat.

hic canis est Argus. Argus in agrō dormit.

ecce! in hāc pictūrā Quīntus agrum intrat et Argum vocat; sed Argus nōn audit; Argus dormit.

QUINTUS HELPS HIS FATHER

Flaccus in agrō labōrat; agrum arat. Quīntus agrum intrat; puer Argum sēcum dūcit; Flaccum videt et vocat; sed pater eum nōn audit; nam labōrat. puer Flaccum iterum vocat. pater fīlium audit et ad eum venit. Quīntus Flaccum salūtat et paulīsper eum iuvat. sed mox fessus est et ad casam redit.

arat is ploughing
sēcum with him; dūcit brings, leads
nam for
iterum again
paulīsper for a little
mox soon; fessus tired

13

G Gender: masculine and feminine

You may know already that in French, nouns are either masculine or feminine. This is called the *gender* of the noun. In Latin also, nouns have genders. Obviously father (**pater**) is masculine and mother (**māter**) is feminine; but also dinner (**cēna**) is feminine and a field (**ager**) is masculine.

Nearly all nouns whose subject case (called *nominative*) ends -**a** are feminine; most nouns whose nominative ends -**us** or -**er** are masculine. So

feminine: Horātia, puella, fīlia, cēna, iānua, casa
masculine: fīlius, Iūlius, ager, puer

The *accusative* (object case) of masculine nouns which you have met so far ends -**um**.

And so we can form a table

	feminine nouns in -**a**	masculine nouns in -**us** and -**er**		
nominative (subject)	puell-a	fīli-us	pu-er	ag-er
accusative (object)	puell-am	fīli-um	puer-um	agr-um

G Verbs

voca-t he calls   (*or* he is calling)
vide-t he sees   (*or* he is seeing)
audi-t he hears (*or* he is hearing)
Note that the ending -**t** is the same in all these verbs, though the vowel before it is in some verbs -**a**, in others -**e** and in others -**i**.

Exercise 2.1

Analyse and translate

1 Flaccus agrum arat.
2 Quīntus agrum intrat.
3 puer Flaccum salūtat.
4 pater labōrat; eum nōn audit.
5 fīlius Flaccum iuvat.
6 Flaccus fīlium laudat.

laudat praises

14

Exercise 2.2

Put the word in brackets into the appropriate case and translate

e.g. Flaccus (fīlius) vocat.   fīlium: Flaccus calls his son.

1 Quīntus (Flaccus) audit.
2 Quīntus (Horātia) videt.
3 Iūlia (puer) vocat.
4 puer (puella) iuvat.
5 Horātia (Quīntus) salūtat.

Exercise 2.3

Translate into Latin
1 Quintus enters the field.
2 The boy calls Flaccus.
3 The father does not hear (his)* son.
4 Quintus calls him again.
5 Flaccus sees his son and greets him.

> *leave out 'his'
> again **iterum**

Exercise 2.4

Analyse and translate
1 Scintilla Quīntum vocat.
2 Quīntus Scintillam audit et casam intrat.
3 puer Scintillam iuvat; cēnam parat.
4 Scintilla puerum laudat.
5 Flaccus casam intrat; Horātiam videt et salūtat.

Exercise 2.5

Translate
1 Quintus calls Horatia.
2 Horatia does not hear Quintus; she is working.
3 Quintus calls again; the girl hears him and replies.
4 The boy helps the girl; the girl praises him.
5 Flaccus enters the house; he praises the girl and boy.

> replies **respondet**

Exercise 2.6

Translate the first paragraph. Answer the questions on the second paragraph without translating

postrīdiē Scintilla Quīntum vocat. mittit eum ad agrum. Flaccus in agrō labōrat; Quīntus cēnam ad eum portat; nam Flaccus diū labōrat et valdē fessus est. puer ad agrum festīnat; valdē ēsurit; in viā cēnam spectat; cēna bona est. sub arbore sedet et cēnam cōnsūmit. deinde ad agrum prōcēdit.

  agrum intrat et Flaccum videt. timet sed Flaccum vocat. Flaccus fīlium audit et salūtat. dīcit: 'ubi est cēna?' puer nihil dīcit sed ad casam recurrit.

> **postrīdiē** the next day
> **mittit** sends
> **portat** carries
> **nam** for; **diū** a long time
> **valdē** very
> **festīnat** hurries; **ēsurit** is hungry; **spectat** looks at
> **sub arbore** under a tree
> **cōnsūmit** eats; **deinde** then
> **prōcēdit** goes on
> **timet** is afraid
> **ubi** where
> **nihil** nothing; **recurrit** runs back

15

1 When Quintus sees Flaccus, how does he feel?
2 When Quintus appears, how does Flaccus react? What does he ask
   him?
3 How does Quintus respond?
4 Give one English word derived from each of the following: **timet**,
   audit, **salūtat**.
5 In what case is each of the following nouns in this paragraph:
   agrum (1. 1); **Flaccus** (1. 2); **cēna** (1. 3); **puer** (1. 3)? Explain why
   these cases are used.

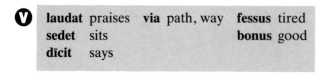

laudat praises	**via** path, way	**fessus** tired
sedet sits		**bonus** good
dīcit says		

LIFE IN THE COUNTRY

Horace's early years in Venusia left him with a deep love for the
country. After he had become a successful poet in Rome, he was
overjoyed to be given a small estate in the Sabine hills to the north
east of the city. Here he would entertain his guests with vegetarian
dinners suitable for the simple country life.

Horace had eight slaves to run his Sabine farm. For his father, on
the other hand, life would have been extremely hard – that is if what
Horace says about him is true. He grew enough food to keep his
family alive, living in a small cottage in Venusia and tramping out to
the country every day to work on his farm as peasants do in modern
Italy. Here he worked for most of the daylight hours through almost
all of the year. The list of farmers' tasks in Roman times shows a
break in the middle of the winter which lasted only a month.

He grew olives, vines and corn on his farm. Oil from the olives
provided the fuel for lamps and was used in soap and in cooking, as in
Mediterranean countries today. The vines produced wine. Italy was
also famous for its honey and Horace's father may well have kept
bees.

The Romans always expressed the highest admiration for the
simple country life, though they were more enthusiastic about praising
it than living it. A typical Roman hero was Cincinnatus who,
according to legend, was called from ploughing a field to become
dictator at a crisis in Rome's history. Sixteen days later, after saving
the state, he resigned the dictatorship and returned to his farm. For

the Romans, farming stood for the qualities of tough simplicity that had made their nation great.

There were vast country estates which belonged to wealthy and important Romans alongside the small-holdings of poor men such as Horace's father. Italian agriculture was at its most productive around the time when Horace was alive, since prisoners of war were cheaply available as slaves. The huge estates were worked by large numbers of men and they were run by bailiffs, usually slaves or freedmen of the owners. The only aim was to bring in as much money as possible.

Many slaves lived a grim life on such farms, where they were housed in dreadful barracks. One ancient writer talks about three types of farm equipment: 'the kind that speaks (i.e. slaves), the kind that cannot speak (i.e. cattle), and the voiceless (i.e. agricultural tools).'

Describe the farming operations illustrated in this picture. How do they resemble or differ from farming methods today?

CHAPTER III

Horātia Scintillam iuvat.

Horātia diū labōrat; fessa est.

Quīntus Argum ad agrum dūcit; Argus canis bonus est.

Quīntus Argum vocat sed canis nōn redit: malus est.

QUINTUS IS LOST

Scintilla in culīnā labōrat. Quīntum vocat. Quīntus culīnam intrat et Scintillam salūtat. Scintilla eum ad agrum mittit. puer hortum intrat et Argum vocat. canis ad puerum currit. laetus est quod Quīntus eum ad agrum dūcit.

     sed in viā Argus leporem videt; ferōciter lātrat. lepus timet et fugit in silvam. puer Argum vocat, sed canis nōn redit. itaque Quīntus silvam intrat et Argum quaerit. diū quaerit et vocat, sed nōn redit malus canis. tandem puer fessus est; sub arbore iacet; dormit.

culīnā kitchen

hortum garden
quod because
dūcit is taking

leporem a hare
ferōciter fiercely; **lātrat** barks

tandem at last

18

diū dormit Quīntus sub arbore. intereā Scintilla
ānxia est. Horātiam vocat et dīcit: 'ubi est Quīntus?'
cūr nōn redit ad cēnam? malus puer est.' Horātia
nescit. Scintilla timet; lacrimat et clāmat. tandem
Horātiam in silvam mittit.

    Horātia ad silvam currit. diū vocat et quaerit; sed
puer nōn respondet; nam dormit. tandem puellam
audit et vocat. sīc Horātia puerum invenit. Quīntus
tūtus est. Horātia gaudet et puerum ad casam redūcit.

    ibi Scintilla ānxia exspectat. tandem fīlium et
fīliam videt. currit ad Quīntum; gaudet et lacrimat et
puerum bāsiat. dīcit: 'ō Quīnte, cūr parentēs sīc vexās?'

intereā meanwhile
ānxia anxious; ubi? where?
cūr? why?
nescit does not know
lacrimat cries; clāmat shouts
tandem at last
currit runs
respondet replies; tandem at
length
sīc thus; invenit finds
gaudet rejoices; redūcit leads
back
ibi there; exspectat waits
bāsiat kisses; parentēs
parents; vexās do you worry?

iacet	lies	**silva**	wood	**nam**	for
timet	fears, is afraid	**canis**	dog	**mox**	soon
adit	goes to, approaches	**malus**	bad	**iam**	now, already
dormit	sleeps	**tūtus**	safe	**diū**	for a long time
fugit	flees				
mittit	sends				
quaerit	looks for; asks				

Exercise 3.1

Give an English word coming from each of the following
ānxius, dormit, exspectat, salūtat, fugit

The verb 'est'

We have already met two basic sentence patterns

  s   *v*   *s*   *o*   *v*
Flaccus labōrat.   Flaccus fīlium vocat.

There is one more basic pattern of sentence

Quīntus est puer   Quintus is a boy.
Quīntus est fessus Quintus is tired.

The verb **est** requires a completing word: **Quīntus est**? The noun or adjective which completes the sense is called a *complement* and is in the same case and gender as the subject.

<pre>   s   v   c</pre>
So: **Quīntus est fessus.** **fessus**, the complement, is, like **Quīntus**, in the nominative case and masculine.

<pre>   s   v   c</pre>
    Scintilla est fessa. **fessa**, the complement, is, like **Scintilla**, nominative and feminine.

Exercise 3.2

Analyse and translate: mark 'c' over complement
1 Flaccus est fessus.
2 puer malus est.
3 Scintilla est fessa.
4 Horātia tūta est.
5 cēna bona est.

Exercise 3.3

Translate into Latin
1 The boy is not bad.
2 Horatia is good.
3 Quintus is safe.
4 Flaccus is tired.
5 The dinner is bad.

Exercise 3.4

Analyse and translate
1 Quīntus Argum vocat; canis nōn redit.
2 puer ānxius est; Argum quaerit.
3 Quīntus magnam silvam intrat.　　　　　　　　**magnam** great, big
4 puella fessa est; dormit.
5 malus puer puellam excitat.　　　　　　　　　**excitat** wakes
6 puella īrāta est; Quīntum reprehendit.　　　　**īrāta** angry
　　　　　　　　　　　　　　　　　　　　　　　reprehendit blames

Exercise 3.5

Either translate the following passage or answer the questions without translating
Flaccus in agrō dormit; fessus est. Scintilla in casā labōrat; cēnam parat. ānxia est; nam Flaccus nōn redit. Scintilla Quīntum vocat et eum ad agrum mittit. Quīntus Argum vocat et festīnat ad agrum. ubi agrum　　**festīnat** hurries; **ubi** when intrat, Flaccum videt; Flaccus tūtus est; sub arbore dormit. fīlius Flaccum vocat et excitat. Flaccus eum　　**excitat** wakes up audit; surgit et cum fīliō ad casam redit.　　**surgit** gets up; **cum fīliō** with his son

1 What is Flaccus doing, and why? What is Scintilla doing?
2 Why is Scintilla anxious?
3 What does she do about it?
4 Where does Quintus find Flaccus?
5 What does Quintus do then?
6 The following English words are derived from Latin words in this passage: agriculture, dormitory, laborious. From what Latin word does each come and what do the English words mean?
7 In what case is each of the following words: **fessus** (1.1); **cēnam** (1.2); **Scintilla** (1.3); **eum** (1.3)? Explain why these cases are used.

WOMEN

A family meal

Horace's mother had to work extremely hard as the wife of a Roman farmer. She got up very early in the morning before it was even light, stirred up the embers of last night's fire, and lit the lamp. Then she began to spin and weave wool in order to make clothes for her family and herself. She continued with this task for most of the day. It is probable that even in a home as humble as hers there were some maidservants, and perhaps she had a daughter to help her. Horace tells us nothing about the women in his household. We have invented a sister for him whom we have called Horatia. The women gossiped as they worked at the wool, which would have made the long hours of spinning and weaving pass more quickly and enjoyably. At some stage of the day, Horace's mother or one of her servants had to go to the spring in the middle of the town to fetch water. Here she would stop for another gossip with the local women before returning home with her full jar.

Horace's mother prepared a simple breakfast for her husband before he went off to the country to his farm. She sent his lunch out to

21

him as he worked in the fields, and provided him with dinner, probably the largest meal of the day, when he returned home in the evening. On top of this, she had to see to all the housework. Her life was difficult and exhausting, even if she did have help. Her duty was to put her husband and sons first because she was a Roman **mātrōna** (older, married woman). Ancient Rome was very much a man's world, and women were only thought important because they would be the mothers of the Romans of the future. Wives and their children were totally under the authority of the father of the family (**paterfamiliās**). Marriages were arranged by the parents of the bride and bridegroom and often took place at a very early age. Marriage was legal for girls at twelve and for boys at fourteen, and most girls had become wives before their sixteenth birthday. Husband and wife would hardly have seen each other before the wedding as with many marriages in non-Western cultures today. There is no reason to believe that this led to an unsuccessful marriage.

A Roman woman's situation appears pretty grim, and yet Roman history is full of the names of women who made their mark because of their strong personalities. Such women came from the upper class, unlike Horace's mother. They could have considerable influence in politics and many of them were well educated and witty. A girl would not go to school for as many years as a boy, but she could be taught at home by her mother or a gifted slave. The household called her '**domina**' (mistress) and she received visitors. At home she dined with her husband and she went out to dinner with him. Outside, she travelled in a litter, a portable couch enclosed by curtains, or walked with an attendant, and people made way for her in the street.

CASTA FUIT, DOMUM SERVAVIT, LANAM FECIT
She was faithful to her husband, she looked after the home, she spun wool

An inscription on a Roman woman's tomb sums up the traditional wifely virtues.

❓ Imagine you are Scintilla; describe a typical day in your life.

What seem to you the most striking differences between the position of women then and now? How would you have liked to be a woman in the Roman world?

puer puellam videt; eam vocat.

puerī puellās vident; eās vocant.

puella puerum audit et respondet.

puellae puerōs audiunt et respondent.

canis bonus est.

canēs malī sunt.

G Singular and plural

Latin, like English, distinguishes between *singular* (one person or thing) and *plural* (more than one) by changing word endings. This applies to verbs, nouns and adjectives. Study the examples on p.23 and see what changes are made.

Changes in noun endings

	singular	*singular*	*singular*
nominative	puell-a	puer	domin-us (master)
accusative	puell-am	puer-um	domin-um

	plural	*plural*	*plural*
nominative	puell-ae	puer-ī	domin-ī
accusative	puell-ās	puer-ōs	domin-ōs

Adjectives change their endings in the same way, so that they agree with the nouns they describe, e.g. puerī fessī sunt; puellae nōn fessae sunt.

Exercise 4.1

Translate the following pairs of verbs
vocat, vocant; videt, vident; quaerit, quaerunt; audit, audiunt; est, sunt; adit, adeunt

Exercise 4.2

Put into the plural and translate
e.g. puer puellam vocat; puerī puellās vocant = the boys call the girls.
1 puella puerum videt.
2 puer fēminam audit.
3 fēmina ad silvam adit.
4 puella fessa est.
5 fēmina puerum vocat; puer nōn respondet.
6 puella puerum quaerit; puella ānxia est.
7 puella puerum videt; puer tūtus est.

ARGUS SAVES HORATIA

Quīntus et Horātia ad agrum eunt. Quīntus Argum dūcit. sed in viā Argus duōs leporēs videt et ferōciter lātrat; fugiunt leporēs in silvam. Argus leporēs petit et currit in silvam. puerī eum vocant et diū quaerunt, sed nōn redit malus canis.

  tandem in silvās eunt et collem dēscendunt; mox ad fluvium veniunt; fluvius, nōmine Aufidus, magnus est et celeriter fluit. puerī ad rīpam adeunt; calidī sunt

eunt go
duōs leporēs two hares
ferōciter fiercely
lātrat barks
puerī the children
tandem at last; collem hill
fluvium river; nōmine by name, called
celeriter quickly; fluit flows;
rīpam bank; calidī hot

et fessī. in rīpā sedent. deinde in aquam ineunt. diū laetī natant.

tandem Quīntus fessus est et in rīpā iacet; sed Horātia in aquā manet et iterum natat. subitō lāpsat; fluvius eam rapit; territa exclāmat. Quīntus clāmōrem audit et surgit. in aquam ruit et Horātiam petit. sed fluvius eam aufert. Quīntus identidem clāmat.

Argus clāmōrēs audit; ad rīpam currit; videt Horātiam et in aquam ruit. tunicam eius dentibus capit et ad rīpam trahit. Quīntus quoque ad rīpam ēvādit. diū in rīpā iacent puer et puella, valdē fessī.

tandem surgunt. Argum laudant; collem lentē ascendunt. per silvās festīnant et tandem ad casam adveniunt. Scintilla eōs ānxia exspectat. ubi eōs videt, accurrit et laeta eōs salūtat. in casam eōs dūcit et magnam cēnam parat.

mox pater ab agrō redit; Scintillam et puerōs salūtat. valdē fessus est. 'parāta est cēna?' rogat. 'cēna est parāta,' respondet Scintilla. omnēs sedent et cēnam laetī edunt. post cēnam Scintilla Horātiae tunicam videt; tunica scissa est. Scintilla rogat: 'cūr tunica est scissa?'

Horātia omnem rem nārrat. Flaccus et Scintilla Argum laudant sed Quīntum reprehendunt, quod Horātiam nōn cūrat.

deinde	then
natant	swim
iterum	again
subitō	suddenly; **lāpsat** slips
rapit	seizes; **clāmōrem** shout
surgit	gets up; **ruit** rushes
aufert	carries away
identidem	again and again
tunicam eius	her tunic
dentibus	with his teeth
trahit	drags; **quoque** also
ēvādit	escapes
lentē	slowly
ubi	when
accurrit	runs up
cēnam	dinner
parāta	ready
omnēs	all
edunt	eat; **post** after
Horātiae	Horatia's
scissa	torn; **cūr** why
omnem rem	the whole thing
nārrat	tells
reprehendunt	blame
quod	because
cūrat	looks after

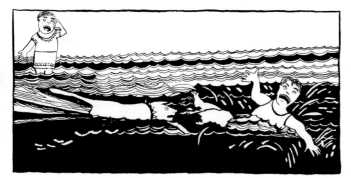

Argus tunicam eius dentibus capit et ad rīpam trahit.

clāmat	shouts	**ascendit**	goes up, climbs		Note: adjectives are now given in masculine and feminine forms
exspectat	waits for	**dēscendit**	goes down, descends		
festīnat	hurries	**currit**	runs		
rogat	asks	**dūcit**	leads		**laetus, laeta** happy
manet	remains	**petit**	seeks, chases; asks		**magnus, magna** great
respondet	answers	**capit**	takes, catches		**territus, territa** terrified
aqua	water	**valdē**	very		

G Prepositions

These are words like 'in', 'to', 'through', 'out of', which expand the action of the verb. They require a noun (or pronoun) to complete their sense, e.g.

Flaccus in agrō labōrat.
in agrō tells you where Flaccus is
working.
Flaccus ad casam redit.
ad casam tells you where Flaccus goes.

Preposition + noun make one phrase and in analysis should be underlined, as in the examples above.

     s   *o*   *v*
Scintilla puerum in casam vocat.

Notice that in this example there are two nouns in the accusative case: **puerum** is in the accusative because it is the object of **vocat**; **casam** is in the accusative because it is governed by the preposition **in**.

Learn the following prepositions

Flaccus ad casam redit.	**ad** + accusative = to
Scintilla puerum in casam vocat.	**in** + accusative = into, to
puella per silvam currit.	**per** + accusative = through

Exercise 4.3

Analyse the following sentences and translate (mark 's', 'o', 'v'; join prepositions to the nouns they govern by drawing a line underneath them)

1 pater puerōs in agrum dūcit.
2 māter puellās in casam mittit.
3 puerī per silvās currunt.
4 puellae in aquam ineunt.
5 Flaccus fīlium in agrum mittit.

Exercise 4.4

Translate into Latin

1 Scintilla calls the boys into the house.
2 The boys lead Argus through the wood.
3 Flaccus goes into the field and works.
4 Flaccus is tired; he returns to the house.
5 The girls run to the field.

G Prepositions (continued)

Some prepositions are not followed by the accusative case, but by another case with a different ending called the *ablative*, which you will meet at present only after these prepositions.

Flaccus in agrō labōrat.   **in** + ablative = in
canis in viā iacet.

ab agrō redit.	**ā/ab** + ablative = from (**ā** is used before consonants: **ā casā** **ab** is used before vowels: **ab agrō**)
ē casā exit.	**ē/ex** + ablative = out of (**ē** is used before consonants: **ē casā** **ex** is used before vowels: **ex agrō**)

Note that the ablative of words whose nominative ends -**a** (**casa**, **via**, etc.) is also spelt **ā**; the nominative is a short **a**: **casa**; the ablative is a long **ā**: **casā**.
The ablative of words whose nominative ends -**us** and -**er** (**fīlius**, **ager**, **puer**, etc.) is **ō** (**fīli-ō**, **agr-ō**, **puer-ō**).

Exercise 4.5

Fill in the blanks with correct endings and translate
1 Flaccus et fīlius in agr– labōrant.
2 canis in vi– iacet; puer– eum vocant.
3 Scintilla ē casā exit et puell– vocat.
4 puerī fess– sunt; ad cas– ab agr– redeunt.
5 puellae laet– sunt; ē cas– exeunt et currunt ad silv–.

Exercise 4.6

Translate
1 The girls are sitting in the field.
2 The dog goes out of the house.
3 The boys lead Argus through the wood.
4 The father leads his sons from the field to the house.
5 Scintilla is tired; she is working in the house.

Exercise 4.7

Using your knowledge of Latin, explain what the words underlined mean
magnifying glass; aquatic sports; filial affection; puerile behaviour; laborious task

G Compound verbs

Prepositions can be put before verbs to form one word; such verbs are called compound verbs, e.g.

it he goes

adit he goes to, approaches; **init** he goes into, enters; **exit** he goes out of.

Note also the prefix **re-** (**red-** before vowels): it means 'back'; **redit** he goes back, returns; **revenit** he comes back.

Exercise 4.8

What do the following mean?
addūcit, indūcit, ēdūcit, redūcit, ēmittit, immittit
(in-mittit), remittit, accurrit (ad-currit), recurrit, incurrit

Exercise 4.9

*Translate the first paragraph, and answer the questions on the second
paragraph without translating*

postrīdiē Quīntus ad lūdum it. Horātia in casā manet et
Scintillam iuvat. amīcula casam intrat et Horātiam
vocat; puellae in hortum exeunt et lūdunt. mox Scintilla
puellās vocat et dūcit eās ad fontem. Horātia et amīcula
laetae sunt, quod Scintillam iuvant. magnās urnās
portant.

    collem dēscendunt et mox ad fontem veniunt.
aquam dūcunt et redeunt ad casam. puellae valdē
fessae sunt, nam urnae gravēs sunt. ubi casam intrant,
Scintilla eās laudat. in hortō sedent, dum Scintilla
fābulam nārrat.

postrīdiē the next day
lūdum school
amīcula friend
hortum garden; **exeunt** go out; **lūdunt** play
fontem spring
quod because; **urnās** water pots
portant carry
collem hill; **dūcunt** draw
gravēs heavy; **ubi** when
dum while
fābulam story; **nārrat** tells

At the spring

1 What way do the girls go to reach the spring?
2 Why are they tired?
3 What does Scintilla do when they get home?
4 The following English words are derived from Latin words in this
   passage: horticulture, vocation, aquatic, porter. From what Latin
   word does each come? Explain the meaning of the English words.

5 Give one example each from this paragraph of: a compound verb; a preposition with the accusative case; a preposition with the ablative case.

6 Translate into Latin: (a) Mother sends (her) son to school.
(b) She leads the girls to the spring.
(c) The girls soon return home.

THE COUNTRY TOWN

The forum at Pompeii

At first, Rome was not the capital of Italy. It was the home of a small tribe which often had to fight for its survival with the other Italian peoples. However, Rome defeated and made alliances with its rivals and had become the leading city of Italy by Horace's time.

The Romans used one especially successful method to build up and to keep their power. They sent out Roman citizens to found towns in various parts of Italy. This meant that they could spread their influence and look after their interests. Later, when the population of Rome became too great, the problem could be eased by sending out the overflow of citizens to create such settlements. In the same way, when Roman soldiers finished their military service and had to be pensioned off, they could be sent to found new towns.

These towns were called colonies, and Horace's home-town Venusia was one of them. **Colōnus** is the Latin for a small-holder like Horace's father, and the word colony (**colōnia**) shows us that these settlements consisted mainly of farmers. The original settlers and their descendants kept their Roman citizenship and the colony was organized on the model of Rome itself. There were annual elections of the **duovirī** (two men) to preside over the local council just as the two consuls, the chief men at Rome, were elected every year to preside over the government in the capital. In addition, the colonies had their own priests. The first colonies were in Italy, but later they were founded throughout the Roman empire. The **colōnī** were envied and respected by their neighbours because they were Roman citizens.

Horace tells us that the original settlers in Venusia had been sent to keep the peace in a remote and violent part of Italy. The local school was attended by the sons of hulking soldiers, and it did not strike Horace's father as a suitable place to send his son. Probably Horace was simply too clever. So his father took him off to Rome to be educated.

Horace's friend and fellow poet Virgil writes of Italian towns 'piled up on cliff tops with rivers flowing beneath their ancient walls'.

Such hill towns remain a feature of the Italian landscape and even today, when viewed from a distance, they probably look much the same as in Horace's time.

The following election poster was found painted on the walls of a street in Pompeii:

> I beg you to elect Marcus Epidius Sabinus duovir; he is a worthy candidate; a defender of your colony, supported by the eminent judge Suedus Clemens and the unanimous voice of the town council, as worthy of our republic because of his services and his honesty. Vote for him.

Explain what office Sabinus hopes to win, whose support he claims to have, and what grounds he has for hoping that the electors will vote for him. Compare this poster with those put out by candidates in a local or national election today.

CHAPTER V

Quīntus amīcum rogat: 'cūr in agrō labōrās?'
amīcus respondet: 'patrem iuvō.'

Quīntus amīcōs rogat: 'cūr in agrō labōrātis?'
amīcī respondent: 'patrem iuvāmus.'

māter Quīntum rogat: 'cūr in viā iacēs, Quīnte?'
Quīntus respondet: 'in viā iaceō quod fessus sum.'

Quīntus puellās rogat: 'cūr in hortō sedētis, puellae?'
puellae respondent: 'in hortō sedēmus, quod fessae sumus.'

Quīntus mātrem rogat: 'quid facis, māter?'
māter respondet: 'cēnam parō.'

Quīntus puellās rogat: 'quid facitis, puellae?'
puellae respondent: 'ad silvam ambulāmus.'

31

G Verb: all persons

Latin changes the verb endings to show which person (I, you, he, we, you, they) is performing the action of the verb.
(English used to do this: I come, thou comest, he cometh; compare also: I am, thou art, he is.)

There are three persons singular: I, you, he
and three plural: we, you, they

In Latin the person endings for all verbs are:

singular	1	**ō**	I		*plural*	1	**mus**	we
	2	**s**	you			2	**tis**	you
	3	**t**	he			3	**nt**	they

Verbs are divided into four groups called *conjugations*; the person endings are the same for all four groups but the vowel before the ending differs. So

1. *First conjugation* (-**a** verbs)

singular		*plural*	
am-ō	I love	**amā-mus**	we love
amā-s	you love	**amā-tis**	you love
ama-t	he loves	**ama-nt**	they love

2. *Second conjugation* (-**e** verbs)

singular		*plural*	
mone-ō	I warn	**monē-mus**	we warn
monē-s	you warn	**monē-tis**	you warn
mone-t	he warns	**mone-nt**	they warn

3. *Third conjugation* (stems end in consonants)

singular		*plural*	
reg-ō	I rule	**reg-imus**	we rule
reg-is	you rule	**reg-itis**	you rule
reg-it	he rules	**reg-unt**	they rule

4. *Fourth conjugation* (-**i** verbs)

singular		*plural*	
audi-ō	I hear	**audī-mus**	we hear
audī-s	you hear	**audī-tis**	you hear
audi-t	he hears	**audi-unt**	they hear

Notice that in the third conjugation, where the stems end in consonants, vowels have to be inserted, which give the same endings as for **-i** verbs.

As the endings change for each person, there is no need to express the subject pronouns; for instance, **monēmus** we warn, **regunt** they rule, **audīs** you hear.

The subject of the third person singular can be either *he*, *she*, or *it*.

Exercise 5.1

Translate the following
1 Flaccum iuvāmus.
2 in agrō labōrant.
3 cēnam parās.
4 Quīntum vidēmus.
5 Scintillam audiō.
6 aquam initis.
7 Argum dūcimus.
8 puerōs exspectant.
9 Quīntum ad agrum mittunt.
10 puellās moneō.

Exercise 5.2

Translate the following into Latin
1 He is helping Flaccus.
2 We hear Quintus.
3 They see the boy.
4 What are you doing?
5 I am staying in the house.
6 You are not working, boys.
7 We are waiting for the girls.
8 They are calling Argus.
9 They quickly arrive at the field.
10 She is preparing dinner.
11 Why are you staying in the field?
12 We run to the house.

THE SCHOOL OF FLAVIUS

Quīntus ad lūdum lentē ambulat; in viā amīcum videt, nōmine Gāium; eum vocat. Gāius ad lūdum festīnat sed ubi Quīntum audit, manet et eum salūtat. 'quid facis, Quīnte?' inquit. 'cūr tam lentē ambulās? sērō ad lūdum venīmus. ego festīnō.' Quīntus respondet: 'errās; nōn sērō venīmus. exspectā mē!' Gāius ānxius est sed Quīntum exspectat. itaque duo amīcī lentē ad lūdum prōcēdunt.

    ubi ad lūdum accēdunt, aliōs puerōs vident. hī puerī magnī sunt et dūrī. ubi Gāium et Quīntum vident, ūnus, nōmine Decimus, 'ecce!' inquit. 'Quīntus et Gāius accēdunt. heus, puerī, quid facitis? cūr tam lentē ambulātis? cūr nōn festīnātis? sērō ad lūdum venītis.'

    Quīntus respondet: 'errātis. nōn sērō venīmus. manēte! exspectāte nōs!' Decimus eōs exspectat sed, ubi ad iānuam accēdunt, Quīntī capsulam rapit et in arborem iacit. Quīntus valdē īrātus est et clāmat: 'cūr

lentē slowly; **ambulat** is walking
nōmine by name, called
ubi when
sērō late
ego I; **errās** you're wrong
exspectā mē wait for me!
duo two
prōcēdunt go on

hī these
dūrī tough
ūnus one
heus hey!

Quīntī capsulam Quintus's satchel; **rapit** snatches
arborem tree

id facis? asinus es.' et Decimum pulsat. Decimus timet; fugit in lūdum.

    Quīntus et Gāius arborem ascendunt et capsulam repetunt; deinde lūdum intrant. cēterī puerī iam in sellīs sedent et magistrum, nōmine Flāvium, spectant. ille, valdē īrātus, clāmat: 'cūr nōn adsunt Quīntus et Gāius? cūr sērō veniunt?'

    intrant puerī et Flāvium salūtant. sed ille clāmat: 'cūr sērō venītis? malī puerī estis. venīte hūc!' ferulam sūmit et puerōs verberat. deinde Quīntus et Gāius in sellīs sedent et magistrum spectant. diū sedent puerī et magistrum audiunt; diū clāmat magister et litterās docet. puerī litterās in tabulīs scrībunt; magister litterās spectat et corrigit.

id that; asinus ass; pulsat hits

repetunt get back; cēterī the other
sellīs chairs
adsunt are here

venīte come
hūc here; ferulam cane
sūmit takes; verberat beats

litterās letters
tabulīs tablets
corrigit corrects

magister clāmat: 'cūr sērō venīs? malus puer es!'

    Decimus est magnus et dūrus sed stultus; litterās aegrē discit. magister ad eum venit et tabulam spectat. 'Decime,' inquit, 'asinus es; litterās nōn rēctē scrībis.' Decimus 'errās, magister,' inquit; 'nōn sum asinus. litterās rēctē scrībō. ecce!' litterās iterum scrībit. sed magister, valdē īrātus, 'impudēns es, Decime, et asinus,' inquit; 'litterās nōn rēctē scrībis.'

    tandem magister puerōs dīmittit; 'abīte, puerī,' inquit; 'domum festīnāte! sed tū, Decime, in lūdō manē et litterās rūrsus scrībe!' abeunt cēterī celeriter et domum laetī festīnant.

    pater, ubi domum redit, Quīntum rogat: 'quid facitis in lūdō hodiē?' Quīntus respondet: 'litterās discimus, pater. ego et Gāius ad lūdum sērō advēnimus, quod Decimus capsulam in arborem iacit; sed Flāvius Decimum verberat, quod litterās nōn rēctē scrībit. Decimus litterās male scrībit, quod magister male docet. et Decimus et magister asinī sunt.' Flaccus valdē īrātus est sed nihil dīcit.

stultus stupid
aegrē with difficulty
discit learns
rēctē correctly

impudēns impertinent

tandem at last; dīmittit sends away; abīte go away
tū you
rūrsus again

hodiē today
discimus we learn
quod because

et ... et both ... and
nihil nothing

34

puerī in sellīs sedent et magistrum audiunt.

Personal pronouns

Latin has personal pronouns (**ego** I, **tū** you, **ille** he, etc.) which are
used to emphasize the subject, e.g.
ego bonus sum, **tū malus** *I* am good, *you* are bad.

Learn		*Compare French, but notice differences in spelling*
ego sum	I am	*je suis*
tū es	you are	*tu es*
ille est	he is	*il est*
nōs sumus	we are	*nous sommes*
vōs estis	you are	*vous êtes*
illī sunt	they are	*ils sont*

From now on in the vocabulary, we show which conjugation a verb
belongs to by a number, e.g. **amō** (1).

spectō (1)	look at	**amīcus**	friend	**alius, alia**	other
doceō (2)	teach	**lūdus**	school	**īrātus, īrāta**	angry
iaciō (4)	throw	**magister**	master, teacher	**celeriter**	quickly
accēdō (3)	go to, approach	**domus**	home	**tam**	so
scrībō (3)	write	**domum eō**	I go home	**quid?**	what?
faciō (4)	do, make			**cūr?**	why?
adveniō (4)	come to, arrive				
inquit	he says				

35

G Adverbs

Adverbs are usually attached to verbs and tell you how the action of the verb is performed, e.g.

We are walking slowly **lentē ambulāmus**.

Many adverbs are formed by changing the ending of adjectives from **-us** to **-ē**.

lentus slow   **lentē** slowly   **malus** bad   **male** badly   **laetus** happy   **laetē** happily

But there are other types of adverb which have no corresponding adjectives, e.g. **iam** now, **iterum** again, **diū** for a long time.

Exercise 5.3

Give one English word derived from each of the following
errō, spectō, exspectō, īrātus, dēscendō, doceō, aqua

Exercise 5.4

Analyse and translate (no mark of analysis is needed over adverbs)

```
         s      o                v
```
e.g. Quīntus Argum ad agrum celeriter dūcit.

1 Quīntus amīcum in viā diū exspectat.
2 amīcī ad lūdum lentē ambulant.
3 cūr nōn festīnās? magister īrātus est.
4 magister Quīntum laudat. Quīntus laetus est.
5 in viā sedēmus; valdē fessī sumus.
6 quid facitis? amīcōs exspectāmus.
7 puer ad casam celeriter currit; sērō redit.
8 quid facis? Argum domum dūcō.
9 diū in lūdō manēmus; litterās scrībimus.

Exercise 5.5

Translate into Latin
1 What are you doing, girls? We are preparing supper.
2 Why are we waiting for Quintus? He is coming late.
3 I run into the wood and look for Argus.
4 Argus is naughty (=bad); I call him but he does not return.
5 We are happy; we run into the wood and play.
6 I do not see the girls. They are sitting in the field, for they are tired.
7 Why are you not hurrying, boy? You are an ass.

36

Exercise 5.6

Translate and answer the questions

magister puerōs exspectat; īrātus est,
iam puerī sērō veniunt. tandem lūdum
intrant et magistrum salūtant. ille, valdē
īrātus, clāmat: 'cūr sērō ad lūdum
venītis, puerī? cūr nōn festīnātis? diū vōs
exspectō. malī puerī estis.' puerī
respondent: 'festīnāmus, magister. nōn
sērō venīmus. cūr tū īrātus es?'

  sedent et magistrum spectant. ille
litterās docet; puerī litterās scrībunt.
magister Quīntum spectat et 'quid facis,
Quīnte?' inquit; 'cūr nōn labōrās?'
Quīntus respondet: 'errās, magister. ego
labōrō et litterās rēctē scrībō. ecce!'
magister litterās spectat et Quīntum
laudat.

1 Give three examples of adverbs
  from this passage.
2 Give one English word derived from
  each of the following: **exspectat** (1.1),
  salūtant (1.3), **respondent** (1.7),
  labōrō (1.14), **scrībō** (1.14)
3 Give one example each of the
  following verb forms in this passage:
  1st person singular, 2nd person plural,
  3rd person plural.
4 Give one example of a preposition +
  accusative.
5 Translate into Latin:
  (a) The boys came late to school.
  (b) The master is waiting for them.
  (c) He is very angry.

EDUCATION

Roman boys and girls were taught at home up to the age of six or
seven. At first they were taught by their mothers, and later by a nurse
and then by a tutor if their parents could afford one. They learned
how to talk Latin with a good accent. This was very necessary since
some Italian dialects would not have been understood at Rome.
Children from wealthy families learnt Greek too, since the great
works of Greek literature were highly important in Roman education.

Scenes in a boy's education

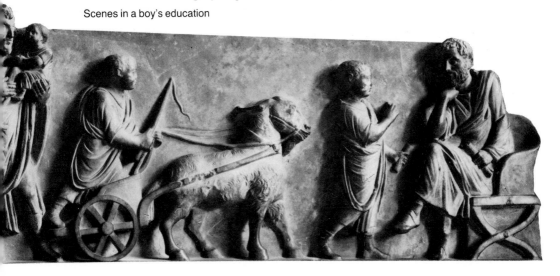

When the children were six or seven, parents who had the money to educate their children had to choose whether to employ a private tutor and educate them at home or to send them away to school. Some fathers tried to get the best of both worlds by starting their sons' education at home and sending them off to school later.

A wealthy family would appoint a slave, often a Greek, as a kind of personal tutor who would take a child to and from school. The two of them would be accompanied by another slave who carried the child's books. In country towns, schoolchildren went to school on their own carrying their satchels and taking along the schoolmaster's pay once a month. But when Horace went to school in Rome, his father took him there and sat in on his lessons.

A Roman writer called Pliny sums up a good school. It should have admirable teaching, firm discipline and high standards of behaviour. The first four or five years of teaching would cover reading and writing in both Latin and Greek, and elementary arithmetic.

For the most part, the lessons were boring and unenjoyable. Pupils sat on uncomfortable benches or chairs, often in noisy surroundings. They endlessly recited the alphabet both forwards and backwards, as well as chanting their multiplication tables again and again. Teaching started very early, soon after dawn, and one Roman poet complained violently at being woken up by the noise of a schoolmaster shouting at his pupils and beating them. Probably lessons started up again after a break for lunch. There would be a holiday every ninth day, short breaks in the winter and spring, and a very long holiday in the summer.

Children would move on to another (secondary) school around the age of eleven or twelve. Here they would learn grammar and literature. The poetry of Horace became part of the literature syllabus, as he had feared!

Arithmetic, geometry, music and astronomy were studied as minor subjects. The curriculum was not wide; there were medical schools in Greece but in Italy there was no scientific education at all. However, when they were about sixteen, upper-class Roman boys went on to a teacher of rhetoric. They received from him a thorough training in speaking and arguing, and this was a good preparation for a career in politics.

Girls dropped out of education after the first (primary) school. They then learnt needlework, dancing, singing and lyre-playing at home.

❓ Imagine that you are going to school with Quintus. Describe your day.

❓ Do you think the teaching in a Roman school would have been very boring compared with the teaching in your school?

puerī prope iānuam stant; magister dīcit:
'intrāte, puerī, et sedēte!'

Quīntus sērō advenit; magister dīcit: 'cūr
sērō advenīs, Quīnte? intrā celeriter et
sedē.'

puerī in subselliīs sedent; magister dīcit:
'tacēte, puerī, et audīte!'

Decimus litterās male scrībit; magister
dīcit: 'venī hūc, Decime, et litterās
iterum scrībe.'

Imperatives

Imperatives are the part of the verb used to give orders;
orders may be given to one person (Come here, boy!) or
to more than one (Come here, boys!); and so Latin has
different forms for singular and plural

	1	*2*	*3*	*4*
singular	**amā** love!	**monē** advise!	**rege** rule!	**audī** hear!
plural	**amāte**	**monēte**	**regite**	**audīte**

Exercise 6.1

Translate

1 intrāte, puerī, et sedēte!
2 respondē, Marce*! cūr nōn dīcis?
3 ubi est Argus? quaere canem, Quīnte!
4 redīte ad agrum, puerī, et patrem iuvāte!
5 venī hūc, Quīnte, et mātrem salūtā!

*NB Words ending in -us change to -e when the person is being addressed or called to (*vocative* case)

Exercise 6.2

Translate into Latin
1 Come here, friends, and look at Quintus.
2 Hurry, Quintus; we are arriving late.
3 Answer, boys. Why are you silent?   are you silent **tacētis**
4 Run to the field, Quintus, and call Flaccus to dinner.
5 Work hard, friends; the master is coming.   hard **dīligenter**

G The third declension

Nouns are divided into groups, called *declensions*. You have already met nouns of the first declension: nominative -a, accusative -am; and nouns of the second declension: nominative -us or -er, accusative -um, e.g. **fīli-us, fīli-um; pu-er, puer-um**.

The nominative singular of the third declension has various forms, e.g. **rēx, nāvis, urbs**; the accusative singular ends -em; the nominative and accusative plural end -ēs (the same ending for both cases).

nominative singular	**urbs** city	**rēx** king	**nāvis** ship
accusative singular	**urb-em**	**rēg-em**	**nāv-em**
nominative plural	**urb-ēs**	**rēg-ēs**	**nāv-ēs**
accusative plural	**urb-ēs**	**rēg-ēs**	**nāv-ēs**

Some words ending -er in nominative singular belong to the third declension, e.g.

nominative	**pater** father	**māter** mother	**frāter** brother
accusative	**patrem**	**mātrem**	**frātrem**

Third declension adjectives have the same endings for masculine and feminine, e.g.

nominative singular	**omnis** all	**trīstis** sad	**fortis** brave
accusative singular	**omnem**	**trīstem**	**fortem**
nominative plural	**omnēs**	**trīstēs**	**fortēs**
accusative plural	**omnēs**	**trīstēs**	**fortēs**

FLAVIUS'S STORY: THE DEATH OF HECTOR

postrīdiē puerī ad lūdum accēdunt. Decimus sērō advenit. amīcōs vocat: 'manēte, amīcī; exspectāte mē.' amīcī manent et Decimum exspectant. sed magister ē iānuā exit et eōs vocat: 'festīnāte, puerī; intrāte celeriter et sedēte.'

    itaque intrant puerī celeriter et sedent in sellīs, sed nōn labōrant. magister īrātus est; 'labōrāte, puerī,' inquit; 'litterās scrībite.'

    sed Decimus nōn labōrat; puellam spectat, quae in viā ambulat. magister valdē īrātus est. 'Decime,' inquit, 'cūr nōn labōrās? venī hūc.' Decimus ad magistrum adit et dīcit: 'errās, magister. ego labōrō. vidē litterās.' magister litterās spectat et 'Decime,' inquit, 'litterās male scrībis. asinus es. dīligenter labōrā.' Decimus ad sellam redit. dīligenter labōrat. omnēs puerī dīligenter labōrant. tandem Marcus 'magister,' inquit, 'omnēs dīligenter labōrāmus et litterās bene scrībimus. itaque nārrā nōbīs fābulam.'

    magister 'ita vērō,' inquit. 'iam vōs omnēs dīligenter labōrātis. bonī puerī estis. iam ego fābulam vōbīs nārrō. attendite et mē audīte.'

Agamemnōn, rēx Mycēnārum, omnēs prīncipēs Graecōrum convocat; nam bellum in Trōiānōs parat. frāter eius, Menelāus, adest; Achillēs venit ē Thessaliā; adest Ulixēs ex Ithacā, et multī aliī. magnum exercitum colligunt et multās nāvēs parant. ad Trōiam nāvigant et urbem oppugnant.

Glossary:
postrīdiē the next day
sellīs chairs
quae who
ambulat is walking
errās you're wrong
dīligenter hard
omnēs all
tandem at last
bene well; itaque and so
nārrā nōbīs tell us
ita vērō certainly
vōbīs to you
Mycēnārum of Mycenae; prīncipēs Graecōrum princes of the Greeks
bellum war; in against
frāter eius his brother
exercitum army
colligunt collect

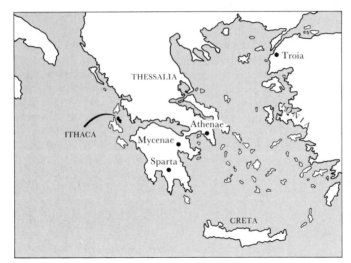

The Lion Gate at Mycenae

sed Trōiānī fortiter urbem dēfendunt. saepe in pugnā Graecī Trōiānōs vincunt sed urbem nōn capiunt. decem annōs Trōiam obsident. tandem Agamemnōn Achillem īnsultat; ille valdē īrātus est; nōn diūtius pugnat sed prope nāvēs manet et cessat. tum Trōiānī Graecōs vincunt et pellunt ad nāvēs.

Agamemnōn amīcōs ad Achillem mittit et auxilium petit; illī dīcunt: 'Achillēs, Trōiānī nōs vincunt et pellunt ad nāvēs. in magnō perīculō sumus. itaque amīcōs iuvā; redī ad pugnam.' sed ille īram nōn compēscit neque ad pugnam redit, sed manet prope nāvēs et cessat.

iam Trōiānī nāvēs oppugnant et incendunt. tum amīcus Achillis, Patroclus, 'Achillēs,' inquit, 'Trōiānī iam nāvēs incendunt. amīcōs iuvā. sī tū īram nōn compēscis, mitte mē in pugnam.' Achillēs invītus Patroclum in pugnam mittit. ille arma Achillis induit et comitēs in pugnam dūcit.

dēfendunt defend
saepe often

decem annōs for ten years
obsident besiege
īnsultat insults; **diūtius** any longer
prope near; **cessat** rests
tum then
pellunt drive
auxilium help; **nōs** us
perīculō danger
compēscit check, abate
neque nor, and not

incendunt set fire to
amīcus Achillis Achilles's friend
sī if
invītus unwilling(ly)
arma Achillis the arms of Achilles; **induit** puts on
comitēs comrades

volat hasta per auram et Hectoris gulam percutit.

Trōiānī, ubi eōs vident in pugnam ruentēs, valdē timent et fugiunt. Patroclus fortiter currit in eōs et multōs interficit. sed Hector, fortissimus Trōiānōrum, resistit et Patroclum in pugnam vocat. hastam iacit et Patroclum interficit.

Achillēs, ubi hoc cognōscit, valdē trīstis est et amīcum lūget. īram in Hectorem vertit. redit ad pugnam et comitēs in Trōiānōs dūcit. illī territī in urbem fugiunt et portās claudunt. Hector sōlus extrā mūrōs manet et Achillem exspectat.

pater Priamus, rēx Trōiae, eum videt ē mūrīs et clāmat: 'urbem intrā, Hector; Achillēs tē petit. festīnā; portās aperīmus. in magnō perīculō es.' sed Hector urbem nōn intrat. Trōiānōs vocat et dīcit: 'portās claudite, Trōiānī; festīnāte. ego sōlus maneō extrā portās et prō patriā pugnō.'

Trōiānī portās claudunt et Hector Achillem exspectat. ille propius accēdit et hastam vibrat. tum Hector valdē timet; tergum vertit et fugit.

ruentēs rushing

interficit kills; **fortissimus Trōiānōrum** bravest of the Trojans
resistit stands firm
hastam spear
hoc this; **cognōscit** learns
lūget mourns; **vertit** turns
claudunt shut; **sōlus** alone
extrā mūrōs outside the walls

rēx Trōiae king of Troy

tē petit is after you

aperīmus we are opening

prō patriā for my country
propius nearer
vibrat brandishes

tergum back

Achilles fights Hector.

Achillēs celeriter currit et Hectorem petit, sed nōn capit eum. ter circum mūrōs urbis fugit Hector; tandem resistit; sē vertit et Achillem in pugnam vocat. Achillēs prōcēdit et hastam vibrat. conicit hastam in Hectorem. sed Hector hastam videt et vītat. tum Hector hastam conicit et Achillis scūtum percutit. sed Achillēs tūtus est; nam scūtum eum prōtegit.

deinde Achillēs propius accēdit; hastam summā vī conicit; volat hasta per auram et Hectoris gulam percutit. ille ad terram cadit mortuus.

ter three times; **circum** round
sē vertit turns round
prōcēdit advances
conicit hurls
vītat avoids
Achillis scūtum Achilles's shield; **percutit** hits
prōtegit protects
deinde then; **summā vī** with all his might
volat flies; **auram** air
Hectoris gulam Hector's throat
cadit falls

43

pugnō (1)	I fight	**mortuus-a**	dead
oppugnō (1)	I attack	**multus-a**	much, many
nāvigō (1)	I sail	**fortis**	brave
vincō (3)	I conquer	**fortiter**	bravely
adsum	I am present	**omnis**	all
		trīstis	sad
		ille, illa	he, she
		tandem	at length, at last

NB The gender of nouns is given thus: *m.* masculine; *f.* feminine.

porta, *f.*	*gate*	**nāvis**, *f.*	ship
pugna, *f.*	*fight, battle*	**rēx**, *m.*	king
īra, *f.*	*anger*	**urbs**, *f.*	city
terra, *f.*	*land, earth*	**prīnceps**, *m.*	chief, leader

NB Many third declension adjectives form adverbs by adding **-ter** to the stem

fortis	brave	**fortiter**	bravely
celer	quick	**celeriter**	quickly
dīligēns	careful	**dīligenter**	carefully

Exercise 6.3

Add the correct ending to the nouns and adjectives ending – and translate

1 Quīntus patr– exspectat.
2 Graecī nāv– ascendunt.
3 puerī mātr– salūtant.
4 omn– puerī et omn– puellae dīligenter labōrant.
5 pater puerum fort– laudat.
6 māter fīliam trīst– cōnsōlat.
7 magister omn– puerōs laudat.
8 puella rēg– diū exspectat.

cōnsōlat comforts

Exercise 6.4

Analyse and translate

1 pater fīlium ad nāvem dūcit.
2 rēx omnēs prīncipēs ad urbem vocat.
3 puella frātrem diū in viā exspectat.
4 quid facitis, amīcī? festīnāte ad urbem.
5 cūr nāvem ascendis, Marce? manē et mē exspectā.

Exercise 6.5

Translate into Latin

1 Why are you waiting? Run quickly to the ship.
2 Fight bravely, friends, and take the city.
3 All the boys are sitting in the school and working.
4 Mother is sad; for (her) daughter is not here.
5 The king prepares many ships and sails to Troy.
6 Hurry to the woods, Quintus, and look for Argus.
7 The master praises the brave boys.
8 What are you doing, friends? Come to the city.

Exercise 6.6

Translate the first paragraph and answer the questions below on the second and third paragraphs

Hector in terrā iacet mortuus. Achillēs accurrit et dīrum facinus facit. Hectorem mortuum ad currum alligat et circum mūrōs trahit, pater et māter ē mūrīs spectant, territī. māter clāmat: 'ō Achillēs,' inquit, 'tandem īram compēsce; fīlium redde.' sed Achillēs Hectorem ad nāvēs trahit; ibi eum relinquit in terrā iacentem.

dīrum facinus terrible deed
currum chariot
alligat ties

compēsce check; **redde** give back
relinquit leaves
iacentem lying

Achillēs Hectorem mortuum ad currum alligat et circum mūrōs trahit.

    diū Priamus fīlium mortuum lūget. tandem, ubi nox venit, ex urbe exit et sōlus ad Graecōrum nāvēs prōcēdit. ad Achillis tabernāculum venit; intrat; ad terram prōcumbit et misericordiam rogat. 'ō Achillēs,' inquit, 'tū victor es. tandem īram compēsce et fīlium mortuum ad mātrem remitte.'

lūget mourns for
sōlus alone
Graecōrum of the Greeks
Achillis tabernāculum Achilles's tent
prōcumbit bows
misericordiam pity

ubi Achillēs Priamum videt, attonitus est.
misericordia animum vincit. Priamum ē terrā tollit,
fīlium mortuum reddit et patrem ad urbem Trōiam
tūtum remittit.

animum mind; tollit raises

1 What does Priam do when night comes?
2 What does he say to Achilles?
3 How does Achilles behave when he sees Priam in his tent?
4 How does his behaviour make you reassess his character?
5 Give one example each from these two paragraphs of: a compound
   verb, an imperative, a preposition with the ablative.
6 Give the nominative singular of the following words: **fīlium** (1.8),
   nāvēs (1.9), **terram** (1.11).

HOMER AND THE *ILIAD* – 1

The first, and some would say the greatest,
poet of Western literature is a Greek
who probably lived before 700 BC. His
name was Homer. We know almost
nothing about him. He came from Ionia
(see map), and according to tradition he
was blind. Most scholars now think that
he composed both the *Iliad* and the
Odyssey, the great poems which have
come down to us under his name, but
even that is uncertain. The *Iliad* is the
tragic story of the terrible events which
led up to the sack of Troy, a city in north-
west Turkey, by the Greeks. The *Odyssey*
tells of Odysseus's return from Troy to
Greece and his recovery of his kingdom,
and the adventures and dangers he met
in the process.

Homer

In this chapter the schoolmaster tells the story of the *Iliad*. We now summarize the events which come before the action of Homer's poem.

The gods held a great wedding feast to celebrate the marriage of Peleus and Thetis. The goddess Strife, however, had not been invited. Furious at this insult, she stormed into the hall where the feast was taking place and flung down a golden apple. Inscribed upon this were the words 'For the most beautiful'.

As Strife had planned, the apple was going to prove the cause of terrible troubles. The obvious candidates for the title of most beautiful goddess were Juno, Minerva and Venus. Understandably, none of the gods was prepared to make the decision between them. The judge would have to face the anger of the two losers, whichever of the three won! Jupiter therefore decided that a mortal must settle the matter, and his choice fell on the Trojan prince Paris. He was extremely good-looking and seemed likely to be highly experienced in such matters.

So the goddesses flew down to Mount Ida near Troy where Paris was tending his flocks. After he had overcome his astonishment and realized what was expected of him, all three of them tried to bribe him to give them the apple. Juno offered him a vast kingdom, Minerva promised him military glory, and Venus said that she would give him the most beautiful woman in the world. This was Helen, the wife of Menelaus, king of Sparta in Greece. Venus's offer seemed the most attractive to Paris and he presented the apple to her.

Paris now went to stay with Menelaus in Sparta. Here he and Helen fell in love with each other and they ran off back to Troy. Menelaus joined with his brother Agamemnon, king of Mycenae, to lead a huge expedition of Greeks against Troy in order to bring the faithless wife home again. Helen's face 'launched a thousand ships'.

But the war that took place around the walls of Troy did not go well for the Greeks. Homer's *Iliad* begins by telling of the disastrous quarrel which arose when King Agamemnon took from Achilles, the greatest of the Greek warriors, a slave girl who had been given to Achilles by the army. This was a devastating blow, not only to the emotions of Achilles, who was very fond of the girl, but far more importantly to his honour. Horace's schoolmaster relates to his pupils the dreadful results of Agamemnon's foolish insult to Achilles.

If you had been in Paris's position, which choice would you have made?

Consider the behaviour of Achilles described in this chapter as a whole. What qualities does he show? The Greeks admired him: do you?

Minerva

Neptune, Apollo, Diana

PS (**post scrīptum**) In this chapter you have met some of the gods of the ancient world. The greatest of these were: Jupiter, god of the sky; Juno, his wife, goddess of women; Neptune, god of the sea; Ceres, goddess of the crops; Minerva, goddess of wisdom and handicraft; Diana, goddess of hunting and childbirth; Venus, goddess of love; Apollo, god of light, music, and prophecy; Mars, god of war; Vulcan, god of fire; Bacchus, god of wine.

puer puellae cēnam rapit.

puella puerī capsulam rapit.

māter tabulās puerōrum spectat.

māter pūpās fīliae spectat.

fīlius equum patris dūcit.

puer canum cēnam portat.

G Genitive case

So far you have learnt the nominative case (subject) and the accusative case (object, and also used after prepositions such as **ad**). Now you must learn the *genitive* case:
puell-ae māter <u>the girl's</u> mother or the mother <u>of the girl</u>.

	1st declension	*2nd declension*	*3rd declension*
singular	**puell-ae** of the girl, the girl's	**puer-ī, amīc-ī** of the boy, of the friend	**patr-is** of the father
plural	**puell-ārum**	**puer-ōrum, amīc-ōrum**	**patr-um**

And so we can continue our table of noun endings

singular	*1st declension*	*2nd declension*	*3rd declension*
nominative	**puell-a**	**domin-us** lord, master	**pater**
accusative	**puell-am**	**domin-um**	**patr-em**
genitive	**puell-ae**	**domin-ī**	**patr-is**

plural			
nominative	**puell-ae**	**domin-ī**	**patr-ēs**
accusative	**puell-ās**	**domin-ōs**	**patr-ēs**
genitive	**puell-ārum**	**domin-ōrum**	**patr-um**

Learn all these endings carefully.

Notice that some endings are the same for two cases – genitive singular and nominative plural of **puell-a** are both **puell-ae** and of **domin-us** both **domin-ī**.
A noun in the genitive always belongs to another noun. 'The girl's . . .' – a noun such as 'mother', 'father', 'house', etc. is needed to complete the sense; and so in analysis join genitives to the nouns they belong to, e.g. **patris-equus** father's horse, **iānua-lūdī** the door of the school. (Note that the genitive can come either before or after the noun it belongs to.)

Translate the following phrases
Iūliae-māter, Quīntī-pater, Graecōrum-prīncipēs, casa-patris, multī-puerōrum

Exercise 7.1

Put the words underlined into the genitive case and translate the sentences

1 fīliī verba <u>patrēs</u> intentē audiunt.   **verba** the words
2 puerī ad iānuam <u>lūdus</u> accēdunt.
3 magister Quīntum, <u>Scintilla</u> fīlium, quaerit.
4 omnēs puerī litterās scrībunt; magister tabulās
   <u>puerī</u> spectat.
5 Decimus nōn labōrat sed manum <u>puellae</u> spectat.   **manum** group
6 magister <u>Decimus</u> tabulam spectat; īrātus est.
7 rēx Agamemnōn prīncipēs <u>Graecī</u> convocat.
8 rēx eōs dūcit ad <u>Priamus</u> urbem.
9 Graecī saepe Trōiānōs vincunt et ad mūrōs <u>urbs</u>
   pellunt.
10 Achillēs Hectorem, <u>rēx</u> fīlium, interficit.

THE FALL OF TROY

decem annōs Graecī Trōiam obsident sed nōn capiunt.   **decem annōs** for ten years
tandem Agamemnōn, rēx Graecōrum, dēspērat; omnēs   **obsident** besiege
prīncipēs convocat et dīcit: 'decem annōs Trōiam   **dēspērat** despairs
obsidēmus; saepe Trōiānōs in pugnā vincimus, sed
urbem nōn capimus. ego iam dēspērō. quid vōs
monētis?' aliī prīncipēs tacent, sed Ulixēs 'ego nōn   **tacent** are silent
dēspērō,' inquit; 'cōnsilium habeō. audīte mē.'   **cōnsilium** plan

   omnēs prīncipēs cōnsilium Ulixis attentē audiunt.   **attentē** attentively
cōnsilium laetī accipiunt. equum ligneum faciunt;   **equum ligneum** wooden horse
equus ingēns est; multōs virōs in ventre capit. virōs   **ingēns** huge; **ventre** belly
fortissimōs ēligunt; illī ascendunt et in ventre equī   **fortissimōs** the bravest
manent. cēterī nāvēs ascendunt et nāvigant ad īnsulam   **ēligunt** select
vīcīnam.   **cēterī** the rest
    vīcīnam neighbouring

The wooden horse

51

Trōiānī nāvēs vident abeuntēs; ex urbe exeunt; ad castra Graecōrum adeunt. lītus dēsertum spectant et equum in lītore stantem. gaudent quod Graecī nōn adsunt, gaudent quod bellum cōnfectum est. equum laetī in urbem trahunt. magnificē cēnant et multum vīnum bibunt.

nox adest. dormiunt Trōiānī. Graecī, quī in īnsulā exspectant, nāvēs ascendunt et iterum ad urbem Trōiam nāvigant. illī, quī in equō cēlātī sunt, tacitī exeunt et festīnant ad portās urbis.

vigilēs Trōiānōrum dormiunt; ēbriī sunt. Graecī eōs celeriter interficiunt. deinde portās aperiunt et comitēs accipiunt. in urbem currunt. Trōiānī vix resistunt. paucī pugnant, sed frūstrā. Graecī tōtam urbem capiunt. rēgem Priamum et fīliōs interficiunt. sīc post decem annōs Graecī tandem Trōiam capiunt et urbem dēlent.

abeuntēs	going away
castra	camp; lītus
dēsertum	the deserted shore
stantem	standing
bellum	the war
cōnfectum	finished
trahunt	drag; magnificē
	magnificently
vīnum	wine; bibunt drink
quī	who; cēlātī hidden
vigilēs	watchmen; ēbriī drunk
aperiunt	open
comitēs	comrades
vix	scarcely
paucī	a few; frūstrā in vain
post	after
dēlent	destroy

The death of Priam

V

cēnō (1)	I eat, dine	collis, collis, *m.*	hill
moneō (2)	I advise, warn	hostis, hostis, *c.**	enemy
gaudeō (2)	I rejoice	*common; i.e. it can be *m.* or *f.*	
habeō (2)	I have	nox, noctis, *f.*	night
interficiō (4)	I kill		
conveniō (4)	I come together	parvus-a	small, little
NB From now on nouns are given with		tōtus-a	whole
the genitive singular and gender		tacitus-a	silent
īnsula, īnsulae, *f.*	island	ibi	there
mūrus, mūrī, *m.*	wall	iterum	again
equus, equī, *m.*	horse	saepe	often
vir, virī, *m.*	man	quod	because

Exercise 7.2

*From what Latin words are the following English adjectives derived
and what do the English words mean?*
virile, total, nocturnal, pugnacious, hostile

Exercise 7.3

Translate
1 rēx prīncipēs Graecōrum convocat.
2 nāvēs parāte, prīncipēs, et nāvigāte ad Trōiam.
3 fortiter pugnāte et urbem Trōiam capite.
4 quid facis, Ulixēs? cūr equum ligneum aedificās?   **aedificās** build
5 audīte mē, prīncipēs; equus ligneus mūrōs Trōiae
   intrat.
6 fortissimī Graecōrum in equum ascendunt.   **fortissimī** the bravest
7 Trōiānī equum in viās urbis dūcunt.
8 Graecī ex equō exeunt et portās urbis aperiunt.
9 Graecī Trōiānōs vincunt; rēgem et rēgis fīliōs
   interficiunt.
10 paucī Trōiānōrum ēvādunt et fugiunt ad collēs.   **paucī** a few; **ēvādunt** escape

Exercise 7.4

Translate into Latin
1 The boy is waiting near the gate of the city.   near **prope** + accusative
2 The mother sees (her) daughter's dog.
3 The son is leading (his) father's horse.
4 The master looks at the boys' tablets.   tablets **tabulae, tabulārum**
5 The boys fear the master's anger.
6 Help (your) father, boy; he is working in the field.
7 We are waiting for mother; she is looking for the
   dog.
8 Run to father's field, Quintus, and call him to
   supper.
9 What are you doing, friends? Why aren't you
   climbing the hill?
10 We are sitting in the road, because we are tired.

Exercise 7.5

Translate the first paragraph and answer the questions on the second paragraph without translating

Trōiānōrum paucī ēvādunt; urbem ārdentem relinquunt et fugiunt in collēs. inter eōs est Aenēās, prīnceps Trōiānus; ille patrem et uxōrem et parvum fīlium e flammīs ēripit et per hostēs ad collēs dūcit. ibi aliī conveniunt. omnēs dēspērant, sed Aenēās 'Trōia incēnsa est,' inquit, 'sed nōs Trōiānī supersumus. venīte mēcum. nōs novam Trōiam in aliā terrā condēmus.'

    sīc dīcit Aenēās; illī verba eius laetī accipiunt. ad mare festīnant; nāvēs inveniunt et mox ab urbe Trōiā in terrās ignōtās nāvigant. septem annōs per mare nāvigant et multa perīcula subeunt. tandem in Italiam veniunt et urbem condunt.

ārdentem burning	
relinquunt leave; **inter** among	
uxōrem wife	
flammīs flames; **ēripit** rescues	
dēspērant despair	
incēnsa burnt	
supersumus survive	
mēcum with me	
condēmus we shall found	
verba eius his words	
mare sea; **inveniunt** find	
ignōtās unknown; **septem annōs** for seven years	
perīcula dangers	
subeunt undergo	
condunt found	

1 How do Aeneas' companions react to his speech?
2 What do they do when they reach the sea?
3 What do you learn about their voyage?
4 Aeneas' loyalties were divided between trying to save Troy and trying to save his family. Do you think he did the right thing?
5 Give one English word derived from each of the following: **urbe** (1.2), **terrās** (1.3), **annōs** (1.3).
6 Give the nominative singular and genitive singular of the same three words.
7 Translate into Latin:
    (a) Aeneas flees from (his) house to the hills.
    (b) A few of the Trojans escape and help him.
    (c) He says: 'Hurry to the sea. Look for the ships.'

THE *ILIAD* – 2

In our last chapter, we briefly told the end of the story of the *Iliad*. We described how Achilles, although he has now taken revenge on Hector for killing his friend Patroclus, nevertheless pushes his hatred beyond his enemy's death. He drags Hector's corpse round Patroclus's tomb again and again in his wild anger and grief.

    It was considered a terrible thing to leave a man unburied in the Greek world, since it meant that his spirit could not find rest in the next life. Most of the gods disapprove of Achilles's treatment of Hector's corpse, and Apollo protects it, making sure that it does not become damaged in any way.

    Jupiter now decides that Achilles must give Hector's body back to his father Priam. He sends Iris, goddess of the rainbow, to tell

Priam to go to the Greek camp at night and to ask Achilles to grant him this request. He also sends Thetis, the mother of Achilles, to see her son and to make sure that he does what he's told.

Priam loads a wagon with a fabulous ransom and sets off for the Greek camp with a single charioteer. As they approach the enemy lines, the god Mercury meets them in disguise and leads them to Achilles's hut. Miraculously they are unnoticed by any of the Greeks. Achilles gazes in amazement as the old man enters, kneels before him and takes hold of the fatal hands which have killed so many of his children.

Priam begs him to accept the ransom and return Hector's corpse, making him imagine the feelings of an old father who has lost his son. The two men, one so young and the other so very old, weep together. Priam remembers Hector and Achilles thinks of his own father Peleus at home in Greece, destined never to see his son again. For Achilles had been given the choice between a short life with immortal fame and a long but obscure existence. He had chosen the former.

The ransom of Hector

As the two enemies weep, the anger of Achilles disappears and he agrees to Priam's request. They eat together and later that night Priam leaves the Greek camp, again under the protection of Mercury. He returns to the city with his son's body on the wagon which had carried the ransom on the way out. The Trojans will be given the opportunity to pay full funeral rites to Hector back at Troy, during a truce guaranteed by Achilles.

Two dreadful events hang over the end of the *Iliad*. One of them is the death of Achilles. He will be mortally wounded by an arrow in his heel, the only part of his body where a weapon can penetrate. The other is the fall of Troy which cannot be avoided now that Hector is dead. So Achilles and Priam will soon join Patroclus and Hector and the countless other victims of the Trojan War in the Underworld.

Explain the causes of Achilles's anger against first the Greeks and then the Trojans.

How do the events described above bring the *Iliad* to a satisfactory conclusion?

magister dīcit: 'celeriter intrāte, puerī!' magister puerōs iubet celeriter intrāre.

puerī lūdere cupiunt; magister dīcit:
'nōlīte lūdere, puerī; labōrāre dēbētis.'

puerī bonī sunt; tacitī sedent et
magistrum audiunt. magister cōnstituit
fābulam nārrāre.

G The infinitive

1 amāre to love **2 monēre** to warn **3 regere** to rule **4 audīre** to hear

The infinitive is used in Latin, as in English, after verbs like

cupiō	I want to
dēbeō	I ought to, I must
cōnstituō	I decide to
iubeō	I order

also after **nōlī** (singular) and **nōlīte** (plural) don't, e.g.

nōlī dormīre, amīce	Don't sleep, friend.
nōlīte lūdere, puerī	Don't play, boys.

Exercise 8.1

*Analyse and translate; join infinitives to
the verb they depend on by a hyphen*, e.g.
lūdere-cupimus; or thus:
iubet puerōs labōrāre.

1 magister puerōs iubet labōrāre.
2 puerī cupiunt domum redīre.
3 rēx cōnstituit omnēs prīncipēs
   convocāre.
4 iubet eōs nāvēs parāre.
5 dīcit: 'ego cupiō Trōiam nāvigāre et
   urbem capere.'

Exercise 8.2

Translate into Latin

1 The girls want to stay in the house.
2 The boys tell (= order) them to come
   to the field.
3 We are arriving late; we ought to
   hurry.
4 The king decides to prepare the ships.
5 He orders all the princes to come
   together.

The verb 'eō'

The stem of this verb is **i** and so it goes basically like **audiō**

eō = I go   *infinitive* **īre**
īs
it   *imperatives* **ī, īte**
īmus
ītis
eunt (only **eō** and **eunt** start **e** instead of **i**)

So also **redeō, redīs, redit**, etc.   go back, return
         adeō, adīs, adit, etc.   go to, approach
         exeō, exīs, exit, etc.   go out
         abeō, abīs, abit, etc.   go away

The mixed conjugation

These are verbs ending in -**iō** which go like **audiō** except for their
infinitive, which is -**ere** (not -**īre**) and imperative, which is -**e** (not -**ī**)

e.g. **capiō, capere** *imperatives* **cape, capite**
You have also met **iaciō** (infinitive **iacere**) and **interficiō** (**interficere**).

In future you will be able to recognize these verbs in the vocabulary
lists because we shall give the infinitive as well as the first person
singular of every verb.

THE WANDERINGS OF AENEAS

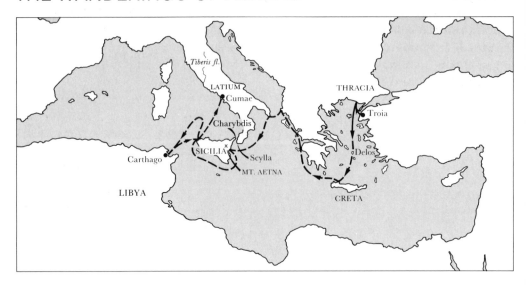

Trōiānī, ubi nāvēs ascendunt, prīmum ad Thrāciam nāvigant. ibi Aenēās eōs iubet urbem aedificāre; sed nōn diū ibi manent. nam portentum immāne eōs terret. itaque Aenēās cōnstituit ā Thrāciā abīre et nāvigāre ad īnsulam Dēlum; nam cupit deum Apollinem rogāre 'ubi dēbent cōnsīdere Trōiānī? quō nōs īre iubēs?' deus respondet: 'ō Trōiānī, dēbētis ad antīquam terram redīre. antīquam mātrem quaerite.' Aenēās ōrāculum nōn intellegit, sed pater Anchīsēs 'audīte mē, prīncipēs,' inquit; 'ego ōrāculum intellegō. antīqua terra Trōiānōrum est īnsula Crēta. deus Apollō nōs iubet in Crētā cōnsīdere. ad Crētam dēbēmus festīnāre.'

itaque ad Crētam Trōiānī fessī nāvigant. ibi urbem aedificāre incipiunt. sed deus morbum in eōs mittit; et hominēs et frūgēs pereunt. Aenēās dēspērat sed in somnō deus eum monet: 'Apollō nōn iubet vōs in Crētā habitāre. nōlīte hīc cōnsīdere. iubeō vōs ad Italiam nāvigāre. ibi Trōiam novam condere dēbētis.'

rūrsus nāvēs ascendunt Trōiānī et nāvigāre incipiunt ad Italiam. sed procul abest Italia. dīrae tempestātēs Trōiānōs afflīgunt. semper perīculum et labōrēs obeunt. saepe dēspērat Aenēās.

tandem ad Italiam accēdunt; obscūrōs collēs procul vident. Italiam laetī salūtant et in portum nāvigant. sed Graecī quīdam in eā parte Italiae habitant. itaque Trōiānī celeriter abeunt et ad Siciliam

ubi when; **prīmum** first
aedificāre to build
portentum immāne a dreadful sign, omen

ubi? where?
cōnsīdere to settle
antīquam ancient

intellegit understands

cōnsīdere to settle

incipiunt they begin
morbum disease
frūgēs crops; **pereunt** perish

condere found
rūrsus again
procul abest is far away; **dīrae tempestātēs** terrible storms
afflīgunt afflict
perīculum danger
obeunt they meet
obscūrōs obscure, dim
portum harbour
Graecī quīdam certain Greeks; **eā parte** this part

nāvigant; sed in itinere magnum perīculum vix vītant; nam saxa vident ubi habitat Scylla, et sonitum ingentem audiunt verticis ubi Charybdis undās ēvomit. pater Anchīsēs eōs monet, 'hīc est illa Charybdis; haec saxa fugite; nāvēs ē perīculō ēripite!' Aenēās patrem audit et saxa vītat. ē perīculō tūtī ēvādunt.

deinde, ubi ad Siciliam veniunt, montem Aetnam vident; nāvēs ad terram dīrigunt et sub noctem ad lītus adveniunt. mōns Aetna per noctem tonat; flammās et lapidēs in caelum prōicit. Trōiānī valdē timent et diem ānxiī exspectant.

in itinere on their journey
vix scarcely; **vītant** they avoid
saxa rocks; **sonitum** sound
verticis of the whirlpool
undās waves; **ēvomit** spews out
haec these
ēripite save!
vītat avoids; **ēvādunt** escape
montem Aetnam Mount Aetna
dīrigunt steer; **sub noctem** towards nightfall; **lītus** shore
tonat thunders
lapidēs stones; **prōicit** flings up

mōns Aetna tonat; flammās et lapidēs in caelum prōicit.

postrīdiē festīnant nāvēs ascendere, sed hominem squālidum et miserum vident, quī ē silvīs exit et currit ad lītus; Trōiānōs vocat; currit ad eōs et ōrat: 'servāte mē,' inquit, 'vōs ōrō; ego Graecus sum, comes Ulixis. cēterī fūgērunt. ego sōlus maneō. fugite, miserī, fugite; nōlīte manēre sed nāvēs celeriter cōnscendite. nam Cyclōpēs hunc montem habitant, gigantēs immānēs, quī hominēs edunt. servāte mē, accipite mē in nāvem.'

squālidum filthy; **quī** who
ōrat begs

cēterī the rest; **fūgērunt** have got away

hunc this; **gigantēs immānēs** huge giants
quī who; **edunt** eat

(V) NB From now on in vocabulary lists the infinitive of verbs will be given; this will show which conjugation they belong to.

Verbs commonly followed by the infinitive

cōnstituō, cōnstituere	I decide	subitō	suddenly
cupiō, cupere	I desire, wish	inter + accusative	among, between
dēbeō, dēbēre	I ought, I must	et ... et ...	both ... and ...
iubeō, iubēre	I order	semper	always
		hīc	here
habitō, habitāre	I live in, inhabit	quō?	where to?
accipiō, accipere	I receive, accept		
servō, servāre	save, preserve		
terreō, terrēre	terrify		

somnus, somnī, *m.*	sleep	Note the following pairs of Latin words
deus, deī, *m.*	a god	
comes, comitis, *c.*	companion	labōrō, labōrāre labor, labōris
diēs, *m.*	day	clāmō, clāmāre clāmor, clāmōris
homō, hominis, *c.*	man	timeō, timēre timor, timōris
labor, labōris, *m.*	work, suffering	What part of speech are the Latin words
		in the first column and what does each
sōlus, sōla	alone	mean? What part of speech are the
miser, misera	unhappy	words in the second column and what
ingēns	huge	does each mean?

Exercise 8.3

Translate

1 nōlīte manēre in viā, puerī; intrāte et sedēte.

2 puellae dormiunt; fessae sunt; nōlī eās excitāre, māter.   **excitāre** wake up

3 Decime, asinus es; dēbēs labōrāre.

4 quid facis, Marce? cūr nōn iānuam claudis?   **claudis** shut

5 Quīntus domum nōn redit; māter eum ānxia exspectat.

6 māter fīlium ad agrum mittit; iubet eum cēnam ad patrem portāre.

7 rēx Agamemnōn omnēs prīncipēs ad urbem Trōiam dūcere cōnstituit.

8 Graecī Trōiam diū oppugnant sed urbem capere nōn possunt.   **possunt** can

9 deus Apollō Trōiānōs monet; 'nōlīte hīc manēre,' inquit; 'iubeō vōs ad prīscam terram redīre.'   **prīscam** ancient

10 Polyphēmus Trōiānōs vidēre nōn potest, sed audīre potest.   **potest** can

Exercise 8.4

Translate into Latin

1 Don't go away, friends; stay and hear me.
2 You ought to lead the dog to the house, Quintus*
3 The daughter wants to help her mother; Scintilla praises her.
4 The boys are tired; they decide to sleep.
5 Wait for me, Quintus. Why are you hurrying?
6 What are you doing, friends? Don't be afraid.
7 The king orders all the men to come together to the city.
8 The master says: 'You are good boys; you are working well.'
9 We are tired, father; don't wake us.
10 The Trojans are very afraid; they wait anxious(ly) for day.

*NB **Quīnte**

wake **excitō, excitāre**
anxious(ly) **ānxiī**
day **diem** (accusative)

Exercise 8.5

Translate the whole of the passage and answer the questions below

subitō Trōiānī Polyphēmum vident, gigantem
ingentem. ille ovēs dē monte dūcit. caecus est; lentē
dēscendit; in viā saepe lāpsat et aegrē prōcēdit. Aenēās
valdē timet. 'currite ad nāvēs,' inquit; 'festīnāte!'
Trōiānī comitem Ulixis accipiunt et fugiunt ad nāvēs.

ovēs sheep; **dē** down from
caecus blind
lāpsat slips; **aegrē** with
difficulty

Polyphēmus dē monte lentē
dēscendit.

Polyphēmus iam ad lītus advenit et in undās
prōcēdit. Trōiānōs vidēre nōn potest sed audit eōs
rēmigantēs. clāmōrem ingentem tollit. cēterī Cyclōpēs
clāmōrem audiunt et currunt dē montibus ad lītus.
conveniunt et Polyphēmum iuvant. saxa ingentia in
nāvēs iaciunt; sed Trōiānī iam ē terrā nāvigant.
Cyclōpēs eōs contingere nōn possunt.

     sīc Trōiānī tūtī ēvādunt et ad aliam partem Siciliae
adveniunt, ubi rēx eōs benignē accipit.

lītus	shore
potest	can
rēmigantēs	rowing;
tollit	raises
saxa	rocks
contingere	reach
ēvādunt	escape; **partem** part
ubi	where

1 In Virgil's description Polyphemus appears not only as a terrifying
    monster but also as a pitiable creature. How does he appear to you?
2 Do you think Aeneas behaved wisely in this crisis? What else could
    he have done?
3 Translate into Latin:
    (a) I do not want to see Polyphemus.
    (b) He is coming slowly down the mountain.
    (c) Run to the ships and sail from the land.

ODYSSEUS AND THE CYCLOPS

All nations have their heroes. We know the famous stories of King
Arthur and King Alfred. The Romans had their legend of Aeneas, the
Trojan Prince who fled from Troy, brought his followers to Italy and
founded the Roman nation.

    Virgil, the greatest of all Roman poets, describes the adventures
of Aeneas in his poem, the *Aeneid*. The first half of this poem tells of
the travels of Aeneas as he tries to find his way from Troy to the site of
Rome. It owes much to Homer's *Odyssey*, which is about the journey
home of the Greek hero Odysseus. The *Odyssey* is the book about
Odysseus. His Latin name is Ulixes, and that is how we have referred
to him in our Latin story.

    On his travels Odysseus meets with many adventures. In one of
them, he has to sail between two rocks. A hideous barking monster
called Scylla lives in a cave on one side. She has six necks and six
heads, and she uses them to snatch victims from passing ships.
Charybdis lurks at the foot of the other rock, a fearful whirlpool which
swallows any vessel that goes near. Odysseus steers closer to Scylla
and gets by safely, though he does lose six men to Scylla's darting
heads. As you can see from what happens in this chapter, Aeneas has
a narrow escape from a similar adventure.

    We now tell the story of Odysseus's adventure with the Cyclops.

    The Cyclopes were a race of one-eyed giants, a savage people
without laws who lived in caves in the mountains of Sicily. Odysseus
and his men had the bad fortune to come to their coast.

Odysseus blinds the Cyclops.

Odysseus was always extremely curious. He decided to take twelve of his followers to investigate this strange race. They set out, taking with them some wonderful wine in a goatskin, and they soon came to the cave of the Cyclops of our story. He was out in the pasture at the time, tending his sheep. Odysseus and his men were able to look undisturbed at all the cheeses, kids and lambs in the cave. The others wanted to take some of these away to their ships and sail off as quickly as possible, but Odysseus wished to meet the Cyclops. It was the custom for guests and hosts to give each other presents, and Odysseus hoped to do well out of such an exchange. He rashly insisted on staying.

At last the huge Cyclops returned with his flocks and, once inside, he rolled an enormous stone in front of the entrance of the cave. This was so vast that twenty wagons could not have moved it. He then noticed his visitors, but he showed no signs of hospitality. On the contrary, he grabbed two of them, dashed their brains out, tore them limb from limb and gobbled them down.

Odysseus had to think of a trick to enable his men to escape, since direct force would achieve nothing against a giant of such size. The next day the Cyclops went out with his flocks, taking care to put the stone back in place once he was outside. Odysseus found a huge staff of olive-wood lying on the ground, and he and his men sharpened it at one end and hardened the point in the fire.

The Cyclops returned in the evening, and gobbled down two more of his visitors. But wily Odysseus, pretending to be friendly, offered him some of the wine he had brought from the ship. The Cyclops accepted and quickly became very drunk. He asked Odysseus his name, and the tricky Greek replied that he was called 'Nobody'. The Cyclops promised that he would eat Nobody last, making a gruesome joke, and collapsed in a drunken sleep. Morsels of the flesh he had eaten dribbled from his mouth.

Odysseus and his men now took hold of the huge olive-wood staff and heated the point in the fire till it glowed. Then they plunged it in the Cyclops's single eye. It made a grisly hissing sound as they twisted

63

it round. The Cyclops awoke in terrible pain and cried out to the neighbouring Cyclopes to help him. They rushed to his cave and asked him who had hurt him. He answered 'Nobody', so they assumed that nothing was the matter and went away. Odysseus laughed to himself at the success of his plan.

However, there remained the problem of how to escape from the cave. Its entrance was still blocked by the huge stone. Odysseus solved this difficulty by tying his men under the bellies of some large rams which the Cyclops would have to let out to pasture. He chose for himself the biggest ram of the flock and clung firmly to its fine fleece. The Cyclops removed the stone at dawn and let out the rams, stroking their backs to see that no-one was on them. Odysseus's ram, weighed down by the great hero, was the last to leave. The Cyclops thought that its slowness was due to its grief over its master's lost eye!

Odysseus and his men escape from the Cyclops' cave.

Odysseus and his men now rushed down to the ships. They took the rams on board with them, and quickly rowed away. (In Virgil's version of the story, which we have followed in this chapter, one of the Greeks is left behind.) Odysseus could not resist shouting taunts at the Cyclops from the ship, gloating over how he had escaped him. The Cyclops flung a great rock into the sea and it landed just ahead of Odysseus's ship. The enormous swell drove the ship back toward the land. However, the crew rowed energetically and they managed to avoid being swept on to the shore.

They were twice their previous distance out to sea when Odysseus, ignoring his crew's pleas to keep quiet, provoked the Cyclops again, letting him know who he really was. The Cyclops prayed to his father Neptune, the god of the sea, to punish Odysseus and flung another huge stone towards the sound of his voice. This time the stone fell short and the swell carried the ship further away from the coast.

Odysseus escaped from the Cyclops, but Neptune did not forget his son's prayer and caused Odysseus to suffer many hardships.

❓ Imagine that you are one of Odysseus' companions. Describe your adventures.

❓ What do you think of Odysseus? Was he a good or a bad leader?

64

dum Trōiānī ad Italiam nāvigant, Aeolus, rēx ventōrum, omnēs ventōs ēmittit.

ubi Neptūnus tempestātem sentit, ex undīs ēmergit.

ventī timent, quod Neptūnus īrātus est, et domum fugiunt.

WRECKED IN LIBYA

dum Aenēās et Trōiānī in Siciliā manent, pater Anchīsēs, quī valdē senex est, perit. Aenēās trīstissimus est et patrem valdē dēsīderat. sed cōnstituit statim ad Italiam nāvigāre. Trōiānī nāvēs cōnscendunt et cursum ad Italiam dīrigunt.

> quī who; **perit** dies
> **trīstissimus** very sad
> **dēsīderat** misses
> **cōnscendunt** board
> **cursum** course; **dīrigunt** steer

statim venit magna tempestās. Aeolus, rēx ventōrum, omnēs ventōs simul ēmittit; ventī magnās undās in nāvēs volvunt. nāvēs aquam accipere incipiunt; nūbēs caelum obscūrant. Aenēās timet et perīre cupit.

> **simul** at the same time
> **volvunt** roll
> **incipiunt** begin; **nūbēs** clouds
> **obscūrant** darken

intereā Neptūnus, rēx Oceanī, tempestātem sentit. ex undīs ēmergit et ventōs vocat. īrātus est quod Aeolus tantam tempestātem excitat. 'quid facitis, ventī?'

> **sentit** feels
> **ēmergit** comes up
> **excitat** stirs up

inquit; 'cūr tantam tempestātem excitātis? iubeō vōs ad
Aeolum statim redīre. ego, nōn Aeolus, sum rēx
Oceanī.' ventī timent et ad Aeolum fugiunt. Neptūnus
nūbēs dispellit et undās sēdat.

dispellit scatters; **sēdat** calms

   sīc Trōiānī ē tempestāte ēvādunt et festīnant ad
proximum lītus. ē nāvibus exeunt et in lītore dormiunt.
postrīdiē Aenēās cōnstituit terram ignōtam explōrāre.
ūnum comitem sēcum dūcit; cēterī prope nāvēs
manent.

ēvādunt escape
proximum lītus the nearest
shore
ignōtam unknown
explōrāre to explore
sēcum with him

   Aenēās et amīcus, nōmine Achātēs, collem
ascendunt et prōspiciunt; multōs hominēs vident, quī
urbem aedificant. Aenēās et Achātēs stupent.

prōspiciunt look down
stupent are amazed

   Aenēās eōs trīstis spectat et dīcit: 'ō fortūnātī, vōs
urbem iam aedificātis; nōs semper in undīs errāmus,
semper Italiam quaerimus.' collem dēscendunt; urbem
intrant et accēdunt ad magnum templum.

trīstis sadly; **ō fortūnātī** o
lucky men
errāmus wander

templum temple

   in templī mūrīs multae pictūrae sunt; Aenēās
pictūrās spectat et stupet; nam pictūrae bellum
Trōiānum dēscrībunt. Achātem vocat; 'ecce,' inquit,
'Achātēs, in hāc pictūrā Priamum vidēre potes et
Achillem. hīc est Agamemnōn. ecce, hīc Achillēs
Hectorem circum mūrōs Trōiae trahit. nōlī timēre. in
omnī terrā Trōiānōrum labōrēs nōtī sunt. in hāc urbe
nōn ignōtī sumus.'

bellum Trōiānum the Trojan
War
dēscrībunt depict; **ecce** look
hāc this

nōtī well-known
ignōtī unknown

Dido welcomes Aeneas.

dum Aenēās pictūrās spectat, ecce, rēgīna, nōmine
Dīdō, ad templum accēdit; multōs prīncipēs sēcum
dūcit. Aenēās nōn timet sed currit ad eam et 'ō rēgīna,'
inquit, 'servā nōs; Trōiānī sumus; Italiam quaerimus;
nam ibi dēbēmus novam Trōiam condere. sed
tempestās nōs ad vestram terram pepulit. comitēs
prope nāvēs manent.'

Dīdō, ubi eum audit, prīmum stupet; deinde 'fāma
Trōiānōrum,' inquit, 'omnibus nōta est. nōlīte timēre.
ego vōs laeta accipiō et libenter vōs iuvō.' sīc eōs
benignē accipit et ad rēgiam dūcit. nūntiōs mittit ad
nāvēs et iubet eōs dūcere Trōiānōs ad urbem. magnam
cēnam parat; omnēs prīncipēs Carthāginis et omnēs
Trōiānōs ad cēnam vocat.

ubi cēna cōnfecta est, Dīdō 'age,' inquit, 'Aenēā,
nārrā nōbīs Trōiae cāsum et omnēs labōrēs
Trōiānōrum.' omnēs tacitī sedent et Aenēam spectant.
ille respondet: 'īnfandum, rēgīna, iubēs renovāre
dolōrem. sed, sī cupis suprēmōs labōrēs Trōiae audīre,
ego nārrābō.'

sēcum with her

vestram your; **pepulit** has
driven

prīmum at first; **fāma** fame
omnibus to all
libenter gladly
benignē kindly; **rēgiam** palace

cōnfecta finished; **age** come
now
nōbīs to us; **cāsum** the fall

īnfandum dolōrem
unspeakable grief;
renovāre renew
sī if
suprēmōs last
nārrābō I shall tell

possum, posse	I am able, I can	**prope** + accusative	near
		statim	immediately
rēgīna, rēgīnae, *f.*	queen	**sīc**	thus
unda, undae, *f.*	wave	**dum**	while
nūntius, nūntiī, *m.*	message;	**ubi**	when
	messenger	**semper**	always
ventus, ventī, *m.*	wind	**intereā**	meanwhile
senex, senis, *m.*	old man		
tempestās, tempestātis, *f.*	storm		
novus-a	new		
ūnus-a	one		
tantus-a	so great		
cēterī, cēterae	the rest		

Revise	*Learn*	
sum	**ad-sum** I am present	**pos-sum** I can
es	**ad-es**	**pot-es**
est	**ad-est**	**pot-est**
sumus	**ad-sumus**	**pos-sumus**
estis	**ad-estis**	**pot-estis**
sunt	**ad-sunt**	**pos-sunt**

G Subordinate clauses

A clause is a group of words containing a verb, e.g. 'Flaccus calls
Quintus'. This clause forms a complete sentence.
'When Quintus enters the field' is a clause (for it is a group of words
containing the verb 'enters'), but it does not form a complete
sentence; it needs another clause to complete it: 'When Quintus
enters the field, Flaccus calls him.'

This sentence consists of two clauses:

1 When Quintus enters the field
2 Flaccus calls him

The two clauses are joined by the word 'when'. The 'when' clause,
which does not form a complete sentence, is called a 'subordinate
clause'. 'Flaccus calls him', which is a grammatically complete
sentence, is called 'the main clause'.

Subordinate clauses are introduced by words such as **ubi** when, **dum**
while, **quod** because.

In analysing, subordinate clauses should be bracketed off; each clause
will contain its own verb and subject. For example

$$s \qquad o \qquad v \qquad s \quad o \quad v$$

(ubi Quīntus agrum intrat,) Flaccus eum vocat.

Exercise 9.1

Analyse the following English sentences.
Bracket off the subordinate clauses and
mark subject, verb, object, etc.

1 When Horatia entered the house, she
  found her mother in the garden.
2 While Quintus went to school,
  Horatia helped her mother.
3 Aeneas is sad because his father died.
4 Neptune is angry, because Aeolus has
  loosed all the winds.
5 When the Trojans reached Carthage,
  Dido received them kindly.

Exercise 9.2

Analyse and translate

1 ubi puerī lūdum intrant, magister eōs
  salūtat.
2 dum Quīntus labōrat, Decimus lūdit.

3 dum Trōiānī in Siciliā manent,
  Anchīsēs perit.
4 ubi Neptūnus tempestātem videt,
  īrātus est.
5 Neptūnus īrātus est, quod Aeolus
  omnēs ventōs ēmittit.

Exercise 9.3

Translate into Latin

1 When Julia sees her mother, she is
  happy.
2 While Scintilla is working in the
  house, Horatia is looking for Quintus.
3 When Dido sees the Trojans, she
  receives them kindly. kindly **benignē**
4 While Aeneas speaks, all listen to
  him.
5 The master is angry, because the boys
  do not work.

68

Exercise 9.4

Give an English word that comes from each of the following and say what each English word means

labor
tempestās
nāvigō
urbs
timeō

Note the following pairs of Latin words

pugnō, pugnāre   pugna
cēnō, cēnāre   cēna
lacrimō, lacrimāre   lacrima

What part of speech (i.e. verbs or nouns) are the Latin words in the first column and what does each mean? What part of speech are the words in the second column and what does each mean?

Exercise 9.5

AENEAS TELLS THE STORY OF THE SACK OF TROY

Translate the first three paragraphs. Answer the questions on the last three without translating

decem annōs Graecī Trōiam oppugnant sed urbem
capere nōn possunt. tandem equum ingentem faciunt.
virōs fortissimōs ēligunt. illī equum ascendunt. cēterī
ad īnsulam vīcīnam nāvigant.

    nōs nāvēs vidēmus abeuntēs. ex urbe eximus.
gaudēmus quod bellum cōnfectum est. equum in urbem
trahimus. tum magnificē cēnāmus et multum vīnum
bibimus.

    nox est. ego dormiō. in somnō Hectorem mortuum
videō. ille 'fuge, Aeneā,' inquit; 'hostēs habent mūrōs.
Trōia corruit. nōn potes patriam servāre. fuge, et
novam Trōiam in aliā terrā conde.'

    somnum excutiō. clāmōrēs audiō. ad tēctum
ascendō et urbem ārdentem videō. arma āmēns capiō et
in viās currō. comitēs, quī in viīs errant, colligō.
Graecōs in tenebrīs oppugnāmus et multōs
interficimus. sed Graecī ubīque vincunt; iam tōta urbs
ārdet.

    subitō patris imāgō in animum venit. domum
recurrō territus. ibi pater et fīlius et uxor ānxiī
exspectant. iubeō eōs urbem ārdentem mēcum
relinquere. patrem senem in umerīs portō; parvum
fīlium manū capiō; uxōrem iubeō pōne īre. per hostēs,
per tenebrās ad portās currimus.

decem annōs for ten years

fortissimōs the bravest
ēligunt select

vīcīnam nearby
abeuntēs going away
bellum war
confectum finished
trahimus we drag; **vīnum** wine
somnō sleep

corruit is falling
patriam your country

excutiō I shake off
tēctum roof
ārdentem on fire
āmēns madly; **arma** arms
quī who; **colligō** I gather
tenebrīs darkness
ubīque everywhere

imāgō thought; **animum** mind
uxor wife
mēcum with me
umerīs shoulders
manū by the hand
pōne behind

ubi ad collem advenīmus extrā portās, cōnsistimus. respiciō, sed uxōrem vidēre nōn possum. patrem et fīlium iubeō ibi manēre, ego in urbem recurrō. ubīque uxōrem quaerō, sed frūstrā. tandem ad patrem fīliumque trīstis reveniō. ubi ad collem adveniō, multōs comitēs inveniō quī ex urbe ārdentī fūgerant. diēs iam lūcet cum patrem et fīlium et comitēs ad montēs dūcō.

extrā outside;
cōnsistimus we stop
respiciō I look back
ubīque everywhere
frūstrā in vain

inveniō I find; **fūgerant** had fled
lūcet is dawning
cum when

1 When Aeneas wakes up, what does he do?
2 'arma āmēns capiō.' Why does he describe his behaviour as mad?
3 What makes him run home?
4 Describe his departure from home.
5 Why does Aeneas run back into Troy?
6 What does he find when he returns to his family?
7 When and where does he lead his companions?
8 Translate into Latin:
   (a) The enemy attack and take the city.
   (b) Aeneas leads his father and son to the gate.
   (c) At last they reach the mountain safe.

Aeneas leaves Troy.

VIRGIL AND THE AENEID

Horace's friend Publius Vergilius Maro, known in English as Virgil, was born in 70 BC and so was five years older than Horace. He was brought up on his father's farm at Mantua in North Italy, and completed his education in Rome and Naples. He belonged to a group of poets who celebrated in their work the first Roman Emperor Augustus. Horace, who described Virgil as 'half of my soul', was also one of the group.

   Virgil's greatest poem was the *Aeneid*. It was in twelve books, begun in 29 BC and still unfinished at his death in 19 BC. Its central figure, as we have seen in Chapter 8, is Aeneas, the son of Venus and the Trojan Anchises. The story tells how he flees from the smoking ruins of

Virgil, flanked by two of the Muses

70

Troy and travels to Italy where Destiny plans that he should found the Roman race.

We now describe the events of that dreadful night in more detail than was possible in the Latin.

On the night when their city fell the Trojans held joyful celebrations, wrongly believing that the Greeks had given up their siege and departed. The whole of Troy was buried in slumber and wine. The ghost of Hector appeared to Aeneas as he lay sleeping. Aeneas was horribly shocked by his appearance, for he was black with the dust through which Achilles had dragged him when he killed him. But Hector paid no attention to Aeneas's reaction, and told him that Troy was now in the enemy's hands. He ordered him to rescue the Trojan gods from the burning city and to sail away to found a new Troy in some other country.

Aeneas was now thoroughly awakened by the noise of the fighting, and climbing to the top of his house he saw the flames which were sweeping through the city. Hector's instructions vanished from his mind and he ran into the streets where he fought with tremendous courage, killing many Greeks. A dreadful sight met his eyes as he rushed along. He saw Achilles's son slaughter King Priam on the step of the altar itself. Aeneas's anger burned fiercely as he sought vengeance for the destruction of Troy.

But now his mother Venus appeared to him and reminded him that his duty was to his family. He must try, she said, to bring them to safety. Aeneas realized that she was right. There was no longer anything he could do for Troy. He rushed back to his house, gathered together his followers and made his way from the city. He bore on his shoulders his father, who carried the little statues of the household gods, and he held his son by the hand. His wife followed them as they set out on this terrifying journey.

Suddenly Aeneas was aware that his wife was no longer behind him. Desperately he ran back into the city, now eerily still, calling her name again and again, but there was no answer. Finally her ghost appeared to him. She told him that she was dead. He must set out for the new land which awaited him. Three times Aeneas attempted to fling his arms around his wife. Three times his wife's ghost dissolved in his embrace like the light winds.

He returned sadly to his companions who were safely hidden in a hollow valley in the mountains by Troy. A dangerous and uncertain future awaited them.

Imagine that you are a Greek hidden in the wooden horse. Describe what happens to you and what you do.

In the first part of the *Aeneid*, Aeneas continually fails to do the right thing. How does he fail in what you have read so far? How does he succeed?

CHAPTER X

Iuppiter īrātus est, quod Aenēās in Libyā cessat.
Mercurium, deōrum nūntium, ad Aenēam mittit.

Mercurius per caelum volat et advenit ad
lītus Libyae.

Mercurius Aenēam monet; omnia
imperia Iovis nūntiat.

ⓖ Neuter gender

In Latin most nouns, as we have seen, are either masculine or
feminine in gender; a smaller number are neuter, that is neither
masculine nor feminine.

1 There are no neuter nouns of the first declension.
2 Second declension neuter nouns end in **-um** in nominative and
   accusative singular; **-a** in nominative and accusative plural;
   otherwise they decline like other second declension nouns. Thus
   bellum declines

	singular	*plural*
nom.	bellum	bella
acc.	bellum	bella
gen.	bellī	bellōrum

In vocabulary lists such words appear:
bellum, **bellī**, *n.* war

Learn the following second declension neuter nouns

caelum sky, heaven **imperium** order
cōnsilium plan **perīculum** danger

3 Third declension; many neuter nouns end **-us**, others **-en** in
nominative singular.

Learn

	singular	*plural*
nom.	lītus	lītora
acc.	lītus	lītora
gen.	lītoris	lītorum

lītus, lītoris, *n.*   shore
tempus, temporis, *n.* time
flūmen, flūminis, *n.* river
nōmen, nōminis, *n.* name
mare, maris, *n.*   sea

Note that in all neuter nouns, nominative and accusative endings are
the same.

Adjectives have all three genders, thus

	singular				*plural*		
	masc.	*fem.*	*neuter*		*masc.*	*fem.*	*neuter*
nom.	bonus	bona	bonum		bonī	bonae	bona
acc.	bonum	bonam	bonum		bonōs	bonās	bona
gen.	bonī	bonae	bonī		bonōrum	bonārum	bonōrum

Revise these endings carefully.

Third declension adjectives have the same endings for masculine and feminine

	masc.	*fem.*	*neuter*		*masc.*	*fem.*	*neuter*
nom.	omnis	omnis	omne		omnēs	omnēs	omnia
acc.	omnem	omnem	omne		omnēs	omnēs	omnia
gen.	omnis	omnis	omnis		omnium	omnium	omnium

Exercise 10.1

*Analyse (joining adjectives to the nouns
they agree with by a hyphen, e.g. **bonus-
rēx**) and translate*

1 Trōiānī multa perīcula subeunt. **subeunt** undergo
2 rēx bonum cōnsilium prōpōnit. **prōpōnit** puts forward

3 Aenēās comitēs iubet ad lītus Italiae
   nāvigāre.
4 labōrāte, puerī; nōn dēbētis tempus
   terere.   **terere** waste
5 puella ad magnum flūmen accēdit sed
   timet trānsīre.   **trānsīre** to cross

Exercise 10.2

Translate
1 omnia bellī perīcula superāmus, amīcī.
2 nōlīte in mare inīre; nōn tūtum est.
3 puerī currunt ad flūmen, quod natāre   **natāre** to swim
   cupiunt.
4 rēx ad caelum spectat et deōs ōrat.   **ōrat** prays to
5 Aenēās dēbet deōrum imperia
   perficere.   **perficere** carry out

Exercise 10.3

Translate into Latin
1 The king prepares war against the   against **in** + **accusative**
   Trojans.
2 We cannot cross the great river.   cross **trānsīre**
3 The girls are approaching the banks of
   the river.
4 Hasten to the sea, comrades, and
   board the ships.
5 Do not listen to the king's plan.   I listen to **audiō**
6 We are overcoming the greatest
   dangers; we must not despair.
7 Sail to the nearest shore; do not waste   nearest **proximus-a-um**
   time.   to waste **perdere**

Exercise 10.4

*In the following phrases put the right
endings on to the adjectives to make them
agree with the nouns*

magn– silvam   rēgem trīst–   magn– flūmen   puerōrum miser–
bon– mātrem   patris fess–   mult– urbēs   hominum mal–
long– bellum   urbis nov–   omn– puerī   tōt– noctem
mult– perīcula   fīliam mortu–   long– lītus

INFELIX DIDO

īnfēlīx ill-starred

ubi Aenēās fīnem dīcendī facit, omnēs tacitī sedent.
tandem Dīdō hospitēs dīmittit. servum iubet Trōiānōs
ad cubiculum dūcere. mox omnēs dormiunt; sed Dīdō
dormīre nōn potest. per tōtam noctem Aenēam et
labōrēs Trōiānōrum in animō volvit.

fīnem dīcendī an end of speaking
hospitēs guests; dīmittit sends away
cubiculum bedroom

volvit turns over

Dido and Aeneas

Aenēās et Trōiānī post tantōs labōrēs valdē fessī
sunt. cōnstituunt in Libyā manēre et quiēscere. intereā
Dīdō Aenēam amāre incipit; semper Aenēam spectat;
Aenēam etiam absentem audit et videt. Aenēās quoque
Dīdōnem amat. itaque per tōtam hiemem in Libyā
manet et Dīdōnem iuvat, dum novam urbem aedificat.
Dīdō Aenēam coniugem vocat; Aenēae fīlium,
Ascanium, cūrat et amat. valdē laetī sunt.

quiēscere to rest
incipit begins
absentem absent; quoque also
hiemem winter
aedificat builds; coniugem husband

sed rēx deōrum, Iuppiter, Aenēam dē caelō
spectat in Libyā cessantem; īrātus est, quod Aenēās,
fātī immemor, in Libyā cessat; nam dēbet ad Italiam
venīre et novam Trōiam condere. itaque Iuppiter
Mercurium, nūntium deōrum, vocat et, 'ī nunc,' inquit,
'Mercurī, et Aenēam monē; non dēbet ille in Libyā
cessāre sed statim ad Italiam nāvigāre.'

cessantem tarrying
fātī immemor forgetful of destiny

Mercurius patris imperia audit; tālāria induit et
statim de caelō ad Libyam volat. Aenēam videt arcem
aedificantem. statim ad eum accēdit et eum monet:
'audī mē, Aenēā,' inquit, 'ego sum Mercurius, deōrum
nūntius; Iuppiter, rēx et pater deōrum, mē mittit. nōlī
diūtius in Libyā cessāre. dēbēs ad Italiam festīnāre et
novam Trōiam condere.'

tālāria winged sandals;
induit puts on
volat flies; arcem
aedificantem building the citadel

diūtius any longer

Aenēās, ubi Mercurium ante oculōs videt monitumque deōrum audit, territus est. fugere cupit sed nōn potest. ad comitēs redit et iubet eōs nāvēs parāre. tum Dīdōnem invītus petit. 'ō rēgīna,' inquit, 'Mercurius mē ante oculōs monet. mē iubet statim abīre. nam Iuppiter īrātus est quod in Libyā cessō. dēbeō ad Italiam festīnāre et novam Trōiam condere.'

Dīdō cōnsternāta est et valdē īrāta. 'quid dīcis, Aenēā?' inquit; 'tu nunc cōnstituis mē prōdere? sīc omnia beneficia mea rependis? sed ego tē nōn retineō. ī nunc. Italiam pete. sed tē moneō; quod tū mē prōdis et amōrem meum spernis, ultiōnem dīram exspectā. sērius ōcius aut ego aut posterī ultiōnem dīram exigent.'

Aenēās trīstis et commōtus est sed imperia deōrum perficere dēbet. postrīdiē prīmā lūce Trōiānī nāvēs solvunt.

Dīdō, ubi diēs venit, ad mare spectat. nāvēs Trōiānōrum videt ad Italiam nāvigantēs. dēspērat. īra et furor animum vincunt. servōs iubet magnam pyram exstruere. pyram ascendit. gladium capit et pectus trānsfīgit. comitēs, ubi Dīdōnem mortuam vident, valdē commōtī sunt. rēgīnam lūgent et trīstēs pyram succendunt. fūmus ad caelum surgit.

intereā Aenēās, dum per mare festīnat, ad Libyam respicit. fūmum videt in caelum surgentem. valdē timet. 'quid accidit?' inquit; 'cūr fūmus ad caelum sīc surgit?' sed nōn potest redīre. trīstis et ānxius Italiam petit.

oculōs eyes; **monitum** warning

invītus reluctantly

cōnsternāta dismayed
prōdere to betray
beneficia kindnesses;
rependis repay;
retineō keep back
spernis reject; **ultiōnem dīram** terrible vengeance
sērius ōcius sooner or later;
posterī my descendants
exigent will exact
commōtus moved, upset
perficere carry out;
prīmā lūce at dawn
solvunt cast off

nāvigantēs sailing
furor madness
pyram pyre
exstruere to build;
pectus heart
trānsfīgit pierces
lūgent mourn for
succendunt light; **fūmus** smoke
respicit looks back;
surgentem rising
accidit is happening

Aenēās fūmum videt in caelum surgentem.

76

amō, amāre	I love	**meus-a-um**	my
regō, regere	I rule, control	**tuus-a-um**	your
amor, amōris, *m.*	love	**etiam**	also, even
animus, animī, *m.*	mind	**nunc**	now
gladius, gladiī, *m.*	sword	**aut ... aut**	either ... or
servus, servī, *m.*	slave	**post** + accusative	after
		dē + ablative	down from; about

Exercise 10.5

Translate the first two paragraphs. Answer the questions on the last two without translating

dum Trōiānī ad Italiam nāvigant, venit magna
tempestās. nūbēs caelum obscūrant; ventī mare tollunt.
gubernātor nāvēs regere nōn potest. Aenēam vocat et
'nōn possumus,' inquit, 'ad Italiam nāvigāre per tantam
tempestātem. dēbēmus ad proximum lītus festīnāre.'
Aenēās respondet: 'pete Siciliam. ego Siciliam libenter
revīsō, terram ubi pater sepultus est.'

    gubernātor nāvēs ad Siciliam dūcit. mox tūtī ad
lītus adveniunt. postrīdiē Aenēās comitēs convocat et
'Trōiānī,' inquit, 'diēs adest quō pater meus in hāc terrā
periit. iam tempus est ad tumulum īre et patris
memoriam colere.'

    sīc dīcit Aenēās et Trōiānōs ad tumulum dūcit. ubi
adveniunt Aenēās vīnum in terram fundit et flōrēs in
tumulum iacit. patrem salūtat: 'salvē, sāncte pater,'
inquit. sacrificia sollemnia facit. comitēs quoque dōna
ad tumulum ferunt.

    sīc Aenēās patris memoriam colit. ludōs etiam facit
et certāmina. aliī spectant, aliī certant. omnēs gaudent
et diem fēstum laetī agunt.

Margin glosses:
nūbēs clouds; **obscūrant** darken; **tollunt** raise
gubernātor helmsman
proximum nearest
libenter gladly
revīsō revisit; **ubi** where; **sepultus** buried
quō on which; **hāc** this
periit died; **tumulum** tomb
colere revere
fundit pours; **flōrēs** flowers
salvē hail; **sāncte** blessed
sollemnia proper
quoque also; **dōna** gifts
certāmina contests; **certant** compete; **diem fēstum** holiday
agunt keep

1 What does Aeneas do when he reaches his father's tomb?
2 What do his companions do?
3 How else does he commemorate his father's death? Does this seem
   to you a strange thing to do?
4 Give one English word derived from each of the following (which
   occur in the last two paragraphs): **vīnum, flōrēs, memoriam, fēstum**.
5 Give the nominative and genitive singular of the following nouns:
   terram, patrem, lūdōs.

6 Translate into Latin;

(a) We must sail to Sicilia.

(b) The Trojans reach the shore of Sicily.

(c) I am leading (my) companions to (my) father's tomb.

AENEAS DESCENDS TO THE UNDERWORLD

Anchises had given his son Aeneas much helpful support and advice while he was alive. Now he was dead, and Aeneas decided to undertake the perilous journey to the Underworld in order to consult him about how he should deal with the dangers which faced him in Italy.

Aeneas landed in South Italy near a place called Cumae where there was an entrance to the Underworld. Here he asked Apollo's priestess what he must do to succeed in his bold adventure. She replied that it was easy enough to go down to the Underworld; the problem was getting back. What Aeneas had to do was to find a golden branch which was hidden in the middle of a shady wood. This would act as a kind of passport. Aeneas would be able to break off the branch easily if the Fates wished him to go on this journey. If not, no efforts he made would succeed in removing it.

When Aeneas tried to find the wood, he was confronted with such a huge forest that he would have given up. But his mother Venus sent two doves, her special birds, to lead him to the branch. Guided by them, he soon saw it glittering through the green leaves. It resisted a little but he had no difficulty in breaking it off. He now took the branch to the priestess who was to act as his guide.

They descend through the gloomy jaws of the entrance to the Underworld and eventually come to the dreadful waters of the river Styx. Here a grim ferryman, the filthy old god Charon, ferries the souls over on his rust-coloured punt. He objects strongly to the idea of taking across the still-living Aeneas, but when the priestess shows him the golden branch, he gives way immediately. As Aeneas climbs on board, Charon's punt, which is designed for carrying weightless souls, groans beneath his bulk and lets in streams of water through its joints. However, it carries him safely across the river.

Aeneas has to face a new problem on the other bank. The monstrous three-headed dog Cerberus is on guard here. Snakes bristle on his three necks and he fills the kingdom of the dead with the barking from his three mouths. The priestess throws him a piece of meat treated with drugs. Greedily Cerberus opens his three throats and gobbles the food down. Immediately his huge frame collapses in unconsciousness and Aeneas is able to get by without danger.

Now he comes to that area of the Underworld where those who have killed themselves dwell. Here he is horrified to see Dido, since she had still been alive when he left Carthage. He realizes that she has been driven to suicide by her love for him, and he again tries to explain that he left her not because he wanted to but because the gods told him to. She is as unmoved by his speech as a rock and goes away from him in everlasting hatred.

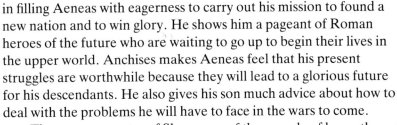
Cerberus

The gloom of Hell gives way after a time to a brighter light and finally Aeneas and his companion come to the Elysian fields. Here those happy souls live who are being rewarded for the good lives they have led on earth. Aeneas at last meets his father Anchises among them. Yet even here is sadness. Three times Aeneas attempts to fling his arms around his father. Three times his father's ghost dissolves in his embrace like the light winds. However, Anchises succeeds in filling Aeneas with eagerness to carry out his mission to found a new nation and to win glory. He shows him a pageant of Roman heroes of the future who are waiting to go up to begin their lives in the upper world. Anchises makes Aeneas feel that his present struggles are worthwhile because they will lead to a glorious future for his descendants. He also gives his son much advice about how to deal with the problems he will have to face in the wars to come.

There are two gates of Sleep, one of them made of horn, through which true spirits make their exit, and one of shining-white ivory, through which false dreams go to the upper world. Aeneas and the priestess leave the Underworld through the gates of ivory, and Aeneas then returns to his ships.

❓ Imagine that you have to descend to the Underworld. Describe your journey.

❓ Aeneas has to desert Dido with terrible consequences. Write two paragraphs, in one of which Aeneas defends his behaviour to Dido and in the other Dido condemns Aeneas for planning to leave her.

CHAPTER XI

Horātia mātrī flōrēs dat.

māter flōrēs fīliae reddit.

Horātia Quīntō flōrēs ostendit.

Quīntus Horātiae 'dā mihi flōrēs,' inquit;
'cupiō eōs comitibus ostendere.'

Quīntus flōrēs puellīs dat.

The dative case

You have already learnt the following cases

nominative   (subject)
accusative   (object, and after many prepositions, e.g. **ad**, **per**, etc.)
genitive   (=of)
ablative   (so far only used after certain prepositions, e.g. **ā**, **ē**)

The last case you have to learn is the *dative* case, which is used with
verbs which mean 'give to', 'say to', 'show to', etc., e.g.

pater fīliō dīcit	The father says to his son.
māter fīliae flōrēs dat	The mother gives flowers to her daughter.
rēx equum prīncipibus ostendit	The king shows the horse to his princes.

These datives are called 'indirect objects' and in analysis they should
be marked 'i.o.'

```
        s    i.o.    o    v
```
e.g. māter fīliae flōrēs dat

Who gives the flowers? **māter** – subject; what does she give? **flōrēs** –
object; who does the give them to? **fīliae** – indirect object.

The dative forms of the first three declensions are

	1st (puella)	*2nd* (dominus, puer, ager)	*3rd* (rēx)
singular	puell-ae	domin-ō, puer-ō, agr-ō	rēg-ī
plural	puell-īs	domin-īs, puer-īs, agr-īs	rēg-ibus

Note also: **mihi** to me, **tibi** to you, **eī** to him, to her

dā mihi flōrēs	Give the flowers to me (or 'give me the flowers')
fābulam tibi nārrō	I tell a story to you (or 'I tell you a story')
equum eī ostendō	I show the horse to him (or 'I show him the horse')

Exercise 11.1

*Analyse and translate each sentence in
two ways*
```
        s    i.o.    o    v
```
e.g. **fīlia mātrī flōrēs dat**
(1) The daughter gives flowers to her
mother
(2) The daughter gives her mother
flowers.

1 māter tibi flōrēs reddit.
2 magister puerīs fābulam nārrat.
3 puer comitibus omnia dīcit.
4 pater fīliō canem dat.
5 fīlius canem amīcīs ostendit.
6 amīcī canem eī reddunt.
7 māter mihi cēnam dat.

G '-que' and

māter paterque mother and father. Note that **-que** is added to the second of the two words joined.

Exercise 11.2

Translate
1 fīlius fīliaque patrem salūtant.
2 magister lūdum intrat puerōsque iubet sedēre.
3 pater Quīntum Horātiamque ad agrum dūcit.

G 'est' and 'sunt'

We have often met these with a complement, e.g.
cēna bona est; puerī laetī sunt.
They can also be used without a complement, e.g.
sunt multī flōrēs prope viam There are many flowers near the road.
est lupus in silvā There is a wolf in the wood.

Exercise 11.3

Translate
1 est equus in agrō.
2 sunt multae nāvēs in portū.
3 parva puella est in hortō.

    portū harbour

Exercise 11.4

Put the words in brackets into the correct case and translate
1 puer equum (amīcus) ostendit.
2 Scintilla (fīlia) aquam dat.
3 puer librum (magister) reddit.
4 Horātia Quīntusque (comitēs) omnia dīcunt.
5 māter (cēna) (vir) (fīlius)que dat.

Exercise 11.5

Translate into Latin
1 Horatia shows the beautiful flowers to her brother.
2 There is a horse in the field; tell father.
3 There are many ships near the shore; come and see them.
4 Mother is telling Horatia a story; they are in the garden.
5 The old man gives the boys advice but they do not listen.

    tell (imperative) **dīc**
    story **fābula, fābulae,** *f.*

HORATIA ARGUM SERVAT

postrīdiē Quīntus ad lūdum nōn it. fēriae sunt. patrī dīcit: 'nōnne mē ad agrum dūcis? nam tē iuvāre cupiō.' Flaccus fīliō respondit: 'libenter tē dūcō. Quīnte. venī mēcum. sed Argum in casā relinque. nam malus canis est. leporēs semper petit nec redit, cum eum vocās. nōn possumus eum quaerere tōtum diem.' itaque Quīntus

    postrīdiē the next day
    fēriae sunt there is a holiday
    libenter gladly
    relinque leave
    leporēs hares
    cum when

Argum in hortō inclūdit et cum Flaccō ad agrum prōcēdit.

    sed Scintilla eum revocat. 'manē, Quīnte,' inquit. 'ego cibum parō tibi patrīque.' itaque Quīntus in hortō cum Argō lūdit, dum māter cibum parat. mox Scintilla ē culīnā exit cibumque Quīntō dat. Quīntus Argum in hortō relinquit lentēque ad agrum prōcēdit. Argus trīstis est, quod Quīntus eum ad agrum nōn dūcit. miserē lātrat et ēvādere temptat, sed nōn potest. tandem sub arbore iacet et dormit.

    intereā Scintilla ligna in culīnam portat furnumque succendit. nam pānem facere dēbet. deinde Horātiae 'venī,' inquit, 'Horātia; ad fontem īre dēbēmus. nūlla aqua est in casā.' duās urnās ē culīnā portat ūnamque fīliae dat. Argum in casā inclūdunt et lentē ad fontem prōcēdunt.

    sunt multī flōrēs prope viam. dum prōcēdunt, Horātia flōrēs carpit corōnamque facit. corōnam mātrī dat. Scintilla eam laudat sed fīliae reddit. 'corōna valdē pulchra est,' inquit, 'sed nōlī eam mihi dare. tū eam indue; nam tū quoque pulchra es.' Horātia gaudet corōnamque induit.

    Horātia amīculam videt in viā, nōmine Pyrrham. accurrit et 'manē, Pyrrha,' inquit; 'quō īs?' illa Horātiae respondet: 'ego ad fontem eō. māter mē ibi exspectat.' Horātia 'nōs quoque ad fontem īmus,' inquit; 'venī nōbīscum.' corōnam Pyrrhae ostendit. 'ecce!' inquit, 'corōnam spectā. nōnne pulchra est?' Pyrrha respondet: 'valdē pulchra est. dā eam mihi.' sed Horātia corōnam Pyrrhae dare nōn vult. Pyrrha temptat eam rapere. corōna frācta est. Horātia Pyrrham pulsat. et illa et Horātia lacrimant. Scintilla eīs 'nōlīte lacrimāre,' inquit. 'sunt multī flōrēs prope viam. duās corōnās celeriter facere potestis.'

    itaque Horātia novam corōnam facit Pyrrhaeque eam dat. Pyrrha corōnam splendidam facit, quam Horātiae dat. puellae corōnas induunt laetaeque ad fontem prōcēdunt.

    ubi adveniunt, multae fēminae iam adsunt. aliae ad fontem urnās ferunt, aliae aquam dūcunt. Scintilla vīcīnam videt salūtatque. illa 'quid agis, Scintilla?' inquit. 'cūr tam sērō ad fontem venīs?' Scintilla eī respondet: 'valdē occupāta eram. vir fīliusque ad agrum eunt; ego cibum eīs parō; deinde ligna portō furnumque succendō; nam pānem hodiē faciō. ergō sērō ad fontem adsumus.'

---

inclūdit shuts in

cibum food; **tibi** for you

lātrat barks; **ēvādere** escape

intereā meanwhile; **ligna** firewood; **furnum** oven **succendit** lights; **pānem** bread **fontem** spring **urnās** water pots **inclūdunt** shut in

carpit picks; **corōnam** garland

indue put on; **quoque** also

amīculam friend

nōbīscum with us

nōn vult refuses **rapere** to snatch; **frācta** broken **pulsat** hits; **lacrimant** cry

quam which

aliae . . . aliae some . . . others

vīcīnam a neighbour; **quid agis?** how are you?

occupāta eram I was busy

ergō and so

Horātia Argum ē casā ārdentī trahit.

illa 'nōnne ānxia es?' inquit; 'nōnne furnum cūrāre
dēbēs?' Scintilla eī respondet: 'nōn ānxia sum. statim
ad casam redīmus.'

sed Scintilla, ubi vīcīnam audit, rē vērā ānxia est.
urnam celeriter complet Horātiamque quaerit. illa cum
Pyrrhā lūdit. Scintilla 'festīnā, Horātia,' inquit; 'nōlī
cessāre. dēbēmus ad casam celeriter redīre furnumque
cūrāre.'

Horātia urnam celeriter complet et post mātrem
festīnat. urna gravis est. Horātia eam in capite portat.
quod festīnat, viam nōn spectat. via līmōsa est. Horātia
lāpsat; urna dē capite cadit in terram; frācta est; omnis
aqua effluit. Horātia in terrā sedet et mātrem vocat.
'ēheu!' clāmat, 'urna frācta est. ō māter, redī.
succurre!'

Scintilla, ubi fīliam audit, celeriter recurrit. ubi
urnam videt frāctam, īrāta est. 'ō fīlia,' inquit, 'quam
neglegēns es! quid facis? cūr in terrā iacēs? surge. curre
ad casam. aliam urnam ad fontem portā. festīnā.'

Horātia surgit et ad casam festīnat. sed ubi accēdit,
fumum videt ad caelum surgentem. cōnsistit territa.
deinde Argum audit miserē lātrantem. currit ad casam.
ubi advenit, fūmus ē iānuā exundat. Horātia Argum
vocat sed canis nōn respondet. statim in casam ruit;
Argum videt prope iānuam iacentem, semimortuum.

rē vērā in fact
complet fills

cessāre idle, dawdle

in capite on her head
līmōsa muddy
lāpsat slips
effluit flows out
ēheu! oh dear!
succurre! help!

quam neglegēns how careless
surge get up!

fūmum smoke; surgentem
rising; cōnsistit she stops
lātrantem barking
exundat is billowing

iacentem lying;
semimortuum half-dead

84

canem ē iānuā trahit et prope viam relinquit. iānuam claudit et recurrit ad mātrem.

    Scintilla ā fonte lentē prōcēdit. subitō fūmum videt. valdē ānxia est. cōnsistit urnamque dēpōnit. sibi dīcit: 'dī immortālēs! quid accidit? fūmus ē casā nostrā surgit?'

    eō ipsō tempore Horātia advenit matrīque omnia nārrat. Scintilla territa est. 'curre ad agrum,' inquit. 'patrem Quīntumque vocā.' Horātia ad agrum quam celerrimē currit. ubi advenit, Flaccus in ultimā parte agrī labōrat. Horātia clāmat et 'ō pater,' inquit, 'venī, succurre! ārdet casa.' Flaccus attonitus est. 'dī immortālēs,' inquit, 'venī, Quīnte. festīnā!' omnēs ad casam currunt.

    ubi adveniunt, multōs hominēs vident discurrentēs. nam vīcīnī conveniunt Scintillamque iuvant. aliī aquam ferunt, aliī aquam in flammās īnfundunt. mox flammās exstinguunt. culīna tōta combusta est, sed relīquam casam servant.

    Scintilla valdē commōta est. virō dīcit: 'mea culpa est, mī vir. neglegēns eram.' Flaccus nōn īrātus est sed Scintillam laudat quod casam tam fortiter servat. deinde Argum quaerunt. ille in hortō est; sub arbore dormit, omnīnō recreātus. omnēs gaudent. Quīntus Horātiae 'tū quoque valdē fortis es,' inquit, 'quae Argum ē flammīs ēripuistī.'

    Horātia rubēscit; valdē laeta est, quod frāter rārissimē eam laudat.

trahit	drags
claudit	shuts
dēpōnit	puts down; **sibi** to herself
dī immortālēs!	immortal gods;
accidit	is happening
eō ipsō tempore	at that very moment
quam celerrimē	at full speed
ultimā	furthest
ārdet	is on fire;
attonitus	astounded
discurrentēs	running about
aliī . . . aliī . . .	some . . . others . . .
īnfundunt	pour on;
exstinguunt	put out
combusta	burnt;
relīquam	the rest of
culpa	fault
mī vir	my husband; **neglegēns** careless; **eram** I was
omnīnō recreātus	completely recovered
quoque	also; **quae** who
ēripuistī	rescued
rubēscit	blushes
rārissimē	very seldom

cūrō, cūrāre	I care for, look after	**pulcher, pulchra, pulchrum**	pretty, beautiful
dō, dare	I give		
temptō, temptāre	I try	**gravis, grave**	heavy
cadō, cadere	I fall	**nūllus-a-um**	no
discēdō, discēdere	I leave, go away	**duo**	two
ostendō, ostendere	I show		
prōcēdō, prōcēdere	I go forward, go on	**contrā** + accusative	against
reddō, reddere	I give back, return	**cum** + ablative	with
ferō (3)	I carry; I bear	**mēcum**	with me
		tēcum	with you
fēmina, fēminae, *f.*	a woman	**itaque**	and so, therefore
flōs, flōris, *m.*	flower	**nec**	nor, and not
frāter, frātris, *m.*	brother	**nec/neque . . .**	neither . . . nor
pars, partis, *f.*	part	**nec/neque**	

Exercise 11.6

Give one English word derived from each of the following
prōcēdō, fēmina, vir, pars, duo

Exercise 11.7

Put the words underlined into the correct case and translate
1 nūlla aqua est in casā. Scintilla Horātia vocat.
2 māter urna fīlia dat et 'cāra fīlia,' inquit, 'curre ad
   fontem et aquam mihi portā.'   **mihi** for me
3 Horātia prōcēdit ad fontem sed in viā Quīntus videt,
   quī redit ab agrō cum patre.
4 Horātia urna Quīntus dat et 'cāre frāter,' inquit,
   'curre ad fontem et aqua mātrī portā.'   **mātrī** for mother
5 Quīntus urnam accipit festīnatque ad fontem. redit
   ad casam ubi comitēs videt. illī eum lūdere iubent. **ubi** where
   sed Quīntus urna comitēs ostendit et 'aquam' inquit
   'dēbeō mātrī portāre.'
6 illī urnam rapiunt aquamque in terram effundunt.   **effundunt** spill
   tum urnam Quīntus reddunt. Quīntus īrātus ad
   fontem recurrit.

ROMULUS AND REMUS

Aeneas left the Underworld and went to the area in central Italy
where Rome now stands. He had to fight a series of terrible battles
with the local tribes, the Latins, but at last he managed to win peace.
His travels were finally over and he married a Latin princess called
Lavinia. The Trojans now called themselves Latins and built a
settlement called Lavinium after Aeneas's new wife. We are now
studying the language and culture of these Italian Trojans.

When Aeneas died, Ascanius, his son by his first marriage,
became ruler. After a time, Ascanius left his step-mother to rule the
now flourishing town of Lavinium and founded his own settlement in
the Alban hills, Alba Longa. Thirteen generations later, the rightful
king Numitor was driven from the throne by his younger brother,
Amulius. Numitor's sons were killed and his daughter, Rhea Silvia,
was made a Vestal Virgin. This appeared to be an honour, but, since it
meant that she was not allowed to marry, it was Amulius's way of
making sure that she had no heirs.

However, the gods took an interest in this new nation, which they
had destined to rule the world. Mars, the god of War, made love to

Rhea Silvia who gave birth to twin boys. Understandably Amulius was furious. He imprisoned the mother and condemned the sons to be drowned in the river Tiber.

However, the river was flooded and it proved impossible to reach its main current. So the boys were left in a basket by the edge of the flood-water which, it was thought, would now sweep them away. But the waters in fact went down and the twins were found by a she-wolf who gave them milk and licked them as if they were her own cubs. The king's herdsman came upon this strange scene and took the boys to his hut. He and his wife brought them up and gave them the names of Romulus and Remus.

Father Tiber with the she-wolf and Romulus and Remus

When they grew up, they killed Amulius and brought back their grandfather Numitor as ruler of Alba Longa in his place. But they wanted to found a new settlement on the spot where they had been left to die and then been saved by the she-wolf. There were seven hills here above the river Tiber.

However, since the young men were twins, it was unclear who should be king of the new settlement and they decided to consult the gods. Remus, standing on the Aventine Hill, received the sign of six vultures, but Romulus, who took his stand on the Palatine Hill, then saw twelve.

The Capitoline Wolf

The matter was not settled, since Remus's sign had appeared first but Romulus's was double his brother's in number. Remus then provoked his brother by jumping over the small wall he was building. Romulus, in a rage, struck him over the head with his spade and killed him. 'May all who leap over my walls perish thus!' he exclaimed.

The new city was called Rome after Romulus, and the traditional date of its founding is 753 BC. It was right that Rome should prove outstanding in war, since Romulus was the son of Mars. But it was likely that much strife would follow, as he had committed the terrible crime of killing his brother.

? Read the story of the birth of Moses in the Bible (Exodus, chapter 2, verses 1 to 10). Compare this story with the story of Romulus and Remus.

CHAPTER XII

Scintilla cēnam parat. Horātia in culīnā sē lavat.

Scintilla 'festīnā, Horātia,' inquit; 'parā tē ad cēnam.'

Quīntus Horātiaque Argum in agrō exercent.

puerī in hortō sē exercent.

Flaccus eōs rogat: 'quid facitis, puerī?' il respondent: 'nōs exercēmus, pater.'

QUINTUS MILITES SPECTAT

A larārium. Three household gods and a sacred serpent

cotīdiē Flaccus prīmā lūce tōtam familiam convocat et ad Larārium dūcit. vīnum in terram ante Larēs fundit flōrēsque iacit. deōs ōrat familiam cūrāre et pecora servāre. deinde ille ad agrōs festīnat, Quīntus ad lūdum. sed hodiē Flaccus 'diēs fēstus est,' inquit. 'Parīlia celebrāmus. vōs parāte.' Quīntus gaudet, quod non dēbet ad lūdum īre, Horātia gaudet quod nōn dēbet mātrem in casā iuvāre.

ubi omnēs parātī sunt, Flaccus familiam in viam dūcit. multī hominēs iam ad agrōs laetī festīnant, virī, fēminae, puerī. Horātia Quīntusque amīcōs vident salūtantque. multī flōrēs prope viam sunt. puerī flōrēs carpunt; corōnās faciunt puellīsque dant.

mox ad locum sacrum adveniunt ubi Parīlia celebrāre dēbent. omnēs tacitī manent, dum sacerdōs vīnum in terram fundit et Palem prō agricolīs ōrat: 'alma Palēs,' inquit, 'servā pecora; morbōs arcē; agnās cūrā.' omnēs carmen sacrum canunt. tum ad lūdōs sē parant. multum vīnum bibunt cibumque edunt. stipulās ferunt magnōsque acervōs faciunt; acervōs accendunt; flammae ad caelum ascendunt multusque fūmus. iuvenēs acervōs fortiter trānsiliunt, dum cēterī clāmant plauduntque.

Quīntus quoque acervōs trānsilīre cupit sed pater eum prohibet; 'nōlī acervōs trānsilīre,' inquit; 'nimis parvus es. in flammās cadēs.' itaque Quīntus tacitus sedet et, dum pater māterque iuvenēs spectant, vīnum bibit.

subitō amīcus ad eum accurrit, nōmine Gāius. 'age, Quīnte,' inquit, 'venī mēcum. mīlitēs ad oppidum contendunt.' Quīntus 'quid dīcis? mīlitēs ad oppidum prōcēdunt? multīne sunt?' 'ita vērō,' eī respondet, 'multa mīlia. venī celeriter.'

cotīdiē every day; **prīmā lūce** at dawn
fundit pours
pecora flocks

hodiē today; **diēs fēstus** feast day

parātī ready

carpunt pick
locum place
sacerdōs priest
prō on behalf of
alma kindly; **morbōs arcē** keep off diseases; **agnās** lambs
carmen song
cibum food; **edunt** eat
stipulās straw
acervōs heaps; **accendunt** light
iuvenēs young men
trānsiliunt jump through
plaudunt clap
quoque also
prohibet stops; **nimis** too
cadēs you will fall
subitō suddenly
age come on!

ita vērō yes indeed
mīlia thousands

Quīntus Gāiusque ad oppidum recurrunt. ubi adveniunt, mīlitēs in oppidum iam intrant et per viās contendunt. prīmus venit imperātor; palūdāmentum purpureum gerit et in equō magnō vectus exercitum dūcit; post eum equitant lēgātī.

trēs legiōnēs post lēgātōs contendunt; signiferī legiōnēs dūcunt, quī signa fulgentia ferunt. post eōs veniunt centuriōnēs mīlitēsque gregāriī. puerī spectant attonitī.

iam multī agricolārum ab agrīs reveniunt mīlitēsque spectant. senex quīdam, quī prope Quīntum stat, 'ecce,' inquit, 'Crassus ad bellum prōcēdit, homō pūtidus. populum Rōmānum nōn cūrat sed suam glōriam augēre cupit. sine dubiō mīlitēs ad mortem dūcit.' in terram īnspuit et domum abit.

Quīntus eum nōn audit sed mīlitēs laetus spectat. iam novissimī mīlitum praetereunt agricolaeque domum abeunt. sed Quīntus plūra vidēre cupit. Gāiō 'venī mēcum,' inquit. Gāium manū capit et post mīlitēs festīnat.

Crassus exercitum ē portīs oppidī dūcit in agrōs apertōs. diū contendunt. tum Crassus manum tollit; exercitus cōnsistit. Crassus imperia lēgātīs dat; illī ad legiōnēs equitant et imperia centuriōnibus dant. centuriōnēs mīlitēs iubent castra pōnere. statim omnēs ad opera festīnant. centuriōnēs castra in terrā signant, mīlitēs vāllum faciunt. ante sōlis occāsum omnia parāta sunt. mīlitēs cēnant et cubitum eunt.

Quīntus Gāiusque omnia ē colle vīcīnō spectant, parentum immemorēs. sed iam nox est. Gāius 'age, Quīnte,' inquit 'domum recurrere dēbēmus. nox est. sine dubiō parentēs ānxiī sunt et īrātī.' puerī iam timent. nox obscūra est, nūlla lūna; viam vix vidēre possunt. sed Quīntus Gāium manū capit et fortiter per umbrās dūcit. tandem tūtī ad portās oppidī veniunt.

Quīntus Gāium valēre iubet et domum currit. ibi

mīlitēs per viās oppidī contendunt.

imperātor general
palūdāmentum purpureum a purple cloak
vectus riding
equitant ride
lēgātī the officers
signiferī standard-bearers
quī who; **signa fulgentia** shining standards
gregāriī ordinary
quīdam a certain

pūtidus rotten
suam his own; **augēre** to increase; **sine dubiō** without doubt
īnspuit spits
novissimī the last
praetereunt are passing by
plūra more
manū by the hand

apertōs open; **tollit** raises
cōnsistit halts

opera work; **signant** mark out
vāllum rampart; **sōlis occāsum** sunset
cubitum to bed
vīcīnō nearby
immemorēs unmindful of

sine dubiō without doubt
obscūra dark; **lūna** moon
vix scarcely

umbrās shadows
valēre iubet bids goodbye

90

Scintillam Horātiamque invenit trīstēs et ānxiās.   **invenit** finds
Scintilla surgit et currit ad eum: 'ō Quīnte,' inquit 'tūtus
es. deīs grātiās agō. pater valdē īrātus est. tē quaerit in   **grātiās agō** I give thanks
agrīs. ubi fuistī?' Quīntus omnia mātrī nārrat et patrem   **fuistī** have you been
ānxius exspectat. Scintilla eum bāsiat Horātiamque   **bāsiat** kisses
iubet cēnam frātrī ferre.   **frātrī** for her brother; **ferre** to
       bring
     tandem revenit Flaccus, īrātus et valdē ānxius.
Scintilla audit eum intrantem; currit ad eum et 'mī vir,'   **intrantem** coming in
inquit, 'Quīntus adest. tūtus est. nōlī nimis īrātus esse.'   **nimis** too
     Flaccus in culīnam festīnat Quīntumque rogat 'ubi
fuistī? cūr parentēs sīc vexās? malus puer es.' Quīntus   **vexās** worry
omnia patrī nārrat veniamque ōrat. Flaccus gaudet   **veniam** pardon
quod fīlius tūtus est et iam minus īrātus est. 'nōlī   **minus** less
unquam,' inquit, 'tāle iterum facere. ī nunc cubitum.'   **unquam** ever; **tāle** such a
       thing; **cubitum** to bed

ōrō, ōrāre	I pray, beg	**centuriō, centuriōnis,** *m.*	centurion
contendō, contendere	I march, hasten	**legiō, legiōnis,** *f.*	legion
gerō, gerere	I carry, wear	**mīles, mīlitis,** *m.*	soldier
pōnō, pōnere	I place, put	**mors, mortis,** *f.*	death
		opus, operis, *n.*	work
agricola, agricolae, *m.*	farmer	**parēns, parentis,** *c.*	parent
familia, familiae, *f.*	household, family	**exercitus,** *m.*	army
glōria, glōriae, *f.*	glory		
cōpiae, cōpiārum, *f. pl.*	forces	**prīmus-a-um**	first
populus, populī, *m.*	people	**sacer, sacra, sacrum**	sacred
oppidum, oppidī, *n.*	town		
vīnum, vīnī, *n.*	wine	**ante** + accusative	before
arma, armōrum, *n.pl.*	arms	**ubi?**	where
castra, castrōrum, *n.pl.*	camp	**domus,** * **domī,** *f.*	home
castra pōnere	to pitch camp	**cum** (conjunction)	when

*NB **domum festīnō** I hurry home; no preposition is used with **domus**.

Further examples of compound verbs (see Chapter 4, page 27)

eō I go; **abeō** I go away; **adeō** I go to, approach; **exeō** I go out of; **redeō**
I go back.

NB **con** together: **convocō** I call together
     dē down: **dēdūcō** I lead down
     prō forwards: **prōdūcō** I lead forward

What is the meaning of the following compound verbs?

addūcō, indūcō, dēdūcō, prōdūcō, redūcō
im (=in) mittō, ēmittō, dēmittō, remittō advveniō, conveniō, reveniō, ēveniō
ac (=ad) currō, incurrō, dēcurrō, concurrō, prōcurrō, recurrō.

Ⓖ Revision

You now know all the cases of the nouns of the first three declensions.
They are set out in the table below, which should be carefully learnt.

singular	1st (f.)	2nd (m.)	2nd (n.)	3rd (m./f.)	3rd (n.)
nominative (subject)	puell-a	domin-us	bell-um	rēx	lītus
accusative (object & after some prepositions)	puell-am	domin-um	bell-um	rēg-em	lītus
genitive (=of)	puell-ae	domin-ī	bell-ī	rēg-is	lītor-is
dative (=to or for)	puell-ae	domin-ō	bell-ō	rēg-ī	lītor-ī
ablative (at present used only after some prepositions)	puell-ā	domin-ō	bell-ō	rēg-e	lītor-e

plural					
nominative	puell-ae	domin-ī	bell-a	rēg-ēs	lītor-a
accusative	puell-ās	domin-ōs	bell-a	rēg-ēs	lītor-a
genitive	puell-ārum	domin-ōrum	bell-ōrum	rēg-um	lītor-um
dative	puell-īs	domin-īs	bell-īs	rēg-ibus	lītor-ibus
ablative	puell-īs	domin-īs	bell-īs	rēg-ibus	lītor-ibus

Exercise 12.1

Make adjectives agree with nouns
1 alt– flūmina
2 omn– prīncipibus
3 miser– senī
4 trīst– puellam
5 mult– hostēs
6 puerīs fort–
7 parv– urbem
8 rēgī īrāt–
9 canum mal–
10 magn– urbe

Ⓖ Pronouns

You learnt the nominative of the personal pronouns in Chapter 5.
Now learn the accusative and the dative

	I	you	he		we	you	they
nom.	ego	tū	ille	*nom.*	nōs	vōs	illī
acc.	mē	tē	illum	*acc.*	nōs	vōs	illōs
dat.	mihi	tibi	illī	*dat.*	nōbīs	vōbīs	illīs

In the nominative they are only used for emphasis e.g.
ego laetus sum sed tū trīstis *I* am happy but *you* are sad.

92

Exercise 12.2

Translate
1 ego corōnam tibi dō sed tū eam mihi reddis.
2 illī nōs iuvant; tū nōs impedīs.
3 ego tē laudō sed illī tē reprehendunt.
4 nōs omnia vōbīs nārrāmus sed vōs audīre nōn cupitis.

impedīs hinder
reprehendunt blame

Exercise 12.3

Translate into Latin
1 We are happy but they are sad.
2 I can see you but you cannot see me.
3 What are <u>you</u> doing? <u>I</u> am helping father.
4 I give you flowers but you give me nothing.　　　　　nothing **nihil**

Reflexive pronouns

Personal pronouns can be used reflexively, i.e. referring back to the subject of the verb, as in French

je me lave	ego mē lavō	(**lavāre** to wash)
tu te laves	tū tē lavās	
il se lave	ille sē lavat	
nous nous lavons	nōs nōs lavāmus	
vous vous lavez	vōs vōs lavātis	
ils se lavent	illī sē lavant	

Note that **sē** = himself *and* themselves.

    s   *o*   *v*
Scintilla cēnam parat　　　　　　　Scintilla prepares supper.

    s   *o*   *v*
Scintilla sē parat　　　　　　　Scintilla prepares herself, gets ready.

  s   *o*   *v*
nautae nāvem ad lītus vertunt　　　　The sailors turn the ship to the shore.
  s   *o*   *v*
naūtae sē vertunt　　　　　　　The sailors turn round.

  s   *o*   *v*
Quīntus canem exercet　　　　　Quintus exercises the dog.
  s   *o* *v*
Quīntus sē exercet　　　　　　Quintus exercises himself, takes exercise.

Note also

meus-a-um	my	**noster, nostra, nostrum**	our
tuus-a-um	your	**vester, vestra, vestrum**	your
suus-a-um	his own	**suus-a-um**	their own

Exercise 12.4

Translate
1 pater sē vertit et fīlium videt.
2 vōs parāte ad cēnam.
3 ego tē reprehendō sed tū tē laudās.
4 mīlitēs sē exercent ante castra.
5 iuvenēs ad lūdōs sē parant.
6 Crassus suam glōriam augēre cupit.
7 puerī suōs loculōs ferunt.

reprehendō blame
loculī   satchel

Exercise 12.5

Translate into Latin
1 Get ready for supper, Quintus.
2 The old man turns and goes away.
3 I don't praise you but I praise myself.
4 The young men are exercising in the fields.
5 Horatia is washing (herself) in the house.

Exercise 12.6

Translate the first two paragraphs and answer the questions below on the last three

postrīdiē ubi Flāvius puerōs ē lūdō dīmittit, Quīntus Gāiō 'age,' inquit, 'venī mēcum et mīlitēs iterum spectā.' Gāium ē portīs oppidī dūcit in agrōs. ad castra mox veniunt mīlitēsque vident in agrō ante castra sē exercentēs.

age come on

diū spectant. deinde Quīntus propius accēdit quod plūra vidēre cupit. subitō lēgātus puerōs videt; equitat ad eōs et 'cōnsistite, puerī,' clāmat; 'quid facitis? quō ītis?' puerī cōnsistunt territī. lēgātus ad eōs accēdit et 'quid cupitis?' inquit. Quīntus fortiter respondet: 'cupimus mīlitēs spectāre sē exercentēs.' ille 'licet vōbīs spectāre,' inquit, 'sed nōlīte propius accēdere.'

propius nearer
plūra more; **subitō** suddenly
lēgātus officer
cōnsistite stop

licet vōbīs you may

lēgātus manet cum puerīs dum mīlitēs spectant. iuvenis cōmis est et multa puerīs explicat. mox Quīntus eum rogat: 'quō contendunt mīlitēs? quis exercitum dūcit? ad bellum ītis?' ille 'nunc Brundisium contendimus. ibi nāvēs cōnscendere dēbēmus et nāvigāre ad Asiam. Marcus Crassus nōs dūcit in Parthōs, quī in Oriente habitant. et tū, Quīnte, tū cupis mīles fierī, glōriam tibi quaerere, imperium populī Rōmānī augēre?'

iuvenis young man; **cōmis** friendly; **explicat** explains
exercitum army

Oriente the East
fierī to become
imperium empire
augēre enlarge
forsitan perhaps

Quīntus eī respondet: 'forsitan. mortem nōn timeō sed pugnam nōn amō.' alia rogāre cupit sed Gāius ānxius est; Quīntī manum capit et 'venī, Quīnte,' inquit; 'tempus est domum festīnāre. hodiē nōn dēbēmus sērō redīre.'

manum hand
hodiē today

Quīntus aegrē dīscēdit. lēgātum valēre iubent domumque festīnant.

aegrē reluctantly

1 What did Quintus ask the officer?
2 What was the officer's answer to Quintus' question?
3 What did the officer ask Quintus?
4 What was Quintus' reply?
5 What do you learn about the officer's character from this passage?
6 From the fourth paragraph, give one example each of: an infinitive, an imperative, an adverb.
7 In what case is each of the following words (all in the fourth paragraph): **eī, alia, Quīntī, Quīnte?** Explain why these cases are used.
8 Translate into Latin:
(a) When the boys leave school, they hurry to the fields and watch the soldiers.
(b) An officer tells the boys to stop; they are terrified.
(c) You must not return home late today, Quintus.

ROMAN RELIGION

The ordinary Romans, especially the country people, were deeply religious. They believed in many gods and their religion had several different aspects. Every family worshipped the **Larēs** and **Penātēs**, the spirits of dead ancestors, and of the farm and the larder. Each morning the father of the family (**paterfamiliās**) would lead his household to the **Larārium**, a little chapel, often no more than a cupboard, which contained the family **sacra** (sacred things), such as little statues of the Larēs. He would offer gifts, incense, flowers or wine, and make prayers on behalf of the family.

Other gods of the home were Vesta, goddess of the hearth (for man cannot survive without fire) and Jānus, spirit of the door (**iānua**), who blessed the family's going out and coming in.

Every important event in life was marked by prayer and sacrifice to the appropriate god or goddess. Birth, death, marriage, sowing and harvest were all celebrated with religious rituals. There was a succession of festivals throughout the year.

In this chapter Quintus and his family celebrate the Parīlia, an ancient festival intended to secure the health and safety of the flocks. It was held on 21 April in honour of Palēs, a deity so old that no one could say whether he/she was male or female or one god or two. The festival began with prayer and sacrifice in the fields at an altar built of turf. This was followed by a feast and a lot of hard drinking. Finally straw was piled up and lit; the company joined hands and jumped through the flames. No-one could say just what the ritual meant but it was all good fun. The essential thing in religion to the Romans was to perform the right rituals and make the right prayers at the proper time. This would secure them the help of the gods. If the flocks were sick, they would suppose that they had not celebrated the Parīlia properly.

Apart from the ancient gods of the family and the farmers, there were the great gods of the state, who formed a family of twelve: Jupiter, father of gods and men and god of the sky, Juno, his wife, the goddess especially worshipped by women, Apollo, Jupiter's son, god of prophecy, of health and of music, Minerva, his daughter, goddess of wisdom, Neptune, his brother, god of the sea, and seven others. The worship of these gods was organized by the state; priests were elected, who made regular prayer and sacrifice. Just as the Romans started the day with prayer in private life, so all state occasions began with prayer and sacrifice.

The Romans were not reluctant to welcome new gods. New cults were continually introduced as the Romans ranged further abroad, from Greece, Asia, Egypt and many other parts of the world. No-one was obliged to worship these gods, but no-one was prevented from joining foreign cults, if they wished. The only religions to which the Romans were sometimes opposed were those which denied the existence of other gods: Judaism, and later Christianity.

In the second part of this chapter Quintus sees a Roman army march through Venusia on its way to Brundisium, the main port in South East Italy. This was part of the army which Marcus Crassus was leading in 55 BC to fight Parthia, the great kingdom which lay beyond the eastern frontiers of the Roman empire.

A sacrificial procession

The Parthians were the only people at this time who might have threatened the Roman empire, but they had not provoked this war. Crassus was one of the wealthiest men in Rome, and at this time he dominated the Roman state together with Pompey the Great and Julius Caesar. Pompey had won great victories in the East, Julius Caesar was even now conquering Gaul (France, Holland and Belgium). Crassus was determined that he too should win military glory and embarked on the invasion of Parthia. A tribune cursed him as he passed out of the gates of Rome to join his army. Two years later his army was surrounded and defeated by the Parthians. Crassus himself was taken prisoner and put to death.

Describe what you see in the picture of the sacrificial procession. Can you find any features of Roman religion which are shared by the religion you practise? Can you think of any features of your religion which might have struck a Roman as strange?

CHAPTER XIII

ōlim Quīntus ad lūdum ambulābat;
subitō Gāium vīdit.

Gāius arborem ascendēbat.

Quīntus ānxius erat; clāmāvit: 'quid
facis, Gāī? dēscende.'

Gāius ad terram dēscendit et Quīntum
salūtāvit.

Ⓖ Past tenses of the verb

So far all the stories have been told in the present tense. You now
have to learn two past tenses:

In English, 'I walk' or 'I am walking' is present tense.
  'I was walking' is imperfect tense.
  'I walked' is perfect tense.

In Latin,   **ambulō**, present tense, 'I walk' or 'I am walking'.
  ambulābam, imperfect tense, 'I was walking' or 'I walked'
  (for a long time).
  ambulāvī, perfect tense 'I walked' (simple past time).

The imperfect tense

	1	2	3	4		
	amō, amāre	moneō, monēre	regō, regere	audiō, audīre	sum	(I am)
I	amā-bam	monē-bam	regē-bam	audiē-bam	eram	(I was)
you	amā-bās	monē-bās	regē-bās	audiē-bās	erās	(you were)
he	amā-bat	monē-bat	regē-bat	audiē-bat	erat	(he was)
we	amā-bāmus	monē-bāmus	regē-bāmus	audiē-bāmus	erāmus	(we were)
you	amā-bātis	monē-bātis	regē-bātis	audiē-bātis	erātis	(you were)
they	amā-bant	monē-bant	regē-bant	audiē-bant	erant	(they were)

Notice that the endings are the same for every conjugation.

The perfect tense

	1	2	3	4	
I	amāv-ī	monu-ī	rēx-ī	audīv-ī	fu-ī
you	amāv-istī	monu-istī	rēx-istī	audīv-istī	fu-istī
he	amāv-it	monu-it	rēx-it	audīv-it	fu-it
we	amāv-imus	monu-imus	rēx-imus	audīv-imus	fu-imus
you	amāv-istis	monu-istis	rēx-istis	audīv-istis	fu-istis
they	amāv-ērunt	monu-ērunt	rēx-ērunt	audīv-ērunt	fu-ērunt

Note that the perfect *endings* are the same for every class of verb but
that the perfect *stem* is different for each class:
thus, from **amō** class, the stem is **amāv-**
       from **moneō** class, the stem is **monu-**
       from **audiō** class, the stem is **audīv-**
       from **sum**, the stem is **fu-**

Exercise 13.1

Say what tense each of the following verbs is in and translate

audiēbāmus, labōrant, pugnāvit, diū
manēbās, mē terruistī, tē rogāvērunt,
bene cēnat, eōs monētis, eōs monuistis,
ad lūdum festīnābat

Exercise 13.2

Form the imperfect and perfect (1st person singular) *of the following verbs and say what each means*

clāmō, intrō, doceō, timeō, dormiō, iaceō

From **regō** class verbs, the perfect stem is formed in various ways, which you will gradually learn. At present *learn the following*

regō, regere, rēx-ī	I rule
dīcō, dīcere, dīx-ī	I say
dūcō, dūcere, dūx-ī	I lead
vīvō, vīvere, vīx-ī	I live
cēdō, cēdere, cess-ī	I give way
mittō, mittere, mīs-ī	I send

Exercise 13.3

Form the imperfect and perfect of the following verbs and say what each means

regō, dīcō, accēdō, mittō

Exercise 13.4

Say what tense each of the following verbs is in and translate

celeriter currēbant, mihi dīxistī, diū vīvēbat, rēgī cessērunt, canem dūcō, canem dūxī, in oppidō manēbat, nūntium mīsī, regunt, rēxistī

TUMULTUS

tumultus riot

Quīntus ad lūdum lentē ambulābat; in viā Gāium vīdit et eum vocāvit. Gāius festīnābat, quod sērō veniēbat; sed, ubi Quīntum audīvit, mānsit et eum salūtāvit. 'quid facis, Quīnte?' inquit; 'cūr tam lentē ambulās? sērō ad lūdum venimus. dēbēmus festīnāre.' Quīntus respondit: 'errās, Gāī. nōn sērō venimus. exspectā mē.' Gāius ānxius erat sed Quīntum exspectāvit.

errās you're wrong

Decimus ruit ad magistrum et iēcit eum ad terram.

cum ad lūdum accēdēbant, multōs puerōs vīdērunt
quī prope iānuam stābant. duo puerī pugnābant. aliī
circumstābant et clāmābant. tum Flāvius ē iānuā lūdī
exiit; vīdit puerōs pugnantēs et valdē īrātus erat. 'quid
facitis, puerī?' inquit; 'intrāte statim et sedēte.'

sed Decimus, puer magnus et dūrus, ad Flāvium
accurrit et dīxit: 'abī, magister. redī in lūdum. nōlī
intercēdere.' ille, valdē attonitus, 'puer impudēns es,'
inquit; 'intrā statim et tacē.' et Decimum saevē
pulsāvit. Decimus valdē commōtus erat; furor et īra
animum vincunt; ruit in magistrum et iēcit eum in
terram. aliī puerī accurrērunt et Decimum
comprehendērunt. Flāvius ē terrā surrēxit; valdē īrātus
erat; nihil poterat dīcere; lūdum tacitus intrāvit et
iānuam clausit.

puerī valdē timēbant. Gāius Decimō dīxit: 'quid
fēcistī, Decime? nōn possumus hīc manēre. dēbēmus
fugere.' itaque omnēs puerī domum celeriter fūgērunt.
Quīntus casam intrāvit et mātrem quaesīvit. māter in
culīnā labōrābat; cēnam parābat. Quīntus eam vocāvit.
illa respondit: 'ecce, Quīnte; in culīnā sum; cēnam
parō. sed quid facis? cūr ā lūdō rediistī?' Quīntus in
culīnam cucurrit et mātrī omnia nārrāvit. illa respondit:
'malī puerī estis. ī nunc, Quīnte. ad agrum curre et
omnia patrī nārrā.'

Quīntus timēbat sed nōn poterat recūsāre. ad
agrum cucurrit. ubi agrum intrāvit, Flaccus in ultimā
parte agrī labōrābat. Quīntus eum vocāvit; ille fīlium
audīvit et ad eum accessit. 'quid facis, Quīnte?' inquit;
'cūr ā lūdō tam mātūre rediistī?' Quīntus timēbat sed
omnia patrī nārrāvit. Flaccus valdē īrātus est. 'ēheu!'
inquit; 'nōn tua culpa est, Quīnte. illī puerī scelestī sunt
et Flāvius est asinus. quid facere dēbēmus? nihil in illō
lūdō discis. redī mēcum ad casam.'

itaque Quīntus paterque celeriter ad casam
rediērunt Scintillamque quaesīvērunt. Scintilla in hortō
erat cum Horātiā; nam fessae erant et quiēscēbant.
Flaccus ad Scintillam accessit et 'Scintilla,' inquit, 'quid
facere dēbēmus? Quīntus nihil discit in illō lūdō. valdē
ingeniōsus est, sed magister docēre nōn potest et puerī
scelestī sunt.'

Scintilla eī respondit; 'vērum dīcis, Flacce; Quīntus
nihil discit; ingenium perdit. cēterī puerī in malōs
mōrēs eum dūcunt. Flacce, Quīntus dēbet Rōmam īre;
dēbēmus eum mittere ad optimum lūdum.'

Flaccus, ubi haec audīvit, cōnsternātus erat; 'quid

circumstābant were standing
around
pugnantēs fighting
dūrus tough

intercēdere interfere;
attonitus astonished;
impudēns impertinent
tacē be quiet
pulsāvit struck; furor frenzy
ruit he rushed
comprehendērunt seized;
surrēxit got up
nihil nothing
clausit shut

recūsāre to refuse
ultimā furthest

mātūre early
ēheu alas
culpa fault; scelestī bad

hortō garden
quiēscēbant were resting

ingeniōsus clever

ingenium intelligence;
perdit is wasting
mōrēs habits; Rōmam to Rome
optimum best
cōnsternātus dismayed

dīcis, uxor?' inquit; 'quōmodo potest Quīntus sōlus
Rōmam īre?' Scintilla eī respondit: 'nōn potest sōlus
īre; tū, Flacce, dēbēs eum Rōmam dūcere.'

    diū rem disserēbant. tandem Scintilla dīxit: 'nōlī
dēspērāre, Flacce. audī mē. dēbēmus agrum vēndere.
tū dēbēs Quīntum Rōmam dūcere; ego et Horātia
possumus hīc manēre et frūgāliter vīvere. sed sēra hōra
est. tempus est dormīre.'

    postrīdiē Flaccus ad vīcīnum accessit et rem diū
disserēbat. tandem cōnstituit dīmidium agrī vēndere,
dīmidium vīcīnō locāre. sīc ipse satis argentī habēbat et
Quīntum Rōmam dūcere poterat; vīcīnus volēbat
vectīgal Scintillae solvere; sīc Scintilla poterat Venusiae
manēre et cum Horātiā frūgāliter vīvere.

quōmodo how?

rem matter;
disserēbant discussed

frūgāliter inexpensively; sēra
hōra late

vīcīnum neighbour
dīmidium half; locāre to lease
ipse he himself; satis
argentī enough money
volēbat was willing
vectīgal rent; solvere pay;
Venusiae in Venusia

nārrō, nārrāre, nārrāvī	I tell	**uxor, uxōris,** *f.*	wife
stō, stāre, stetī	I stand	**saevus-a-um**	savage, cruel
moveō, movēre, mōvī	I move		
commoveō, commovēre,	I move	**vērus-a-um**	true
commōvī	violently,	**vērum, vērī,** *n.*	the truth
	disturb	**nihil**	nothing
fleō, flēre, flēvī	I weep	**tum**	then
ineō	I go into, begin		
discō, discere, didicī	I learn		
vēndō, vēndere, vēndidī	I sell		
vīvō, vīvere, vīxī	I live		
argentum, argentī, *n.*	silver, money		

NB

parō	I prepare	**parātus-a-um**	prepared, ready
terreō	I terrify	**territus-a-um**	terrified
armō	I arm	**armātus-a-um**	armed
commoveō	I move	**commōtus-a-um**	moved, upset

Exercise 13.5

Translate into English

1 Scintilla et Flaccus in Apūliā
  vīvēbant.

2 ūnum fīlium habēbant, nōmine
  Quīntum.

3 puer ingeniōsus erat, sed nihil
  discēbat in lūdō Flāviī.

4 pater eum Rōmam dūxit et mīsit ad
  optimum lūdum.

5 Scintilla et Horātia in Apūliā
  manēbant.

6 quid faciēbātis, puerī? cūr in viā
  pugnābātis?

7 frātrēs lentē ambulābant; sērō ad
  lūdum advēnērunt.

8 ad magistrum accessimus et omnia eī
  dīximus.
9 puerī tacitī sedēbant; magister
  cōnstituit fābulam eīs nārrāre.
10 puerum vīdistī, quī arborem
   ascendēbat?

Exercise 13.6

Translate into Latin
1 We said nothing.
2 They were leading the horse to the
  water.

3 I heard the boys.
4 We were dining in the house.
5 The messenger warned the king.
6 The king was angry.
7 Why did you not sail to Troy?
8 You were not brave.
9 I was working in the field.
10 You were preparing dinner.

Exercise 13.7

*Translate the first paragraph and answer the questions below on the
second and third paragraphs*

per tōtam hiemem Quīntus domī manēbat et parentēs
iuvābat. omnēs dīligenter labōrābant. Quīntus in agrō
labōrābat; Flaccus coāctōris partēs agēbat et sīc
multum argentum comparābat. vēr accēdēbat cum
Flaccus uxōrī dīxit: 'iam tempus est Quīntum Rōmam
dūcere; iam satis argentī comparāvimus.' paucīs post
diēbus omnia parāta erant. Flaccus Quīntusque
Scintillam et Horātiam et Argum valēre iussērunt.

hiemem winter; domī at
home
dīligenter hard
coāctōris partēs
agēbat worked as an
auctioneer
comparābat earned
vēr spring
satis enough; paucīs post
diēbus in a few days
valēre iussērunt said goodbye
to

Flaccus Quīntusque Horātiam et
Argum valēre iubent.

māter flēbat et deōs ōrābat: 'ō deī, servāte fīlium meum; reddite eum mihi incolumem. ō Flacce, Quīntum cūrā! ō Quīnte, bonus puer estō! dīligenter studē et mox domum redī.' fīliō virōque ōsculum dedit et rediit in casam, valdē commōta.

incolumem safe
estō be
studē work; ōsculum kiss

Horātia et Argus cum patre et frātre ad prīmum mīliārium iērunt; tum Horātia eōs valēre iussit et Argum domum redūxit. illī, et trīstēs et laetī, viam iniērunt, quae Rōmam dūcēbat.

mīliārium milestone

quae which

1 What was Scintilla's prayer to the gods?
2 What did she tell Flaccus to do?
3 What did she tell Quintus to do?
4 In the last sentence Flaccus and Quintus are described as 'et trīstēs et laetī'. Explain why they had these conflicting feelings.
5 Do you approve of his parents' decision to take Quintus to Rome?
6 The following English words are derived from Latin words in the second paragraph; say from what Latin word each comes and explain the meaning of the English word: oratory, conservation, diligence.
7 From the second paragraph, give one example each of an imperfect tense, a perfect tense, an imperative.
8 Translate into Latin:
(a) Flaccus decided to lead his son to Rome.
(b) When Quintus and his father went away, mother was very sad.
(c) 'Work hard,' she said, 'and come home soon.'

STORIES FROM THE EARLY HISTORY OF ROME

Rome was governed by kings for the first 244 years of its history. The names of six of these after Romulus are recorded, and some of them came from a talented race which lived to the North of Rome, the Etruscans. The last king, Tarquin the Proud, was one of these. He was a valiant leader in war but a cruel tyrant among his people. He added to the greatness of Rome by carrying out vast building projects, but the common people complained bitterly about the labour involved, especially in the construction of a great sewer system for the whole city.

Tarquin attacked the rich neighbouring town of Ardea in order to pay for these works. But Ardea proved extremely difficult to capture and a long siege followed. One day, Tarquin's sons were whiling away the hours drinking with their cousin Collatinus. They began to talk about their wives, each of them claiming that his own was the most virtuous and faithful. Collatinus pointed out that the only way to settle the matter was to make a sudden journey to Rome, visit their wives unexpectedly and see for themselves what they were doing.

The young men had all drunk a great deal of wine and Collatinus's idea struck them as a very good one. They mounted their horses and galloped to Rome, arriving there in the evening. The princes' wives were taking advantage of their husbands' absence to enjoy a lively dinner party. But they found Collatinus's wife Lucretia working with her maidservants by lamplight at her spinning. Lucretia thus was the clear winner of the competition in wifely virtue.

However, events now took a disastrous turn. One of the princes, Sextus Tarquinius, had been so overcome by the sight of the virtuous and beautiful Lucretia that he fell passionately in love with her. A few days later he paid her a visit without telling Collatinus. She received him hospitably, gave him dinner, and took him to the guest chamber. But Tarquinius made his way to Lucretia's bedroom at dead of night, with drawn sword. He persecuted her with dreadful threats, raped her, and then rode away, proud of his shameless deed.

Lucretia now proved that she was as courageous as she was virtuous. She summoned her father and her husband and told them what had happened. She made them swear to take vengeance on Sextus Tarquinius. Then, declaring that she could not live now that she had lost her honour, she drove a knife into her heart. Her father and husband were too shocked to do anything but weep. But Collatinus's companion Brutus drew the knife from Lucretia's body, held it up and vowed that he would drive the impious family of the Tarquins from Rome.

The dreadful story of Lucretia caused such widespread horror and indignation that Brutus found his threat easy to fulfil. The Tarquins were driven into exile, but they tried to regain their power, first through a conspiracy and later by force. Brutus's two sons joined in the conspiracy to bring back the tyrant, and their father had no alternative but to order their execution and watch them being beheaded. His terrible distress was obvious to all. Nevertheless, his love of the liberty which had been so recently

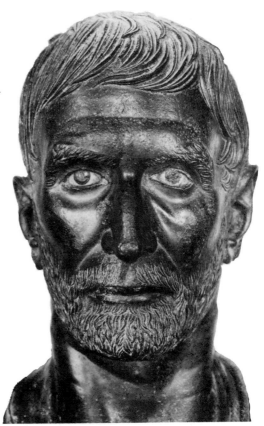

Brutus

105

won overcame his feelings as a father.

The stern example of Brutus was very much in the mind of his descendant Marcus Junius Brutus 500 years later. It looked as if Julius Caesar was about to become king and bring back the hateful form of government which his ancestor Brutus had brought to an end. So he led a conspiracy to murder Caesar, his close friend.

Tarquin then persuaded the Etruscan king Porsenna to use open force to bring about his return. Porsenna advanced on Rome and indeed it looked as if his forces would sweep over the wooden bridge across the Tiber.

The story of how Horatius Cocles prevented them is famous. The Roman troops fled in a panic back across the river, and Horatius shouted to them that if they left the bridge standing the enemy would soon be in Rome. He declared that he would hold back the enemy single-handed to give them time to destroy the bridge. He proudly took his stand at the entrance to the bridge and, first helped by two brave companions and then on his own, he fought off innumerable Etruscans. He astonished them so much by his courage that they were paralysed at first. When they recovered enough to shower weapons at him, he brushed them aside with his shield.

Finally, just as it looked as if he would be overwhelmed by the huge number of the Etruscans, a great crash accompanied by a cry of triumph from the Romans showed that the bridge was now down. Horatius plunged fully armed into the Tiber with a prayer to the river god to protect him, and swam amid a hail of weapons. The Etruscan king was impressed by his enemy's bravery and an English poet, Thomas Macaulay, describes him as hoping that Horatius will get safely across:

'Heaven help him!' quoth Lars Porsenna,
    'And bring him safe to shore;
For such a gallant feat of arms
    Was never seen before.'

Needless to say, he succeeded in reaching the other bank.

Porsenna was frustrated by this and other such acts of courage on the part of the Romans, and stopped supporting the Tarquins. The end of the monarchy in Rome was guaranteed. The city became a republic governed by two consuls who were elected every year. The word **rēx** was from now on a hateful one to Roman ears.

ENEMIES OF ROME   1 The Gauls

The new republic of Rome constantly strengthened her leading
position in central Italy. Her struggles with neighbouring tribes
continued at intervals for centuries, but two foreign enemies involved
the city in her greatest danger. The first were the Gauls who came
from what is now North Italy and France.

They inflicted a shattering defeat in about 386 BC upon the
Roman army only eleven miles from the city. More than half of the
Romans fled in utter terror to the neighbouring town of Veii and
Rome appeared to be totally at its enemy's mercy. But the
determination and courage of this tough nation were seen at their best
at such moments. The inhabitants left most of the city undefended and
abandoned the old and helpless to face whatever fate the Gauls had in
store for them. All the city's able-bodied men occupied the Capitol,
the hill that was Rome's main fortress. It was a difficult decision, but it
seemed wrong to use up the limited supplies on the Capitol on people
who could not contribute actively to Rome's defence. This hill was the
home of the gods who protected Rome, and here the younger
members of the senate determined to preserve their government and
their religion.

The older senators, left in the city below and doomed to death in
company with the humbler citizens, put on their finest clothes in order
to meet their end with dignity. They sat in the courtyards of their
magnificent houses with a grave and calm majesty. The Gauls entered
the eerily empty city and, looking curiously around them, made their
way to the Forum. When they saw the senators, they were so
impressed by their dignified stillness that they thought they must be
gods. They wondered if they were stone images. One of the Gauls
stretched out his hand and touched a senator's beard to see whether it

A Gaul pulls a senator's beard

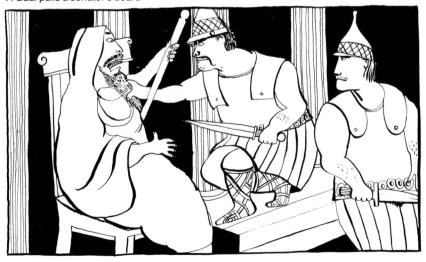

was real or not. The senator, enraged, hit him over the head with his ivory staff. The silence now ended in horror as the Gauls slaughtered everyone they could lay their hands on and plundered and burned the city.

The garrison on the Capitol was appalled as they looked down and saw what was happening to their fellow citizens below. It was indeed a grim sight. Yet they themselves were soon to be even closer to danger than they imagined, for the Gauls had spotted a way by which they could clamber up a rocky slope of the Capitol and surprise the Roman fort. It was a dangerous climb, but one night they undertook it and achieved their aim so silently that they neared the top without being noticed by a single guard. The Romans were saved by their own piety, for some geese sacred to the goddess Juno were on the Capitol. They had been left unkilled despite the dreadful shortage of food. These geese were alarmed by the Gauls and cackled and beat their wings, thus awaking Marcus Manlius. He seized his sword and gave the alarm. The leading Gaul was already on the top but Manlius pushed him over the side with his shield. His fall knocked other Gauls down the slope and they tumbled to the bottom of the cliff.

This hair's-breadth escape did not save the besieged Romans from near starvation, and eventually they decided to buy off the Gauls with 1,000 pounds' weight of gold. But the Gauls used especially heavy weights in order to cheat the Romans. When they complained, the barbarian leader threw his sword into the scale making it even heavier, and exclaimed, 'Vae victīs!' ('Woe to the conquered!'). At this moment an army gathered by the exiled general Camillus suddenly appeared on the scene and the Gauls' forces were wiped out. Thus a terrifying moment in their history ended with a Roman victory.

❓ The Roman historian Livy who tells these stories was well aware that they are legends rather than a factual account of the early days of Rome. What qualities of the Roman character do you feel that these legends bring out? Do you find these qualities admirable?

CHAPTER XIV

Quīntus Flaccusque domō discēdunt et Rōmam iter faciunt.

tōtum diem contendunt; eā nocte valdē fessī sunt.

Quīntus patrī 'tōtum diem contendimus,' inquit; 'nōnne possumus noctem hīc manēre?'

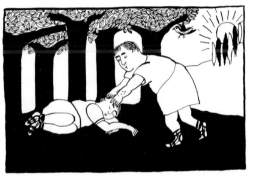

prīmā lūce Flaccus fīlium excitat; 'satis dormīvistī, fīlī,' inquit; 'tempus est viam Rōmam iterum inīre.'

Revision

Revise verbs **dō** to **videō** from the Grammar Section, pages 182–3, and learn the perfect stems carefully.

The numerals: one to ten and first to tenth

			prīmus-a-um	first
ūnus	one	The declension	**secundus-a-um**	second
duo	two	of **ūnus**, **duo**,	**tertius**	third
trēs	three	**trēs** will be	**quārtus**	fourth
quattuor	four	learnt later; the	**quīntus**	fifth
quīnque	five	others do not	**sextus**	sixth
sex	six	decline.	**septimus**	seventh
septem	seven		**octāvus**	eighth
octō	eight		**nōnus**	ninth
novem	nine		**decimus**	tenth
decem	ten		These all decline like **bonus-a-um**.	

G Expressions of time and place

1 Time

ūnum diem mansērunt They stayed for one day.
Time *how long?* goes into the *accusative* case.
trēs hōrās ambulābāmus We were walking for three hours.
posterō diē abiērunt On the next day they went away.
Time *when?* goes into the *ablative* case.
prīmā lūce surrēxerunt At first light they got up.

2 Place

ad urbem festīnāvērunt They hurried to the city.
But: **Rōmam festīnāvērunt** They hurried to Rome.
ab urbe discessērunt They went away from the city.
But: **Rōmā discessērunt** They went away from Rome.

The names of towns do not have a preposition in expressions of place.
The *accusative* case is used to express motion towards and the *ablative*
case to express motion from.

The same applies to **domus** home: so **domum festīnāvērunt** They
hurried home; **domō discessērunt** They left home.
Note also: **domī** at home; **domī manēbant** They stayed at home.

Exercise 14.1

Translate into English
1 trēs diēs ad iter sē parābant; quārtō diē domō discessērunt.
2 novem annōs Graecī Trōiam obsidēbant; decimō annō urbem cēpērunt.
3 Quīntus paterque Venusiā discessērunt Rōmamque contendēbant.
4 prīmā lūce Flaccus surrēxit familiamque ad Larārium dūxit.
5 septem diēs in urbe manēbant; octāvō diē domum rediērunt.

Exercise 14.2

Translate into Latin
1 They remained at home for five days.
2 On the first day Quintus and his father walked for six hours.
3 On the seventh day they arrived at Capua and stayed the night in an inn (**caupōna-ae**, *f.*).
4 At dawn they left the town and walked all day.
5 You have slept for ten hours; it is time to go to school.

QUINTUS ROMAM ADVENIT

Quīntus paterque in viā Appiā prōcēdēbant. iam
quīnque diēs contenderant. Venusiā longē aberant.
collem ascendēbant. Quīntus valdē fessus erat.

contenderant they had
travelled

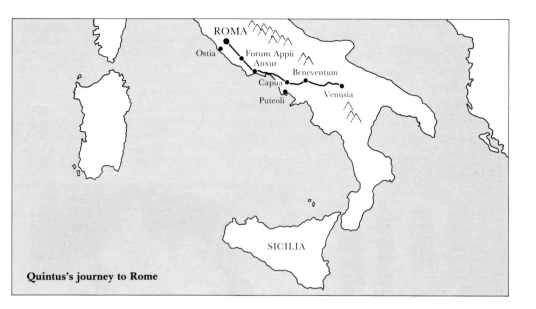

Quintus's journey to Rome

mīliārium prope viam vīdit. accessit et īnscrīptiōnem lēgit: 'Rōma centum et quīnquāgintā mīlia passuum.' patrī dīxit: quīnque diēs contendimus. montēs et flūmina trānsiimus; sed Rōma adhūc centum et quīnquāgintā mīlia passuum abest. ego valdē fessus sum. ecce! vesper adest. quid facere dēbēmus? ego nōn longius contendere possum.'

    pater fīliō respondit: 'nōlī dēspērāre, Quīnte. Capua nōn longē abest, sed sī tam fessus es, possumus hīc pernoctāre.'

    nūllus vīcus erat in cōnspectū, nūlla casa; silvae ubīque et collēs. Flaccus 'venī, Quīnte,' inquit; 'nōn tūtī sumus in viā. in silvam īre dēbēmus.' Quīntum in silvam dūxit.

    mox locum idōneum invēnērunt. Quīntus ligna quaesīvit et ignem accendit. cēnam celeriter parāverunt. tum Quīntus sub arbore cubuit et mox dormiēbat. subitō sonus eum excitāvit; lupōs audīvit procul ululantēs. sed Flaccus eī dīxit: 'nōlī timēre, fīlī. lupī longē absunt; praetereā ignem timent. nōn audent accēdere.'

    itaque Quīntus iterum dormīvit. nox obscūra erat; nūlla lūna lūcem dabat. nōn dormīvit Flaccus sed ignem cūrābat. subitō sonum audīvit; hominēs per umbrās ad ignem accēdēbant. Flaccus fīlium celeriter excitāvit; 'tacē,' inquit; 'hominēs hūc accēdunt. venī mēcum.' Quīntī manum cēpit et celeriter dūxit per umbrās in

mīliārium milestone
īnscrīptiōnem inscription
centum et quīnquāgintā mīlia passuum 150 miles
trānsiimus we have crossed
adhūc still
vesper evening
longius further

sī if
pernoctāre spend the night
vīcus village; **cōnspectū** sight
ubīque everywhere

idōneum suitable; **ligna** wood
ignem fire; **accendit** lit
cubuit lay down
sonus sound; **lupōs** wolves
ululantēs howling
praetereā besides

obscūra dark

umbrās shadows

tacē quiet!; **hūc** here
manum hand

virgulta; ibi sē cēlāvērunt et ānxiē spectābant.

trēs hominēs, gladiīs armātī, ad ignem accessērunt. statim impedimenta Flaccī rapuērunt. tum diū quaerēbant, sed ipsōs invenīre nōn poterant. tandem abiērunt, īrātī et spē dēiectī. Flaccus fīliō 'nōlī timēre,' inquit; 'iam abiērunt. deīs grātiās agere dēbēmus. illī hominēs sunt servī fugitīvī, hominēs audācēs et scelestī. ē magnō perīculō ēvāsimus. iam dēbēmus hīc manēre, in virgultīs cēlātī.'

virgulta undergrowth; **sē cēlāvērunt** they hid themselves
impedimenta baggage
rapuērunt seized
ipsōs them
spē dēiectī disappointed
grātiās agere to give thanks
fugitīvī runaway; **scelestī** bad
ēvāsimus we have escaped
cēlātī hidden

trēs hominēs gladiīs armātī ad ignem accessērunt.

prīmā lūce Flaccus Quīntum excitāvit. 'surge, Quīnte,' inquit; 'tempus est Capuam contendere. venī.' ad viam rediērunt, laetī quod ē tantō perīculō ēvāserant. merīdiē Capuam advēnērunt. Quīntus numquam tantum oppidum vīderat. plūrimī hominēs viās frequentābant, servī cīvēsque, virī, fēminae, puerī. Quīntus paterque per turbam festīnābant et tandem ad forum advēnērunt. Quīntus attonitus erat; numquam aedificia tam magnifica vīderat. omnia spectāre cupiēbat. sed Flaccus eī dīxit: 'venī, Quīnte. nōn tempus est forum spectāre. dēbēmus caupōnam quaerere et cenāre.'

surge get up

ēvāserant they had escaped
merīdiē at midday
vīderat had seen
plūrimī very many
frequentābant crowded
turbam crowd
aedificia buildings
vīderat had seen

caupōnam inn

fīlium ē forō dūxit in vīcōs angustōs; mox ad parvam caupōnam advēnērunt. Flaccus intrāvit et caupōnem rogāvit cēnam et cubiculum. ille Flaccō respondit: 'intrāte; cēna parāta est. post cēnam, potestis in solō dormīre.' Flaccus caupōnī grātiās ēgit. pater fīliusque, ubi bene cēnāvērunt, cubuērunt in solō et mox dormiēbant.

vīcōs angustōs narrow streets
caupōnem inn-keeper
cubiculum bedroom

solō floor
cubuērunt lay down

postrīdiē surrēxērunt prīmā lūce. pater caupōnī argentum solvit et Quīntum ex oppidō dūxit. trēs diēs

surrēxērunt they got up
solvit paid

contendērunt. quārtō diē, ubi vesper aderat, Anxur accessērunt; oppidum in summō colle stat; ubi collem ascendērunt, oppidum intrāvērunt et sedēbant in forō. valdē fessī erant. Flaccus fīliō 'fortis estō, Quīnte,' inquit; 'iam nōn longē abest Rōma.' sed Quīntus patrī respondit: 'nōn longius contendere possum, pater. cōnfectus sum.'

    Flaccus 'nōlī dēspērāre, mī fīlī,' inquit. 'sī tam fessus es, possumus iter facere in nāve.' Quīntus 'quid dīcis?' inquit; 'ubi est nāvis?' in summō colle sumus. nūlla nāvis, nūllum flūmen in cōnspectū est.' Flaccus nihil respondit sed Quīntum ex oppidō dūxit. collem dēscendērunt et mox ad canālem vēnērunt. ibi nāvem vīdērunt ad rīpam religātam.

- **summō colle** top of a hill
- **estō** be
- **longius** further
- **cōnfectus** worn out
- **mī fīlī** my son; **sī** if
- **canālem** canal
- **rīpam** the bank
- **religātam** tied

audeō, audēre	I dare	**longus-a-um**	long, far
absum	I am absent, distant	**longē**	far
legō, legere, lēgī	I read, gather, choose	**tantus-a-um**	so great
inveniō, invenīre, invēnī	I find	**audāx, audācis**	daring, rash, reckless
lūna, lūnae, *f.*	moon	**numquam**	never
nauta, nautae, *m.*	sailor	**procul**	far, far off
locus, locī, *m.*	place	**hodiē**	today
cīvis, cīvis, *c.*	citizen	**postrīdiē**	the next day
lūx, lūcis, *f.*	light	**bene**	well
arbor, arboris, *f.*	tree	**sub** + ablative	under
iter, itineris, *n.*	journey, march		

The meanings of the perfect tense

amāvī usually means 'I loved' (simple past time), but it can also mean 'I have loved'.

So, in this chapter, Quintus says: '**quīnque diēs contendimus**' we *have marched* for five days. '**montēs et flūmina trānsiimus**' we *have crossed* mountains and rivers.

Flaccus says to Quintus: '**nōlī timēre; hominēs abiērunt**' don't be afraid; the men have gone away.

Exercise 14.3

Translate into English. Make sure that you translate all perfect tenses appropriately, choosing between the two possible meanings

1 in viā Appiā ambulābam; subitō lupum vīdī.
2 pater dīxit; 'nōlī timēre; lupus abiit.'
3 novem diēs contendēbāmus; decimō diē Rōmam advēnimus.
4 decem diēs contendimus; tandem pater dīxit: 'Rōmam advēnimus.'
5 Quīntus et pater domō discessērunt et Rōmam contendēbant.
6 Quīntus cupiēbat domum redīre, sed pater dīxit: 'fortis estō, Quīnte; iam montēs trānsiimus; Rōma nōn longē abest.'
7 nāvis tōtam noctem prōcēdēbat; prīmā lūce ad Forum Appiī advēnit.
8 māter ānxia erat, nam fīlius domō aberat. 'trēs hōrās,' inquit, 'exspectāvī sed puer domum nōn rediit.' tandem quīntā noctis hōrā puer domum rediit.
9 māter īrāta erat; 'fīlī,' inquit, 'cūr sērō rediistī? quattuor hōrās tē exspectāvī; iam sextā hōrā tandem rediistī.'
10 puer respondit: 'cum amīcīs duās hōrās lūdēbam. tum domum festīnāvī. ecce, tertiā hōrā noctis rediī. nōlī tē vexāre.'

hōra, hōrae, *f.* hour
vexāre trouble

Exercise 14.4

Translate into Latin

1 We left (= went away from) home at first light and walked on the Appian Way; on the sixth day we reached Capua.
2 We stayed in the town three days; on the fourth day we left Capua and hurried to Rome.
3 I waited for you for five hours in the forum but you did not come.
4 We have waited for the girls for one hour, but they have not come.
5 Don't despair, Quintus. We have almost reached the city.
6 They stayed all night in the hills and at first light they hurried home.
7 What are you doing? Why are you staying at home? Why have you not gone to school?
8 The master has given the boy six books because he can read so well.

almost **paene**

Exercise 14.5

Translate the first paragraph and answer the questions below on the second

multī hominēs nāvem cōnscendēbant; nautae clāmābant et viāticum rogābant. Quīntus gaudēbat. 'festīnā, pater,' inquit; 'nāvis discessūra est.' celeriter cucurrērunt et nāvem cōnscendērunt. diū exspectābant, dum nautae viātica colligēbant. tandem mūla ad nāvem religāta erat, et nāvis lentē prōcēdēbat. Quīntus paterque in ponte cubuērunt sed dormīre nōn poterant, quod viātōrēs tantum clāmōrem faciēbant et malī

viāticum fare
discessūra about to leave

colligēbant collected
mūla mule
religāta tied
ponte deck; **cubuērunt** lay down
viātōrēs travellers

culicēs semper eōs vexābant.

    iam diēs aderat, cum ad Forum Appiī advēnērunt. ē
nāve descendērunt et lentē ad forum ambulāvērunt. ibi
diū manēbant. tandem Flaccus fīliō 'venī,' inquit; 'iam
Rōmā nōn longē absumus. illūc crās advenīre
possumus.' Quīntus gaudēbat. via facilis erat. postrīdiē
sub noctem ad portam Capēnam accessērunt. tandem
Rōmam advēnerant.

culicēs mosquitoes
vexābant troubled

illūc there; crās tomorrow
facilis easy
sub just before
advēnerant they had arrived

1 When did they reach Forum Appii?
2 What did they do when they got there?
3 'Quīntus gaudēbat'. Why was he glad?
4 How long did it take them to get from Forum Appii to Rome?
5 Give one English word derived from each of the following (all in the
   second paragraph): **ambulāvērunt, facilis, accessērunt**.
6 Give the first person singular of the present of the following (all in
   the second paragraph): **aderat, manēbat, accessērunt**.
7 In what case is each of the following words in the second paragraph:
   nāve, fīliō, Rōmā, via. Why are these cases used?
8 Translate into Latin:
(a) We are making a journey to Rome.
(b) On the third day we were tired; my son wanted to return home.
(c) And so we boarded a ship and slept all night.

ENEMIES OF ROME   2 Carthage

You read at the end of the last chapter how Rome came within a hair's
breadth of being captured by the Gauls. Rome's other dark time came
in the third century BC when the city of Carthage came close to
destroying her. As you may remember, Queen Dido had laid a
terrifying threat of revenge upon Rome when Aeneas, the founder of
the Roman nation, had abandoned her. Her words were fulfilled in a
dreadful way.

    The conflict with the Carthaginians was renewed three times in
what are called the three Punic Wars (Punic = Carthaginian). In the
first the Romans achieved victory and showed their usual rugged
determination. When Horace was told about it, he was particularly
impressed by the courage of Regulus, a Roman general. Regulus was
captured by the Carthaginians and sent by them to Rome to negotiate
an exchange of prisoners and, if possible, peace. When he arrived in
Rome, he said the exact opposite of what the Carthaginians wanted
him to. He told the Romans on no account to exchange prisoners but
to fight on until they won. He then refused to remain in the city since
he had promised to return to the place of his captivity. He was cruelly
tortured to death when he arrived back in Carthage.

The Romans gained the victory, but they by no means broke the might and ambition of their enemy. One of the Carthaginian generals of this war took his son to the altar and made him swear over the sacrifice undying hatred of everything that was Roman. The boy's name was Hannibal, and when he grew up he did not forget his oath.

Hannibal's march upon Rome, which began the Second Punic War (218–202 BC), has caught the imagination of the world. He decided to fight his enemy by land, attacking them by crossing the huge natural barrier of the Alps from Spain. It proved an appalling experience. He set out with 102,000 men and he arrived in Italy with only 26,000.

Hannibal's march

But he showed great heroism and skill throughout the ordeal. He placed his elephants precariously on rafts and transported his army across the swirling waters of the wide river Rhone. Then they had a nine days' journey which took them through hostile tribes, terrible storms and a most frightening landscape. At last they came to the top of one of the Alpine passes, which one we shall never know for sure. Here Hannibal pointed out to his men the plains of Italy which lay below. He said that by crossing the Alps they had climbed the very walls of Rome. The city was now in their hands.

At first it seemed as if Hannibal was right. He won a series of crushing victories over the Romans whom he simply out-generalled.

116

Then in 216 BC he inflicted upon them the most severe defeat they had ever known, at Cannae. Perhaps 70,000 Romans were killed in this battle, and their city again seemed to be totally at the mercy of a cruel enemy.

Yet Hannibal hesitated. The leader of his cavalry, Maharbal, begged him to send him ahead to Rome. If Hannibal did so, Maharbal told him, he would be dining on the Capitol three days later. Hannibal would not let him go, however, thinking that his men had earned a rest. 'You know how to win, Hannibal,' replied Maharbal sadly, 'but you do not know how to use your victory.'

The Romans refused to admit defeat, as so often happened amid disaster. Their stubbornness was rewarded and a stalemate developed. Hannibal moved round Italy unopposed, but the Roman army sensibly refused to engage him in a pitched battle, which he would almost certainly have won. Instead, they followed him at a distance and made it difficult for him to get supplies and reinforcements.

In 207 BC the Carthaginians attempted to turn the tide of war by sending Hannibal's brother Hasdrubal over the Alps to Italy to join him. But the Romans succeeded in defeating and killing Hasdrubal before the two armies could combine. They flung his severed head into Hannibal's camp. Hannibal exclaimed, looking sadly at this grim object, 'Carthage, I see your fate!' Yet Hannibal stayed in Italy for another four years, more and more resembling a lion at bay.

Eventually the Romans made a decisive move. They sent a large Roman army to Africa to threaten Carthage itself. This meant that Hannibal had to be recalled to defend his city, and in 202 BC the Carthaginians were defeated in a great battle at Zama. The war was over and Carthage's might was shattered. Hannibal fled and some twenty years later committed suicide rather than fall into Roman hands.

Rome was now the leading power in the western Mediterranean and had won the beginnings of an empire. Yet a later generation of Romans was not content with this victory. 'Dēlenda est Carthāgō!' ('Carthage must be destroyed!') The city of Carthage was razed to the ground at the end of the Third Punic War in 146 BC.

In 1985, 2,131 years later, the Mayors of Carthage and Rome signed a peace treaty, committing the two cities to an 'exchange of knowledge and the establishment of common information, cultural and artistic programmes'.

Trace the map on p. 116 and on your copy mark Hannibal's route from Spain to Italy and the sites of the principal battles.

Do you admire Hannibal? Give reasons for your answer.

iter tandem cōnfectum erat, Quīntus paterque Rōmam advēnerant.

postrīdie ad forum contendērunt; Quīntus numquam aedificia tam magnifica vīderat.

tandem Flaccus fīliō 'iam satis spectāvistī,' inquit; 'venī ād lūdum Orbiliī.'

Quīntus nōn satis spectāverat, sed pater eum ē forō dūxit.

Ⓖ Revision

Revise verbs **dīcō** to **mittō** from the Grammar Section, page 183, and learn the perfect stems carefully.

Ⓖ The pluperfect tense

1 **amāv-eram** I had loved   3 **rēx-eram** I had ruled
2 **monu-eram** I had advised   4 **audīv-eram** I had heard

This tense is used as in English: **vesper vēnerat cum domum rediērunt** evening <u>had come</u> when they returned home.

Quīntus numquam aedificia tam splendida vīderat Quintus <u>had</u> never <u>seen</u> such splendid buildings.

The tense is formed by adding the endings to the perfect stem as follows

1	2	3	4	
amō	moneō	regō	audiō	sum
amāv-	monu-	rēx-	audīv-	fu-
amāv-eram	monu-eram	rēx-eram	audīv-eram	fu-eram
amāv-erās	monu-erās	rēx-erās	audīv-erās	fu-erās
amāv-erat	monu-erat	rēx-erat	audīv-erat	fu-erat
amāv-erāmus	monu-erāmus	rēx-erāmus	audīv-erāmus	fu-erāmus
amāv-erātis	monu-erātis	rēx-erātis	audīv-erātis	fu-erātis
amāv-erant	monu-erant	rēx-erant	audīv-erant	fu-erant

Exercise 15.1

Translate
vēnerant, mānseram, responderat, laudāverās, nuntiāveram, dīxerat, dormīverant
we had seen, they had led, I had worked, you had called, he had ruled, they had climbed

◗ Questions

You have already met questions introduced by **cūr?** why? and **quid?** what?

cūr id facis?   Why are you doing that?
quid facis?   What are you doing?

Learn the following asking words

ubi? where?   **ubi est lūdus Orbiliī?** Where is the school of Orbilius?

quandō? when?   **quandō domum rediit?** When did he return home?

quis? who?   **quis hoc fēcit?** Who did this?

-ne may be tacked on to the first word of a sentence to show that it is a question, e.g.

domum īmus We are going home (statement).
domum-ne īmus? Are we going home? (question).

nōnne is used to introduce questions expecting the answer 'yes', e.g.
nōnne domum īmus? Aren't we going home? (or 'We are going home, aren't we?')

Exercise 15.2

Translate

1 venīs-ne ad lūdum?
2 quis tē iussit hoc facere?
3 quandō domō discessistī?
4 ubi est canis?
5 nōnne cupis eum domum dūcere?

6 Where is father?
7 Didn't you see him in the field?
8 When did he return home?
9 Is mother anxious?
10 Haven't you told her everything?
11 Who is helping her?

ROMA

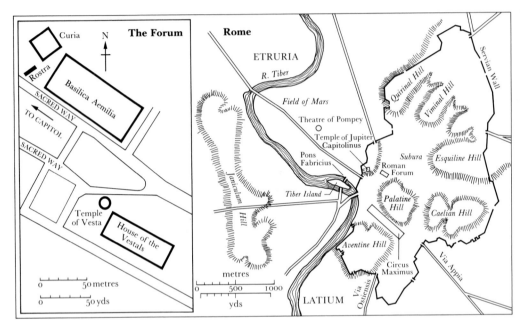

nox iam vēnerat cum Quīntus paterque Rōmam
intrāvērunt. caupō malam cēnam eīs dedit et iussit eōs
in cubiculō parvō et sordidō dormīre. valdē fessī erant
sed nōn bene dormiēbant; nam lectī sordidī erant et
cīmicēs eōs vexābant. prīmā lūce Flaccus Quīntum
excitāvit et 'venī, Quīnte,' inquit, 'dēbēmus lūdum
Orbiliī quaerere.'

lentē prōcēdebant per viās urbis. tandem in Viā
Sacrā ambulābant et mox ad forum vēnerant. Quīntus
numquam aedificia tam magnifica vīderat; diū stābat
attonitus, deinde omnia spectābat. hīc erat templum
Vestae, ubi Virginēs Vestālēs ignem perpetuum
cūrābant; illīc erat Basilica Aemilia, ubi magistrātūs iūs
dīcēbant; hīc erant rōstra, ubi magistrātūs apud

caupō inn-keeper
cubiculō bedroom
sordidō dirty
lectī beds
cīmicēs bed-bugs
vexābant annoyed

attonitus astonished
ubi where; ignem
perpetuum everlasting fire
illīc there
magistrātūs magistrates; iūs
dīcēbant administered justice

populum cōntiōnēs habēbant; illīc steterat Cūria; iam
ruīnīs iacēbat, a populāribus ambusta. ā fronte erat
mōns Capitōlīnus, ubi stābat ingēns templum Iovis.

ubi omnia diū spectāvērunt, Flaccus iuvenem quī
praeterībat rogāvit: 'dīc mihi, sī vīs, ubi est lūdus
Orbiliī?' ille Flaccō respondit: 'nōn longē abest.
prīmum prōcēde ad summum collem, deinde ad
dexteram dēscende.' Flaccus eī grātiās ēgit
Quīntumque ad summum collem dūxit.

mox extrā iānuam lūdī stābant. puerōs audīre
poterant recitantēs et Orbilium eōs corrigentem. sed
nōn intrāvērunt. Flaccus Quīntō 'venī, Quīnte,' inquit;
'prīmum dēbēmus nova vestīmenta emere
domiciliumque condūcere.' Quīntus paterque ē mediā
urbe discessērunt et prōcēdēbant ad Subūram ubi
pauperēs habitābant. ibi nūllae erant aedēs magnificae
sed altae īnsulae, in quibus multae familiae habitābant.
viae sordidae erant et olentēs; multī hominēs hūc illūc
festīnābant; ubīque clāmor et tumultus.

apud populum before the
people; **cōntiōnēs**
habēbant gave speeches
steterat had stood
ruīnīs in ruins
ambusta burnt down
ā populāribus by the lefties; **ā**
fronte in front
praeterībat was passing by; **sī**
vīs if you please
ad dexteram to the right
grātiās thanks
extrā outside
recitantēs reciting
corrigentem correcting
vestīmenta clothes
domicilium lodgings
condūcere hire
aedēs houses
īnsulae blocks of flats; **in**
quibus in which
olentēs smelly
ubīque everywhere
tumultus uproar

The house of Diana, a block of flats at Ostia

A reconstruction of a five-storey
block of flats at Ostia

tandem Flaccus īnsulam intrāvit et iānitōrem
quaesīvit. invēnit eum in angulō aulae dormientem;
ēbrius erat. Flaccus eum excitāvit et dīxit: 'ego fīliusque
nūper Rōmam advēnimus; vīs-ne domicilium nōbīs
locāre?' ille nōn surrēxit sed Flaccō respondit: 'nūllum
domicilium habeō vacuum; omnia opplēta sunt. abī.'
sīc dīxit et redormīvit.

Flaccus ad eum accessit et ōrāvit: 'nōn magnum
domicilium rogāmus,' inquit; 'nōnne ūnum cēnāculum
habēs vacuum?' iānitor oculōs aperuit et clāmāvit:
'nōnne audīvistī, caudex? nūllum domicilium habeō
vacuum.' sīc dīxit et oculōs clausit. pater fīliusque
trīstēs in viam exierant, cum iānitor, quī iam
experrēctus erat, eōs vocāvit: 'stāte, manēte. errāvī.
ūnum cēnāculum habeō vacuum. nōn magnum est, in
summō tabulātō. venīte.'

Flaccus Quīntusque celeriter rediērunt ad
iānitōrem, quī eōs ad cēnāculum dūxit. multōs gradūs
ascendērunt; quattuor tabulāta praeterierant cum
tandem ad summum advēnērunt. ibi parvum erat
cēnāculum, sub tegulīs situm. iānua frācta erat; nūlla
sēdes; grabātus vetus in angulō stat.

iānitor, quī iam ānxius erat, 'nōn lautum est,'
inquit, 'nec cārum. vīs-ne id condūcere? quīnque
dēnāriōs rogō.' Flaccus īrātus erat; 'nimis rogās,'
inquit; 'cēnāculum est parvum et sordidum. trēs
dēnāriōs tibi dare volō.' ille respondit: 'trēs dēnāriōs
dīcis, furcifer? nōlī nūgās agere. dā mihi quattuor
dēnāriōs, sī domum condūcere cupis.'

Flaccus aegrē concessit et argentum iānitōrī
trādidit. mox iānitor abiit.

iānitōrem door-keeper
angulō aulae corner of the courtyard
ēbrius drunk
nūper recently; **vīs-ne** are you willing
locāre to let
surrēxit got up
vacuum empty
opplēta occupied
redormīvit went back to sleep
cēnāculum garret
caudex blockhead
clausit shut
experrēctus awakened
errāvī I was wrong
summō tabulātō the top storey

gradūs steps
tabulāta storeys
praeterierant had gone up
sub tegulīs beneath the tiles
situm situated; **frācta** broken
sēdes seat; **grabātus** camp-bed
lautum elegant, smart
condūcere hire, rent
dēnāriōs denarii
nimis too much
volō I am willing
furcifer scoundrel
nūgās agere play the fool
aegrē reluctantly
concessit gave in

agō, agere, ēgī	I do, drive	**summus-a-um**	highest, greatest; top
emō, emere, ēmī	I buy	**cārus-a-um**	dear
aperiō, aperīre, aperuī	I open	**medius-a-um**	middle
apertus-a-um	open	NB **media urbs**	the middle of the city
		vetus, veteris	old
oculus, oculī, *m.*	eye	**pauper, pauperis**	poor
Iuppiter, Iovis, *m.*	Jupiter	**pauperēs**	poor men
iuvenis, iuvenis, *m.*	young man		
forum, forī, *n.*	forum	**prīmum** (adverb)	first
templum, templī, *n.*	temple	**deinde**	then, next
		anteā (adverb)	before
altus-a-um	high, deep	**hīc**	here

illīc there	**hūc** to here, hither	**illūc** to there, thither

NB The imperatives of the following verbs should be carefully learnt

dīcō	dīc, dīcite	ferō	fer, ferte
dūcō	dūc, dūcite	faciō	fac, facite

Exercise 15.3

Translate

1 ad forum ambulābāmus. ad forum ambulāverant. ad forum ambulō. ad forum ambulāvit.
2 cūr in forō manēs? vīdistī-ne omnia aedificia? nōnne cupis templum Vestae spectāre?
3 Quīntus numquam aedificia tam splendida vīderat. diū stābat attonitus. tandem domum rediit.
4 nōnne anteā Rōmam vēnistī? dēbēs ad forum īre et omnia spectāre.
5 quis Quīntum ad lūdum dūxit? quandō domō discessit? cūr sērō advēnit?
6 Quīntus paterque per viam festīnābant. nam domō sērō discesserant. tandem ad lūdum advēnērunt.

Exercise 15.4

Translate into Latin

1 We were walking to Rome; I had never gone to Rome before. When we arrived, father led me to the forum.
2 On the fifth day we arrived at Capua. We stayed the night in an inn. I had never stayed at an inn before.
3 Gaius was climbing the wall. Quintus was anxious. He called him and said: 'Come down, Gaius; you are not safe.'
4 What have you done? Why are you running home? Ought you not to go to school?
5 Who said that to you? Didn't you hear the master? He ordered you to work.

inn **caupōna, caupōnae**, *f.*
that **id**

Exercise 15.5

Translate the first two paragraphs and answer the questions below on the third paragraph

Quīntus Flaccusque sōlī erant. Quīntus cēnāculum circumspectāns flēbat, sed pater 'nōlī dēspērāre, Quīnte,' inquit; 'prīmum dēbēmus nova vestīmenta emere; deinde possumus cēnāculum pūrgāre. fortis estō. venī.'

circumspectāns looking around
vestīmenta clothes
pūrgāre clean
estō be

In the clothes shop

iterum dēscendērunt et in viam exiērunt. mox ad
vestiārium vēnērunt. Flaccus togam praetextam et
tunicam Quīntō ēmit, sibi ipsī duās tunicās candidās.
Quīntus numquam vestīmenta tam splendida habuerat;
patrī grātiās ēgit; laetī ad īnsulam rediērunt. aquam
dūxērunt ē fonte pūblicō et lentē gradūs ascendērunt.

primum sē lāvērunt; deinde Flaccus dīxit: 'ego
dēbeō ad lūdum īre et rēs expedīre; tū, Quīnte, hīc
manē et cēnāculum pūrgā.' itaque Quīntus sōlus
manēbat et dīligenter labōrābat. paene omnia
pūrgāverat, cum pater rediit et 'Orbilium vīdī,' inquit;
'omnia expedīta sunt. crās ad lūdum tē dūcam.'

vestiārium	clothes shop
togam praetextam	toga bordered with purple
tunicam	tunic
Quīntō	for Quintus; **sibi**
ipsī	for himself
candidās	white
pūblicō	public
lāvērunt	they washed
rēs expedīre	arrange matters
pūrgā	clean
paene	almost
expedīta	arranged; **crās**
	tomorrow; **dūcam** I shall take

1 What did Flaccus say he had to do?
2 What did Quintus do while Flaccus was away; how did he get on?
3 What did Flaccus say when he got back?
4 From this paragraph give one example each of a verb in the present,
  imperfect, perfect and pluperfect tenses (in this order).
5 From this paragraph give one example each of: a reflexive pronoun;
  an adverb; an imperative; an infinitive; a conjunction.
6 Translate into Latin:
(a) When Quintus saw the garret, he wept.
(b) Flaccus said, 'Don't cry; we can soon clean everything.'
(c) When Flaccus returned, Quintus had already brought water from
    the spring.

ROME

You read at the end of Chapter 13 about a grim episode in the history
of Rome. The city was sacked by the Gauls and lay half in ruins. It
seemed a good idea to many to abandon the site and to emigrate to
the neighbouring city of Veii. The general Camillus strongly urged the
citizens to stay. 'It was with good reason,' he said, 'that the gods and
men chose this location for founding the city. The hills cause a healthy
climate; the river is admirably placed to bring us produce from inland
regions as well as supplies from abroad; though we have the
advantages of being near to the sea, we are not too close to it and for
that reason exposed to dangers from foreign fleets; we are in a central
position in Italy. Our location is in fact an ideal one for a city destined
to become great.'

Rome was built on the left bank of the River Tiber about sixteen
miles from where it flows into the sea. A small island in the river
breaks up the strong current here and the water is shallow and easy to

ford. A bridge to this island, the Pōns Fabricius, had been built by Horace's time (in 62 BC). This is still standing and is in fact used by traffic. Rome's control of this part of the Tiber was of great importance since anyone travelling along the western side of Italy would almost certainly cross the river at this point. Thus Rome became a key centre for inland trade. Dangerous shoals in the river for a long time stopped Ostia, the port at the mouth of the Tiber, from becoming as important a harbour as the more distant Puteoli near Naples. But Rome was still able to engage in a flourishing trade abroad.

The famous seven hills of the city, especially the rocky Capitoline hill, made it comparatively safe from attack. The Roman orator and politician Cicero, who is soon to enter our story, praised the city's natural strength. 'Romulus and the other Roman kings,' he wrote, 'showed great wisdom in laying out the course of the wall along a line of hills which are high and sheer at every point. The one approach, which is between the Esquiline and Quirinal hills, is protected by a huge rampart and ditch. The Capitoline hill is so well fortified by its steep walls of rock that, even in the terrible time when the Gauls invaded, it remained safe and undamaged. The place chosen by Romulus was in addition plentifully supplied with springs, and even if the surrounding marshes were a breeding-ground for malaria, Rome is in fact a healthy site. For the hills channel the breezes and give shade to the valleys.'

Camillus won the argument and the Romans stayed in Rome. It was also the home of their gods, and in this chapter we have seen Horace and his father walking along the Sacred Way, the only road of any size in Rome, to the Forum.

The Forum
(a) The temple of Vesta

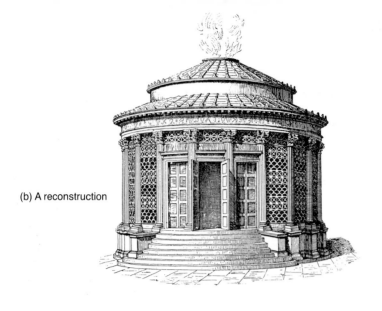

(b) A reconstruction

Here Horace sees the Temple of Vesta where a flame was always kept alight by the Vestal Virgins in honour of the goddess of the hearth, and the great temple of Jupiter on the Capitoline Hill, built by Tarquin the Proud. He also passes by the law courts and the platform (**rōstra**) where magistrates stood to address the people. The senate-house (**Cūria**), the seat of government, had stood close to them on the north side of the Forum. It had recently been burnt down by rioters. Horace has arrived in Rome at a very troubled time, as you will see.

The Forum was certainly no longer the humble market-place which it had once been. Bankers and money-lenders had replaced the shop-keepers and it was now the busy heart of city life. Rome had almost a million inhabitants in Horace's day and it became a city of the greatest splendour. The first emperor, Augustus, boasted that he had found it brick and left it marble. But many squalid areas remained and Horace and his father find a room in one of these, the Subūra.

A bend in the Tiber enclosed the Campus Martius (Field of Mars), on the other side of the Capitoline Hill, to the north west. This was a huge open space used for military and athletic exercises. The Theatre of Pompey was nearby, the first stone theatre in Rome. This was completed in 55 BC and could seat an audience of 9,000 to 10,000. Plays, both comic and tragic, were performed here. The huge Circus Maximus stood between the Palatine and Aventine hills. Here chariot races took place for the amusement of a vast and uncritical audience. The taste of the average Roman was for the violent, sensational and crude.

❓ Summarize briefly the advantages of the site of Rome.

❓ Rome was the capital city of a great empire. Suggest modern equivalents, e.g. in London, for the buildings described above. What other public buildings would you have expected to find in such a city?

CHAPTER XVI

Orbilius barbam longam habēbat et vultum sevērum;
in manū ferulam gerēbat.

Orbilius multōs versūs recitāvit; Quīntus
eōs in tabulā scrīpsit.

Orbilius Quīntum in medium dūxit.
'ecce, puerī,' inquit, 'novum discipulum
vōbīs commendō; nōmen eī est Quīntus
Horātius Flaccus.'

LUDUS ORBILII

postrīdiē Flaccus Quīntum māne excitāvit. Quīntus sē
lāvit et novam togam induit. pater fīliusque in viam
dēscendērunt. Flaccus capsulam Quīntī portābat et
partēs paedagōgī agēbat. multī hominēs per viās iam
festīnābant. Flaccus Quīntusque per turbam
prōcēdēbant et ante lūcem ad lūdum Orbiliī
advēnērunt.

māne early

partēs paedagōgī the part of a
tutor
turbam crowd

127

iānua aperta erat. itaque intrāvērunt et Orbilium
quaesīvērunt. invēnērunt eum in aulā sedentem. vir
gravis erat; barbam longam habēbat et vultum
sevērum; in manū ferulam gerēbat. Flaccus accessit et
'ecce!' inquit, 'magister, fīlium meum Quīntum ad tē
dūcō.' ille Quīntum īnspexit et 'venī hūc, Quīnte,'
inquit, 'et pauca mihi respondē.'

non pauca sed multa Quīntum rogāvit, prīmum dē
rēbus Rōmānīs. Quīntus ad omnia respondēre poterat,
nam pater eī multa dē rēbus Rōmānīs nārrāverat.
'euge!' inquit Orbilius; 'age, potes-ne legere litterās?'
librum Quīntō trādidit et iussit eum legere. Quīntus
librum facile legere poterat. Orbilius patrī 'puer bene
legere potest,' inquit. 'age, Quīnte, iam scrībe hōs
versūs.' Quīntus tabulam stilumque parāvit et Orbilium
audīvit. ille versūs recitāvit, quōs Quīntus scrīpsit in
tabulā.

ubi litterās īnspexit, Quīntum mathēmatica
quaedam rogāvit dē triangulīs et circulīs. Quīntus
haesitābat; non poterat intellegere. Orbilius īrātus erat;
ferulam vibrābat. 'puer dē mathēmaticīs,' inquit, 'nihil
scit. age, potes-ne Graecē dīcere?'

Flaccus, quī iam ānxius erat, prōcessit. 'magister,'
inquit, 'fīlius meus Graecē nec dīcere nec scrībere
potest. propter hanc causam eum ad tē dūcō, quod tū
linguam Graecam bene docēre potes.' Orbilius valdē
īrātus erat. 'quid?' inquit, 'quid? puer Graecē nec
dīcere nec legere potest? mīrum est. dēbet statim
litterās Graecās discere. plānē barbarus est.' librum
Graecē scrīptum Quīntō trādidit et iussit eum omnēs
litterās discere.

iam cēterī puerī advēnerant. Quīntus eōs audīre
poterat inter sē colloquentēs. Orbilius Quīntō dīxit:
'venī, puer. tempus est studēre.' Quīntum patremque
in scholam dūxit. ubi scholam intrāvērunt, omnēs puerī
surrēxērunt et magistrum salūtāvērunt. Flaccus ad
extrēmam partem scholae iit, ubi cēterī paedagōgī
sedēbant post puerōs.

Orbilius Quīntum in medium dūxit et 'ecce, puerī,'
inquit, 'novum discipulum vōbīs commendō. nōmen eī
Quīntus Horātius Flaccus est. barbarus est; Graecē nec
dīcere nec scrībere potest.' puerī rīdēbant. ille 'tacēte,
puerī. Quīnte, ad angulum ī et litterās Graecās disce.'
itaque Quīntus in angulō scholae miserē sedēbat et
litterīs Graecīs studēbat.

aulā courtyard
sedentem sitting
barbam beard
sevērum severe; ferulam cane

īnspexit looked at

dē rēbus Rōmānīs about
Roman history

euge! well done!; age come
now

hōs versūs these verses
tabulam writing-tablet
stilum pen
recitāvit recited; quōs which

mathēmatica mathematical
questions
haesitābat hesitated
vibrābat brandished
Graecē (in) Greek

propter hanc causam for this
reason
linguam language

mīrum extraordinary
plānē totally
barbarus barbarian
scrīptum written

colloquentēs talking

scholam school room

extrēmam back

commendō introduce; eī his

angulum corner

Orbilius cēterōs Iliadem Homērī docēbat; omnēs
discipulī Graecē legere poterant; omnēs Homērum
facile intellegēbant; omnēs versūs Graecōs rēctē
recitābant. Quīntus nihil intellegēbat. interdum ūnus
puerōrum sē vertit et nārēs fastīdiōsē corrūgāvit.
Quīntus valdē miser erat; domum redīre cupiēbat.
omnēs puerī magnī et lautī erant, fīliī senātōrum
equitumque.

rēctē correctly

interdum from time to time

nārēs fastīdiōsē corrūgāvit
turned up his nose scornfully

lautī elegant, smart

equitēs equites, knights

interdum ūnus puerōrum sē vertit et nārēs fastīdiōsē corrūgāvit

merīdiē Orbilius eōs dīmīsit et iussit in aulā
paulīsper lūdere.omnēs ē scholā festīnāvērunt. Quīntus
ultimus exiit et in angulō aulae sōlus stābat. nēmō cum
eō lūdēbat, nēmō eī quicquam dīxit.

tandem, ubi Orbilius eōs in scholam revocāvit,
ūnus puerōrum ad eum accessit; rīdēbat et 'nōlī
dēspērāre, Quīnte,' inquit; 'nōn malī puerī sunt. et
Orbilius sevērus est, sed doctus. malōs puerōs saevē
pūnit sed, sī dīligenter studēs, cōmis est. nōs eum
plāgōsum Orbilium appellāmus.'

Quīntus eī respondēre cupiēbat sed Orbilius eōs
iterum in scholam revocāvit.

merīdiē at midday
paulīsper for a little
ultimus last
quicquam anything

doctus learned
cōmis kind; **plāgōsum** the
flogger
appellāmus we call

intellegō, intellegere, intellēxī	I understand
pūniō, pūnīre, pūnīvī	I punish
rīdeō, rīdēre, rīsī	I laugh, smile
studeō, studēre, studuī + dat.	I study, I am keen on
studium, studiī, *n.*	study; keenness
sciō, scīre, scīvī	I know
littera, litterae, *f.*	letter
liber, librī, *m.*	book

senātor, senātōris, *m.*	senator	
manus, manūs, *f.*	hand	**Some English abbreviations**
nēmō	no one	
		a.m. **ante merīdiem**
facilis, facile	easy	p.m. **post merīdiem**
facile	easily	N.B. **notā bene**
difficilis, difficile	difficult	i.e. **id est**
gravis, grave	heavy; serious	e.g. **exemplī grātiā**
paucī, paucae, pauca	few	etc. **et cētera**

Ⓖ The fourth declension

	singular	*plural*
nom.	gradus	gradūs
acc.	gradum	gradūs
gen.	gradūs	graduum
dat.	graduī	gradibus
abl.	gradū	gradibus

Nouns of this declension have stems in -**u**; they decline very like the third declension, but **u** predominates in all cases except the dative and ablative plural

You have so far met the following nouns in this declension

exercitus, exercitūs, *m.*	an army	**versus, versūs**, *m.*	a verse
gradus, gradūs, *m.*	a step	**vultus, vultūs**, *m.*	face, expression
cursus, cursūs, *m.*	course, race	**manus, manūs**, *f.*	hand

NB 1 Nearly all nouns of this declension are masculine; **manus** is feminine.

2 Nominative and genitive singular and nominative and accusative plural all end in -**us**; in the nominative singular **u** sounds short, but in the other three cases long: **ū**.

3 Second declension nouns like **fīlius** end in -**us** in the nominative singular and so do fourth declension nouns, but their genitives are different. So in vocabulary lists you know which declension they belong to by their genitive; so **dominus, dominī** – second declension; **versus, versūs** – fourth declension.

Ⓖ Revision

Revise verbs **nōscō** to **dēserō** from the Grammar Section, page 183, and learn the perfect stems carefully.

Exercise 16.1

Put the nouns in brackets into the right case and then translate

1 puer multōs (versus) recitāvit.
2 Trōiānī (cursus) ad Italiam dīrigunt.
3 magister ferulam in (manus) gerēbat sed (vultus) mītem habēbat.
4 rēx in (gradus) templī stābat.

    dīrigunt steer
    ferulam cane
    mītem gentle

Exercise 16.2

Analyse the following sentences and then translate

1 Quīntus paterque multōs gradūs dēscendērunt et in viam exiērunt.
2 pater capsulam Quīntī in manū portābat.
3 ante lūcem ad lūdum advēnērunt; Quīntus tantum lūdum numquam vīderat.
4 magister vultum sevērum habēbat sed eōs cōmiter salūtāvit.

    cōmiter kindly

Exercise 16.3

Translate into Latin

1 All the boys had arrived; Quintus could hear them talking.
2 His father led Quintus to the master; he had a serious expression and carried a book in his hand.
3 He handed over the book to Quintus and told the boy to read it.
4 He recited verses and soon asked: 'Have you written all the verses?'
5 'I wrote the verses and gave you back the book.'
6 Quintus had not learnt Greek letters; the other boys could read and write in Greek.
7 We had already left school and were walking home.
8 When we reached the forum, we climbed the steps of the temple.
9 The general led the army back to camp and sent a message to the king.
10 They boarded the ships and held course to the open sea.

    talking **loquentēs**
    recite **recitō**
    in Greek **Graecē**

Exercise 16.4

Translate

post merīdiem Orbilius Latīnē docēbat. puerī poētae veterī Latīnō studēbant, Līviō Andronīcō nōmine. poēma frīgidum erat et difficile, sed Quīntus aliquantum intellegere poterat. tandem Orbilius puerōs dīmīsit. omnēs laetī discessērunt et cum paedagōgīs domum rediērunt.

    Quīntus cum patre trīstis ad regiōnēs pauperum ambulābat. 'ō pater,' inquit; 'omnēs aliī puerī magnī et lautī et ingeniōsī sunt; ego parvus sum et pinguis.

    Latīnē in Latin

    poēma poem; **frīgidum** dull
    aliquantum some of it
    paedagōgīs tutors

    lautī elegant, smart
    ingeniōsī clever; **pinguis** fat

numquam poterō cum eīs contendere.' ille fīliō respondit: 'nōlī dēspērāre, cāre fīlī. tū et ingeniōsus es et dīligenter studēre cupis. mox omnēs aliōs superābis. bonō animō estō.'

poterō will I be able
contendere compete
superābis you will beat
bonō animō estō cheer up

Imagine that you are Quintus; describe your first day in Orbilius' school.

The other boys all went off home 'laetī', but Quintus 'trīstis'. Does this surprise you?

SPQR (Senatus Populusque Romanus)

The new republic of Rome was governed by the Senate after the kings had been driven out in 510 BC. The Senate was a council of elders which numbered between 300 and 600. The chief magistrates were the two consuls who were elected to hold office for a year. Because there were two of them it made it unlikely that one consul would seize all the power and become another king. They were able to veto each other's proposals (i.e. stop them being carried out), but the Romans were a practical people and the consuls usually worked out a way of managing affairs in harmony.

The consul's attendants carry the *fascēs*.

The consuls commanded Roman armies operating in Italy. They were accompanied when on official business by twelve attendants carrying **fascēs**, bundles of rods which were the emblems of their authority. From the end of the first century BC men who had served as consuls could be sent out to govern Rome's increasing number of provinces abroad. Here the bundle of rods carried by their attendants contained an axe, which signified their power to pass the death sentence.

There were other officials, but one group had very different powers from the rest. These were the ten tribunes of the people (**plēbs**), who were appointed to support the authority of the common people against the upper classes. They could veto the Senate's measures and it was illegal to lay a finger on them. The Senate was a conservative body – that is to say, it preferred to keep things as they always had been –, so in the early days the tribunes of the people proved a valuable force in winning justice for the lower classes of Rome.

The common people had voting rights, but they had no real influence on events. Elections were rigged and they were only allowed to vote for members of the upper classes. The many conquests which were expanding the empire brought more and more slaves to Rome and they did more and more of the work. There was, therefore, an increasing number of unemployed citizens who had to be supported by subsidized or free corn. There was no good reason for voting for one candidate rather than another except for their short-term promises, so the common people's vote tended to go to those who gave them the most corn or put on the best shows in the theatre. A Roman poet was to remark, with considerable truth, that the only things that interested the **plēbs** were 'bread and circuses' ('**pānem et circēnsēs**').

A middle class, between the senators and the **plēbs**, but far closer to the former, developed increasing power. This class consisted of the equestrians or knights, the **equitēs**. These had to have a large sum of money to qualify for membership. They tended to be the financiers of Rome, the bankers, money-lenders and collectors of taxes.

Marcus Tullius Cicero, the great statesman of the first century BC whom Quintus meets in the next chapter, tried to bring about harmony between knights and senators. But this was an unreal though noble wish. At the time of our story, each class seemed only interested in what appeared to be best for itself, and the most powerful class, the Senate, was hopelessly divided. In the last decades of the republic a succession of individuals set out to establish their own authority and gain supreme power. The kings had been driven out in the sixth century BC. Five hundred years later, it looked as if they were on the way back.

After reading this section, see if you can answer the following questions:

1 Who were the chief magistrates? What was the emblem of their authority?
2 Who were the officials especially elected to protect the **plēbs**?
3 Why were the **plēbs** so powerless in a republic where every citizen had the vote?
4 Who were the **equitēs**?
5 Why was unemployment so serious a problem in this period?

CHAPTER XVII

Quīntus domum cum patre ambulābat.

accurrit Marcus et 'Quīnte,' inquit, 'nōnne cupis mēcum ad Campum venīre?'

ubi ad Campum advēnērunt, multī iuvenēs lūdēbant; Quīntus laetus spectābat.

Marcus in equum saltāvit et ad ultimam partem Campī equitāvit.

G Revision

Revise verbs **cadō** to **resistō** from the Grammar Section, page 183, and learn the perfect stems carefully.

G The meaning of the imperfect tense

It should be clear by now that you cannot always translate the imperfect tense the same way; this tense is used for any action which is continuous, incomplete or repeated; so

Marcus cum patre ambulābat	Marcus was walking with his father.
Marcus cotīdiē ad lūdum ībat	Marcus used to go to school every day.
Marcus tōtum diem in lūdō manēbat	Marcus stayed all day in school.
Marcus portam claudēbat	Marcus was shutting the door.

You must look at the sense and choose the appropriate meaning.

Exercise 17.1

Translate the first five sentences of the Latin story in this chapter.
Make sure that you choose the appropriate meaning for the imperfect
tenses.

Compound verbs

*Revise what was said about compound verbs in Chapter 4 (p. 27) and
Chapter 12 (p. 91).*
Other prefixes which change the meanings of verbs are

con- (1) together **convocō** I call together
     (2) it can strengthen the meaning of the verb without changing
        it, e.g. **iaciō** I throw; **coniciō** I hurl
             moveō I move; **commoveō** I move violently

circum- round, e.g. **circumspectō** I look round; **circumveniō** I
        surround

dis/dī- in different directions, away, e.g. **discurrunt** they run in
        different directions; **dīmittō** I send away, dismiss

prō- forward, before, e.g. **prōpōnō** I put forward, propose
                       prōcēdō I go forward

prōd- before vowels, e.g. **prōdeō** I go forward

trāns- across, e.g. **trānseō** I go across; **trānsiciō** I throw across

NB Changes in spelling: **faciō** but **cōnficiō**; **iaciō** but **coniciō**;
                      capiō but **accipiō**; **cadō** but **dēcidō**.

Exercise 17.2

What is the meaning of the following compound verbs?
1 prōiciō, dēiciō, trānsiciō, circumiciō, iniciō.
2 dēpōnō, compōnō, prōpōnō, impōnō, dispōnō.
3 afferō (= ad-ferō), īnferō, cōnferō, dēferō, prōferō.
4 accurrō (= ad-currō), incurrō, dēcurrō, prōcurrō, concurrō.
5 dīmittō, dēmittō, immittō (= in-mittō), trānsmittō.

QUINTUS AD CAMPUM MARTIUM ADIT

cotīdiē Flaccus fīlium ad lūdum Orbiliī dūcēbat.
Quīntus celeriter discēbat et mox Graecē et dīcere et
scrībere poterat; Orbilius eum laudābat; nam bonus
discipulus erat et studiīs gaudēbat. prīmum Quīntus
valdē miser erat; cēterī puerī eum vītābant nec cum eō

cotīdiē every day

discipulus pupil; **gaudēbat** +
dat. enjoyed
vītābant avoided

lūdere volēbant.

sed decimō diē is quī prīmō diē eum cōmiter
salūtāverat ad eum accessit, dum sōlus in angulō aulae
sedet, et 'Quīnte,' inquit, 'nōlī sōlus in angulō
sedēre. mihi nōmen Marcus est. venī mēcum et comitēs
salūtā.' sīc dīxit et Quīntum ad comitēs dūxit. illī lūdō
dēsistunt et Quīntum tacitī spectant.

Marcus 'ecce, amīcī,' inquit, 'Quīntum ad vōs
dūxī; nōn dēbet ille sōlus in angulō sedēre, dum vōs
lūditis. salūtāte eum.' cēterī puerī Marcum timēbant;
nam puer magnus erat et lautus; et pater eius erat vir
valdē īnsignis, quī cōnsul fuerat et clārus ōrātor. itaque
cum Quīntō cōmiter loquentēs multa rogābant dē patre
domōque. ille verēcundus erat et pauca respondit.

sīc paulātim cēterī puerī Quīntum accipiēbant et
cum eō lūdēbant. nam Quīntus puer cōmis erat et
facētus; Orbilium poterat imitārī ad unguem; vultum
sevērum simulābat; magnā vōce comitēs castīgābat, eōs
caudicēs appellāns; illī impotenter rīdēbant.

ōlim ubi Orbilius eōs dīmīsit, Marcus ad Quīntum
accurrit et 'age, Quīnte,' inquit, 'quō īs? domum-ne
iam redīs? nōnne vīs ad Campum venīre et iuvenēs
spectāre dum lūdunt?' Quīntus numquam ad Campum
ierat; itaque libenter Marcum sequēns, mox ad viam
Triumphālem advēnit; theātrum Pompēiī praeteriērunt
et celeriter ad Campum aderant.

Campus lātus erat, prope rīpās Tiberis situs.
ubīque iuvenēs lūdēbant; aliī iacula iaciēbant, aliī
discōs; aliī ad ultimam partem campī equitābant. paucī
in flūmen inierant et fortiter natābant.

Marcus iuvenēs quōsdam seniōrēs cōnspexit, quī
iacula iaciēbant. ad eōs accessit et salūtāvit. ūnus
iaculum eī trādidit, quod ille longē prōiēcit. alter
amīcus accessit, equō vectus; equō dēscendit
Marcumque salūtāvit; 'salvē, Marce,' inquit, 'vīs-ne
equitāre?' Marcus nihil respondit sed in equum saluit et
ad ultimam partem Campī equitāvit.

iuvenis Marcum īrātus spectāvit, dum ille ē
cōnspectū ēvānēscit. 'ecce,' inquit, 'Marcus semper
cupit aliōs superāre, semper cupit victor esse. iam
equum meum fatīgat, quod vōbīs, putō, sē fortem
praebēre cupit.' Quīntus amīcum spectāvit,
admīrātiōne plēnus.

tandem rediit Marcus equumque sūdantem iuvenī
reddidit. omnēs ad urbem lentē rediērunt. ubi ad forum
advēnērunt, Quīntus comitēs valēre iussit et domum

volēbant were willing
is the one; **cōmiter** kindly
angulō aulae a corner of the
courtyard

dēsistunt + abl. stop

eius his
īnsignis distinguished
fuerat had been
loquentēs talking
verēcundus shy
paulātim gradually
cōmis pleasant
facētus amusing; **imitārī**
imitate; **ad unguem** perfectly
simulābat put on; **magnā**
vōce in a loud voice
castīgābat told off
caudicēs blockheads
apellāns calling
impotenter helplessly
vīs you want
libenter gladly; **sequēns**
following
Triumphālem Triumphal
praeteriērunt they passed
lātus wide; **situs** situated
ubīque everywhere; **iacula**
javelins
discōs the discus
equitābant were riding
natābant were swimming
quōsdam certain
seniōrēs older
cōnspexit caught sight of
quod which; **alter** a second
equō vectus riding on
horseback
vīs-ne do you want?
saluit leapt
ultimam furthest
cōnspectū sight
ēvānēscit vanishes
fatīgat tires out
sē praebēre to show himself
admīrātiōne plēnus full of
admiration
sūdantem sweating

136

festīnāvit, et laetus et fessus.

postrīdiē, ubi puerī lūdō discessērunt, Marcus Quīntō 'age, Quīnte,' inquit, 'vīs-ne domum mēcum venīre patremque vīsere?' Quīntus erat verēcundus; 'rē vērā,' inquit, 'mē domum tuam vocās? nōnne pater tuus nimis occupātus est?' ille Quīntō respondit: 'venī, Quīnte. semper occupātus est meus pater, sed semper cupit amīcōs meōs vidēre.'

vīsere to visit; **verēcundus** shy
rē vērā really
nimis too; **occupātus** busy

forum trānsiērunt et montem Palātīnum ascendērunt. mox ad Marcī aedēs advēnērunt. Marcus iānuam pulsāvit; iānitor iānuam aperuit et Marcum salūtāvit: 'salvē, domine,' inquit; 'intrā.' Marcus eum rogāvit: 'ubi est pater?' ille respondit: 'pater tuus est in tablīnō, domine. occupātus est; nam epistolās scrībae dictat.'

aedēs house (*f.pl.*)
iānitor door-keeper

tablīnō study; **epistolās** letters; **scrībae** secretary **dictat** is dictating

Marcus Quīntum in ātrium dūxit.

Marcus Quīntum in ātrium dūxit. ille numquam aedēs tam magnificās vīderat. ātrium erat et lātum et altum; in omnibus lateribus erant magnae iānuae. Marcus Quīntum dūxit ad iānuam quae ā fronte stābat. iānuam pulsāvit. aliquis vōce blandā 'intrā,' inquit. Marcus iānuam aperuit et Quīntum in tablīnum dūxit.

pater Marcī prope mēnsam stābat; vultum gravem habēbat et ānxium sed benevolum; togam praetextam gerēbat tabulamque in manū tenēbat. ubi Marcus intrāvit, eī arrīsit et 'manē paulīsper,' inquit; 'ego

ātrium hall

lateribus sides
quae which; **ā fronte** in front of them
aliquis someone; **vōce blandā** with a pleasant voice
mēnsam table
benevolum kindly
praetextam bordered with purple
arrīsit + dat. he smiled at

epistolam dictō ad Atticum dē rēpūblicā.' Marcus
Quīntō susurrāvit: 'Atticus est amīcus intimus patris
meī; pater, ubi ānxius est, semper eī scrībit dē
rēpūblica.' iam Marcī pater epistolam cōnfēcerat et
scrībae dīxit: 'epistolam statim signā et cursōrī trāde.
iubē eum epistolam ad Atticum statim ferre.'

paulīsper a little
rēpūblicā public affairs, politics
susurrāvit whispered
intimus closest
signā seal; **cursōrī** courier
ferre to take

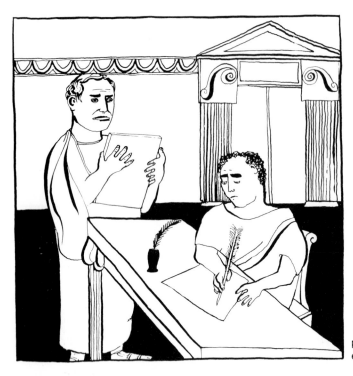

pater Marcī prope mēnsam stābat;
epistolam dictābat.

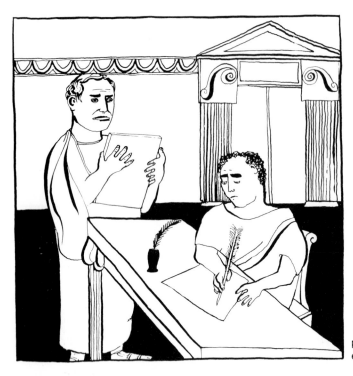

putō, putāre, putāvī	I think, suppose	**lātus-a-um**	wide
superō, superāre, superāvī	I overcome, surpass	**clārus-a-um**	clear; famous
		aliī . . . aliī	some . . . others
lūdō, lūdere, lūsī	I play		
lūdus, lūdī, *m.*	game; school	**quis? quid?**	who? what?
cōnficiō, cōnficere, cōnfecī	I finish	**quō?**	whither, (to) where?
		eō	thither, (to) there
epistola, epistolae, *f.*	letter		
dominus, dominī, *m.*	master, lord	**quantus-a-um?**	how great?
campus, campī, *m.*	plain	**tantus-a-um**	so great
cōnsul, cōnsulis, *m.*	consul		
victor, victōris, *m.*	victor		
ōrātor, ōrātōris, *m.*	speaker, orator		
pes, pedis, *m*	foot		
vōx, vōcis, *f.*	voice		

Revision of adjectives

singular

	m.	f.	n.
nom.	bonus	bona	bonum
acc.	bonum	bonam	bonum
gen.	bonī	bonae	bonī
dat.	bonō	bonae	bonō
abl.	bonō	bonā	bonō

plural

	m.	f.	n.
nom.	bonī	bonae	bona
acc.	bonōs	bonās	bona
gen.	bonōrum	bonārum	bonōrum
dat.	bonīs	bonīs	bonīs
abl.	bonīs	bonīs	bonīs

NB The masculine goes like **dominus**, the feminine like **puella**, the neuter like **bellum**.

So also **miser, misera, miserum**; masculine like **puer**, feminine like **puella**, neuter like **bellum**.

Third declension adjectives

singular

	masc. and *fem.*	neuter
nom.	trīstis	trīste
acc.	trīstem	trīste
gen.	trīstis	trīstis
dat.	trīstī	trīstī
abl.	trīstī	trīstī

plural

	masc. and *fem.*	neuter
nom.	trīstēs	trīstia
acc.	trīstēs	trīstia
gen.	trīstium	trīstium
dat.	trīstibus	trīstibus
abl.	trīstibus	trīstibus

NB Unlike 3rd declension nouns, the ablative ends in **ī**; note also the
neuter plural **-ia**, nom. & acc.
genitive plural **-ium** all genders.

Exercise 17.3

In the following phrases make the adjectives agree with the nouns
(altus) flūminis, puerōs (fortis), senum (trīstis), (omnis) puellīs,
(magnus) urbis, viās (facilis), (multus) hominum, mātrī (cārus),
carmina (laetus), (omnis) mīlitum, rēge (fortis), cōnsilia (audāx)

Exercise 17.4

Translate

1 hodiē tē in Viā Triumphālī vīdī. quō ībās, Quīnte?
2 ad Campum Martium ībam cum amīcīs. ubi eō advēnimus, diū in Campō manēbāmus.
3 multī iuvenēs ibi lūdēbant; aliī iacula coniciēbant, aliī in flūmen incurrēbant.
4 iuvenēs ad campum cotīdiē ībant et sē strēnuē exercēbant.
5 ubi puerī tablīnum iniērunt, Marcī pater epistolam dictābat.
6 Marcī pater cōnsul fuerat et clārus ōrātor erat.
7 ubi epistolam cōnfēcit, scrībam iussit eam cursōrī trādere.
8 quantum est flūmen? flūmen lātum et altum est. nēmō id trānsīre potest.
9 quid in lūdō hodiē fēcistī? litterīs studēbāmus et librum difficilem lēgimus.
10 nōnne librum intellēxistī? nēmō librum tam gravem intellegere potest.

tablīnum study   **scrībam** secretary   **cursōrī** courier

Exercise 17.5

Translate into Latin
1 We went to school every day.
2 The schoolmaster was a serious man and used to punish bad boys.
3 I could not always understand him but I studied hard.
4 When we worked well, he smiled and praised us.
5 Where are you going now? Who told you to open the door?

The ātrium

140

Exercise 17.6

NB Cicero is Marcus's father.

Translate the first two paragraphs and answer the questions below on the last two paragraphs

Cicerō ad puerōs sē vertit. 'venī hūc, Marce,' inquit, 'et amīcum tuum mihi commendā.' Marcus Quīntum ad Cicerōnem dūxit et 'ecce, pater,' inquit, 'volō amīcum meum Quīntum Horātium Flaccum tibi commendāre. puer valdē ingeniōsus est, quī omnēs aliōs studiīs superat.'

    Cicerō ad Quīntum sē vertit et eī arrīsit; 'salvē, Quīnte,' inquit; 'gaudeō quod fīlius meus amīcum tam doctum habet. dīc mihi, quid hodiē in lūdō didicistī?' Quīntus verēcundus erat quod tantō virō respondēre dēbēbat, sed studia bene exposuit.

    ille 'Marcus vērum dīcit. puer valdē ingeniōsus es. Marce, dūc eum ad bibliothēcam et ostende eī meōs librōs. Quīnte, sī vīs, licet tibi librōs meōs legere. audī; hoc tē moneō: cotīdiē aliquid novī lege, cotīdiē aliquid novī scrībe. quis scit? forsitan poēta eris, cārus Mūsīs.' sīc dīxit et librum dē mēnsā sūmpsit. Marcus et Quīntus ē tablīnō tacitī exiērunt.

    ubi in ātrium rediērunt, Marcus Quīntō dīxit: 'Quīnte, bibliothēca ingēns est; sescentī librī Graecī, sescentī Latīnī. num vīs hodiē bibliothēcam spectāre? satis in lūdō studuistī. quid dīcis? venī mēcum in hortum et cum canibus lūde.' Quīntus librōs spectāre cupiēbat sed Marcō concessit, quī eum in hortum dūxit canēsque vocāvit.

commendā introduce

volō I want

studiīs at work

doctum learned

verēcundus shy
exposuit explained

bibliothēcam library
sī vīs if you want; **licet**
tibi you may
aliquid novī something new
forsitan perhaps; **eris** you will be; **Mūsīs** to the Muses
sūmpsit took
ātrium hall

sescentī countless
num vīs do you really want?

satis enough

concessit gave in to

1 What does Cicero tell Marcus to do?
2 What advice does he give Quintus?
3 Did Marcus do what his father had told him to do?
4 What do you learn from this passage about the characters of Marcus and Quintus?
5 Give one English word derived from each of the following (all in the last paragraph): **librōs, spectāre, canibus, concessit**.
6 Give one example each from the last paragraph of: a compound verb, an infinitive, an imperative, a preposition with the ablative case.
7 In what tense is each of the following verbs in the last paragraph: **dīcis, cupiēbat, studuistī?**
8 Translate into Latin:
(a) The boys learnt many things in school today.
(b) Quintus could tell Marcus' father everything.
(c) Don't go into the library; come into the garden and play.

CICERO

Marcus Tullius Cicero, the father of Quintus's friend Marcus, was born in 106 BC near Arpinum, a little hill town about sixty miles from Rome. His father was a wealthy member of the local nobility, but his family had never played any part in politics in Rome. Cicero proved a very bright child and his father sent him to the best teachers in Rome and then to university in Greece, where he studied law, oratory (rhetoric) and philosophy.

A series of terrible wars was tearing the Roman world apart for much of Cicero's life. When he was seventeen, he himself fought in one of these wars, Rome's conflict with her Italian allies. Rome emerged victorious from this, but now a bloody succession of civil wars was to begin. These were fought between the great generals in a struggle for power. Some of these generals claimed to be supporting the rule of the senate against the attacks of popular politicians. Others thought that the present system of government no longer worked and wished to reform it in the interests of the people. Cicero tried throughout his life to prop up the old system, but it was doomed to collapse.

The young Cicero was ambitious and decided to make his way by practising in the law courts as a barrister. He did well from the start and in 70 BC leapt to fame when the people of Sicily asked him to prosecute their ruthless Roman governor, Verres, who had plundered the island for personal gain. Verres had said when he had been elected that he needed to govern Sicily for three years. One year was to cover his election expenses (he had bribed the electors), one year was to get enough money to secure acquittal when he was prosecuted for misgovernment (he intended to bribe the jury), and one year was to make some profit!

Cicero was taking a big risk since Verres was a noble, and had many powerful friends. But he conducted the case so brilliantly that Verres fled into exile before it was even over. So Cicero was acknowledged to be the leading barrister in Rome at the age of thirty-six.

He had already started on a political career and had become a senator in 76 BC. But he was always looked on with suspicion by the old Roman nobility because he was born a member of the equestrian class (a knight). No one could become a consul until he was forty-three, since much experience was necessary for the post. Cicero became consul at the earliest possible age in 63 BC, but the nobility still despised him as a 'novus homō', a self-made man who was not one of them.

While Cicero was consul, a young noble called Catiline, who had failed in his attempts to become consul himself, tried to overthrow the government by force. Cicero acted decisively. He arrested and executed Catiline's chief supporters in Rome – which was illegal, since no Roman citizen could be put to death without a trial – and defeated his army in Etruria. He was hailed by the people as 'pater patriae' (father of his country); he was never tired of reminding others of this great day and wrote a poem 'On my consulship' (*Dē Cōnsulātū Meō*), which included the much-ridiculed line:

ō fortūnātam nātam mē cōnsule Rōmam!

O blessed Rome, reborn when I was consul!

The senators and knights had drawn closer together while they united against the conspiracy, and Cicero hoped to keep this alliance working. His political aim was to maintain the 'concordia ordinum' (the harmony of the senatorial and equestrian classes), but this was a dream never to be fulfilled.

The three most powerful men in the Roman world were now Gaius Julius Caesar, Marcus Licinius Crassus (whom we saw in Chapter 12 leading an army through Venusia), and Gnaeus Pompey, whom Cicero admired as a man and supported as the champion of the knights. In 60 BC these three formed a political alliance called the First

Triumvirate and brushed the authority of the Senate aside. You will
be reading more about this in Chapter 19. Cicero would have nothing
to do with them, but this did not worry them much; all the power was
in their hands.

Caesar was consul in 59 BC and then went out to govern Gaul,
where he achieved famous conquests. Meanwhile Rome was
becoming a dangerous and frightening place to live. Political gangs
were carrying on a reign of terror and the leader of one of them,
Clodius, prepared to prosecute Cicero for executing Catiline's
supporters illegally. Cicero panicked and fled to Greece. He was
allowed back the next year and given a warm welcome by the people
of Italy, but he soon realized that it was the Triumvirs who had let him
return and that he had to do what they told him. He was no longer
independent and was deeply ashamed of the fact.

Then the Triumvirate began to fall to pieces. Caesar and Pompey
drifted apart and Crassus was defeated and killed at Carrhae in 53 BC
by the Parthians, against whom he was marching in Chapter 12 with
high hopes of conquest. Cicero himself was sent in 51 BC, very much
against his will, to govern a remote province called Cilicia. Here he
governed fairly but not very firmly and won a minor military victory of
which he was extremely proud, although no one at Rome took it very
seriously.

He returned home in 50 BC to find that civil war between Caesar
and Pompey could not be long delayed. For a time he sat on the fence.
Caesar took the trouble to visit him to try to win him over, but in the
end he decided to join Pompey's army in Greece. Here he was given
nothing to do. When Caesar defeated Pompey at the battle of
Pharsalus (48 BC), Cicero was stunned and his political hopes were
destroyed. He returned to Italy and was soon reconciled to Caesar,
but he now lived largely in retirement. He entered upon the political
scene again four years later, however, after the murder of Julius
Caesar. As we shall see, this resulted in his death.

Cicero was one of the most remarkable men who ever lived. He
was a brilliant orator, barrister and writer, a philosopher and a
capable, if uninspired, poet. He stuck to his principles as a statesman
and gave up his life for them. He was famous for his sense of humour.
His secretary Tiro published three books of his jokes after his death,
and Julius Caesar used to jot down his latest witty sayings in his Book
of Jests.

He was also a great letter writer. After his death, his letters were
collected and published in thirty-five books. Sixteen of these are to his
family and friends (some with replies from men such as Caesar and
Pompey); sixteen are to his closest friend Atticus, to whom he was
writing when Quintus met him; and three are to his brother Quintus.
Cicero's letters throw an extraordinarily vivid light on the Rome of his day.

Here is part of a letter written to his brother Quintus in February

144

56 BC, the year after he had returned from exile to find the political gangs at work. Clodius's gang had destroyed Cicero's house on the Palatine Hill during his exile, but he received compensation by decree of the Senate and quickly rebuilt it. The letter describes a meeting of the people, before whom Clodius was prosecuting the rival gang-leader Milo for using violence in politics. Pompey came forward to speak for Milo.

On 6 February Milo appeared in court. Pompey spoke, or rather tried to. For as soon as he got up, the gangs of Clodius raised a shout, and this went on throughout his whole speech – he was interrupted not only by uproar but by insults and abuse. When he had finished his speech (for he was extremely brave: he said the lot and at times even amid silence), but when he had finished, up got Clodius. There was such a shout from our side (for we had decided to return the compliment) that he lost all control of his thoughts, his tongue and his expression. This went on for two hours while every insult and even obscene verses were shouted against Clodius and his sister.

Clodius, furious and pale, in the middle of all this shouting asked his supporters, 'Who wants to starve the people to death?' 'Pompey!' answered the gang. Then, at the ninth hour, as if a signal had been given, Clodius's supporters all began to spit at ours. Tempers flared. Clodius's gang shoved, to push us from our place. Our side made a charge; his gang fled; Clodius was thrown from the platform, and then we fled too, in case we should have trouble from the crowd. The Senate was summoned to the Senate House. Pompey went home.

The following year Clodius was killed in a brawl outside Rome by Milo and his supporters. In the rioting which followed, Clodius's gangs burned his body in the Senate house, which was burnt to the ground and had not been rebuilt when Quintus arrived in Rome.

Here is another letter, which Cicero wrote to a friend when his beloved daughter Tullia died in February 45 BC:

In this lonely place, I don't talk to anyone at all. In the morning I hide myself in a thick, thorny wood and I don't come out of it until the evening. After yourself, my best friend in the world is my solitude. When I am alone, all I talk to is my books, but I keep on bursting into tears. I fight against them as much as I can, but so far it has been an unequal struggle.

After reading this section, compose a date chart outlining Cicero's life.

What does the first of the two letters quoted above suggest about the state of politics in Rome at this time? On what occasions might similar scenes occur today?

CHAPTER XVIII

Quīntus lūdō discesserat domumque ambulābat. Marcus eum magnā vōce vocāvit.

Marcus Quīntō 'venī mēcum' inquit 'ad balnea; ā forō nōn longē absunt.'

in balneīs aliī in piscīnam ingentī clāmōre saliēbant. aliī pilīs lūdēbant.

Ⓖ Revision

Revise verbs **ascendō** to **veniō** in the Grammar Section, page 183, and learn the perfect stems carefully.

Ⓖ Uses of the ablative case

So far you have met the ablative case
1 after some prepositions (**in** in, **ē/ex** out of, **ā/ab** from, **cum** with, **prō** in front of, **dē** about, down)
2 expressing <u>time when</u> (**quīntō diē discessit** he left on the fifth day).

The ablative case can also mean: by, with, from, in, on,

e.g. **puer clāmōribus territus erat** The boy was terrified by the shouts.

pilā lūdunt They are playing with a ball.

urbe discessērunt They went away from the city.

Orbilius Marcum lūdō expellit Orbilius expels Marcus from the school.

magnā vōce clāmant They shout in a loud voice.

Viā Sacrā ambulant They are walking on the Sacred Way.

Exercise 18.1

Translate

1 pater Quīntum magnā vōce vocat.
2 prīmā lūce Quīntus domō discessit et Sacrā Viā festīnāvit.
3 Flaccus Quīntī capsulam manibus portat.
4 Quīntus amīcum magnō gaudiō salūtāvit.
5 septimā hōrā Quīntus lūdō cum patre discessit.
6 pater fīlium vultū benignō spectat.

gaudiō joy **benignō** kindly

Exercise 18.2

Translate into Latin

1 Quintus called Argus in a loud voice.
2 The dog greeted the boy with great joy.
3 On the fifth day they left Capua and hurried to Rome on the Appian Way.
4 The men, armed with swords, were approaching through the wood.
5 Quintus was terrified by the storm.
6 They marched to Rome by the longest road.

longest **longissimus-a-um**

Verbs taking the dative

The following verbs are followed by the *dative* case; there is nothing in their English meaning to warn you of this. They must be carefully learnt.

crēdo, crēdere, crēdidī	I believe, trust
persuādeō, persuādēre, persuāsī	I persuade
pāreō, pārēre, pāruī	I obey
placeō, placēre, placuī	I please
resistō, resistere, restitī	I resist

Exercise 18.3

Translate

1 mihi crēde, patrī tuō facile persuādēre possum.
2 Quīntus patrī pāruit, quod semper eī placēre cupiēbat.
3 duo iuvenēs Quīntum oppugnāvērunt, sed ille fortiter eīs restitit.
4 Aenēās comitēs iussit fortiter pugnāre; illī ducī pāruērunt et hostibus resistēbant.
5 Quīntus ad lūdum īre nōlēbat, sed pater eī persuāsit.   **nōlēbat** didn't want

147

QUINTUS LUDO ORBILII DISCEDIT

iam Quīntus tōtum mēnsem in ludō Orbiliī mānserat. celeriter discēbat studiīsque excellēbat. multōs amicōs habēbat. ōlim ubi Orbilius puerōs dīmīsit, Marcus Quīntō 'ego,' inquit, 'ad balnea eō; nōnne tibi persuādēre possum mēcum venīre?' Quīntus ōtiōsus erat Marcōque libenter pāruit. itaque ad balnea ambulābant. Flaccus cum Marcī paedagōgō post eōs ībat.

    mox advēnērunt, nam balnea nōn longē aberant; intrāvērunt et circumspectābant; multī hominēs in ātriō erant; clāmor undique circumsonābat; aliī in piscīnam ingentī sonō saliēbant; aliī pilīs lūdēbant; botulāriī crustulāriīque mercem suam magnā vōce laudābant. Marcus manum iuvenum cōnspexit; inter eōs amīcus erat; accessit et eum salūtāvit.

mēnsem month	
excellēbat excelled	
ōtiōsus at leisure	
libenter gladly	
paedagōgō tutor	
ātriō hall	
undique everywhere	
circumsonābat sounded	
piscīnam bath	
sonō noise; **saliēbant** leapt	
pilīs balls; **botulāriī** sausage-sellers **crustulāriī** cake-sellers	
mercem merchandise	
manum group	

The baths at Pompeii

Quīntus nōn audēbat ad iuvenēs accēdere sed sōlus ad apodȳtērium discessit. vestīmenta exuit et in armāriō posuit. prīmum in tepidārium iniit et paulīsper in aquā tepidā iacēbat; deinde in calidārium iit, sed ibi nōn diū manēbat, quod aqua valdē calida erat; dēnique in piscīnam saluit et aliquamdiū sē exercēbat.

ubi exiit vestīmentaque induit, Marcum in ātriō quaerēbat. subitō clāmōrem audiit et Marcum in ultimā parte ātriī cōnspexit. ille cum manū iuvenum stābat; ūnum magnā vōce vituperābat; plānē in rixam inierant.

Quīntus Marcum nōn dēseruit sed auxilium ferēbat; cum patre et paedagōgō accurrit. iam Marcus iuvenisque pugnābant; Marcus iuvenī fortiter resistēbat sed eō ipsō tempore iuvenis Marcum pulsāvit; ille ad terram cecidit. Quīntus, quī iam aderat, eum tollere temptābat, sed Marcus stāre nōn poterat; multum vīnum biberat; plānē ēbrius erat.

Flaccus et paedagōgus cōnsternātī erant. Marcum manibus tollunt et portant ad iānuam; ibi eum in pavīmentum dēpōnunt. Quīntus ad forum currit et lectīcam hominēsque comparat. Marcum in lectīcam impōnunt; paedagōgus eum domum dūcit. Flaccus valdē īrātus erat Quīntumque domum celeriter dūxit.

postrīdiē Marcus ad lūdum nōn vēnit. Orbilius eum lūdō expūlerat. nec posteā Quīntus eum vīdit. parentēs eum domī retinēbant; Cicerō ipse studia eius cūrābat.

tempus fugit. iam Quīntus trēs annōs in lūdō Orbiliī mānserat. optimus erat discipulōrum Orbiliī; cotīdiē aliquid novī legēbat, aliquid novī scrībēbat, sīcut Cicerō eum monuerat.

hiems praeterierat; vēr aderat. Quīntus in scholā sedēbat dum Orbilius dē Naeviō dīcit, poētā vetere et valdē frīgidō. Quīntus, quī poētās Graecōs mālēbat, nōn audiēbat sed ipse carmen scrībēbat; hōs versūs iam fēcerat:
'diffūgērunt nivēs, redeunt iam grāmina campīs,
    arboribusque comae . . .'
Orbilius eum vīdit scrībentem. 'Quīnte,' inquit, 'quid facis?' Quīntus respondit: 'ego, magister? nihil faciō. tē audiō.' sed Orbilius, quī nōn stultus erat, dīxit: 'nōn tibi crēdō, Quīnte. venī hūc et dā mihi illam tabulam.'

Quīntus aegrē magistrō pāruit; surrēxit et tabulam eī trādidit. Orbilius valdē īrātus erat, sed, ubi tabulam īnspexit, etiam magis īrātus erat; nam in angulō tabulae

apodȳtērium undressing room; **vestīmenta** clothes
exuit he took off
armāriō cupboard;
tepidārium warm room
calidārium hot room
dēnique finally
aliquamdiū for some time
ultimā furthest

vituperābat he was abusing
plānē clearly; **rixam** quarrel

eō ipsō tempore at that very moment; **pulsāvit** struck

ēbrius drunk
cōnsternātī alarmed

pavīmentum the floor
lectīcam litter; **comparat** gets

expūlerat had expelled
posteā afterwards
ipse himself

optimus the best

cotīdiē every day; **aliquid novī** something new
sīcut just as
praeterierat had passed
vēr spring
frīgidō boring; **mālēbat** preferred
ipse himself
nivēs snows; **grāmina** grass (*n.pl.*)
comae leaves
scrībentem writing

stultus stupid

aegrē reluctantly

magis more; **angulō** corner

Quīntus imāginem scrīpserat Orbiliī.

    ille Quīntum ferōciter īnspexit. 'quid?' inquit, 'quid? dum ego Naeviī poēmata expōnō, tū lūdis? tu imāginēs magistrī scrībis et malōs versūs?' ferulam vibrābat. 'vidē, hī versūs nē rēctī quidem sunt. ecce, scrīpsistī "fūgērunt"; dēbuistī scrībere "diffūgēre nivēs". nec mē audīs nec bonōs versūs scrībis. venī hūc.' sīc dīxit et sex plāgās Quīntō dedit, trēs quod magistrum nōn audīverat, trēs quod malōs versūs scrīpserat.

    Quīntus ad sēdem rediit, et dolēns et īrātus.

imāginem picture
ferōciter fiercely
expōnō explain
ferulam cane
vibrābat brandished
nē rēctī quidem not even correct
dēbuistī you ought to have
plāgās blows

sēdem seat; **dolēns** smarting

teneō, tenēre, tenuī	I hold
retineō, retinēre, retinuī	I hold back
dēserō, dēserere, dēseruī	I desert
pōnō, pōnere, posuī	I put, place
dēpōnō, dēpōnere, dēposuī	I put down
impōnō, impōnere, imposuī	I put on
compōnō, compōnere, composuī	I put together, compose
nōscō, nōscere, nōvī	I learn, get to know
cognōscō, cognōscere, cognōvī	I learn, get to know
tollō, tollere	I raise, lift
cōnspiciō, cōnspicere, cōnspexī	I catch sight of
īnspiciō, īnspicere, īnspexī	I look at, inspect
poēta, poētae, *m.*	poet
annus, annī, *m.*	year
auxilium, auxiliī, *n.*	help
carmen, carminis, *n.*	song, poem
lēx, lēgis, *f.*	law
ōrātiō, ōrātiōnis, *f.*	speech
hiems, hiemis, *f.*	winter
ōlim	once; at some time

❻ The declension of 'is' and 'ille'

is (he, she, it, that) and **ille** (he, she, it, that) decline basically like **bonus**.
NB In the singular, the neuter nominative and accusative are irregular, and the genitive and dative are irregular; the plural is completely regular.

singular				plural		
	m.	*f.*	*n.*	*m.*	*f.*	*n.*
nom.	is	ea	id	eī	eae	ea
acc.	eum	eam	id	eōs	eās	ea
gen.	eius	eius	eius	eōrum	eārum	eōrum
dat.	eī	eī	eī .	eīs	eīs	eīs
abl.	eō	eā	eō	eīs	eīs	eīs
nom.	ille	illa	illud	illī	illae	illa
acc.	illum	illam	illud	illōs	illās	illa
gen.	illīus	illīus	illīus	illōrum	illārum	illōrum
dat.	illī	illī	illī	illīs	illīs	illīs
abl.	illō	illā	illō	illīs	illīs	illīs

NB **eius** is used to mean 'his', 'her'.
   eōrum, **eārum** are used to mean 'their'.

Flaccus capsulam <u>eius</u> portābat	Flaccus was carrying his (i.e. Quintus's) satchel.
But **Quīntus capsulam suam portābat**	Quintus was carrying his own satchel.
paedagōgī capsulās <u>eōrum</u> portābant	The tutors were carrying their (i.e. the boys') satchels.
But **puerī capsulās suās portābant**	The boys were carrying their own satchels.

Exercise 18.4

Replace the nouns underlined in the following sentences with the correct part of the pronouns **is** *or* **ille** *and then translate*

e.g. **pater fīlium vocāvit; <u>puer patrī</u> respondit. pater fīlium vocāvit; ille eī respondit** the father called his son; he replied to him.

1 Orbilius Quīntum iussit tabulam sibi trādere; <u>Quīntus Orbiliō</u> aegrē pāruit.
2 Quīntus tabulam magistrō trādidit; <u>magister</u> tabulam <u>Quīntī</u> īnspexit.
3 magister versūs lēgit; <u>versūs magistrō</u> nōn placēbant.
4 in tabulā Quīntus magistrī imāginem scrīpserat; <u>magister imāginem</u> īrātus īnspexit.
5 cēterī puerī rīdēbant; magister <u>puerōs</u> iussit tacēre.

Exercise 18.5

Translate

1 Flaccus post Quīntum ambulābat et capsulam eius manibus portābat.

2 Quintus ad balnea īre nōlēbat sed Marcus eī persuāsit.

    nōlēbat did not want

3 Marcus iuvenem vituperābat; ille eum pulsāvit.

    vituperābat abused

4 Marcus iuvenī resistēbat sed ille facile eum superāvit.

5 crēde mihi, Marce, nimis vīnī bibistī.

    nimis vīnī too much wine

6 magister magnā vōce puerōs vocāvit sed illī nōn pāruerunt eī.

7 Quīntus magistrō 'nihil faciō, magister,' inquit; sed Orbilius eī nōn crēdidit.

8 magister Quīntum ad sē vocāvit et tabulam eius īnspexit.

9 magister tabulam vultū sevērō spectāvit; tabula eī non placēbat.

10 magister omnēs puerōs iussit ad sē venīre tabulāsque eōrum diū spectābat.

Exercise 18.6

Translate the first two paragraphs and answer the questions below on the third paragraph

Quīntus, ubi domum rediit, omnia patrī nārrāvit. Flaccus respondit: 'Quīnte, iam trēs annōs in lūdō Orbiliī mānsistī; optimē studuistī; omnēs aliōs puerōs doctrīnā superāvistī. iam iuvenis es. iam dēbēs togam virīlem sūmere. tempus est studia puerīlia dēpōnere. tempus est ad rhētorem īre.' postrīdiē Quīntus, quī iam septendecim annōs nātus erat, togam virīlem sūmpsit.

    optimē very well
    doctrīnā in learning
    togam virīlem man's toga
    sūmere take on; **puerīlia** a boy's
    rhētorem rhetor
    septendecim 17; **nātus** old

      pater eum ad Hēliodōrum dūxit, quī optimus erat rhētorum. Hēliodōrus multa eum rogāvit; Quīntus ad omnia facile respondēre poterat. Hēliodōrus patrī dīxit: 'iuvenis valdē doctus est. ego libenter eum in discipulōs meōs ascīscō.'

    doctus learned; **libenter** gladly
    ascīsco take, enrol

      itaque cotīdiē Quīntus ad scholam Hēliodōrī ībat et cum iuvenibus nōbilibus rhētoricam discēbat. ōrātiōnēs facere discēbat; contrōversiīs intererat; multa dē iūre et lēgibus cognōscēbat. studia longa et difficilia erant nec Quīntum multum dēlectābant; mālēbat litterīs studēre et carmina compōnere. sed dīligenter studēbat, quod patrī placēre cupiēbat.

    nōbilibus noble
    rhētoricam rhetoric
    contrōversiīs arguments, debates; **intererat** he took part
    iūre justice; **multum** much
    dēlectābant pleased; **mālēbat** he preferred; **litterīs** literature

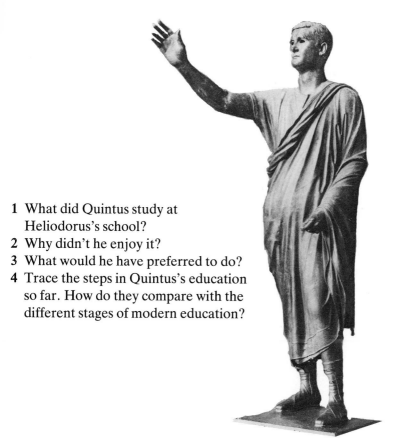

1. What did Quintus study at Heliodorus's school?
2. Why didn't he enjoy it?
3. What would he have preferred to do?
4. Trace the steps in Quintus's education so far. How do they compare with the different stages of modern education?

A Roman orator

A DAY AT ROME

Let us now follow the daily round of an ordinary Roman who wishes to climb to a higher social level.

He gets up very early in his simply furnished bedroom and splashes some water on his face and hands. He has slept in his tunic and, before he leaves the house, he puts on his toga. He drapes over himself this large woollen garment, roughly semi-circular in shape, winding it round his shoulders and waist. To wear the toga marked a man out as a Roman citizen.

If he bothers with breakfast, it is a light one, consisting of bread with cheese or with honey, washed down with some milk. Then he sets off to visit his *patron*, a man of higher rank who he hopes will help him to success. He is his patron's *client* and as such will have to do him favours in return.

He presents himself at his patron's house between daybreak and the second hour (see the note at the end of this chapter). He hopes for a small present of money or an invitation to dinner that evening. His patron might well insist that he accompanies him to the Forum where business begins at the third hour. One Roman writer complained about how many things there were to do there. 'I attended a coming-of-age ceremony,' he wrote, 'I went to an engagement or a wedding, one man called me to witness a will, another to give legal advice.' This may well be an exaggeration, but the morning was certainly the time for business, both political, legal and financial.

Roman meals

Lentils, nuts, and eggs

Bread

There would be a welcome interval after the sixth hour for lunch. This was a light meal consisting of fish, eggs or pork with vegetables, followed by fruit. After a rest, a tradition still kept up by the Italians with their siestas, our Roman would probably take some exercise.

He may well pay a visit to the Campus Martius (Plain of Mars) like Quintus in our last chapter. This broad plain, enclosed on its western side by a bend in the river Tiber, was the playground of ancient Rome. Its vast expanse of green was the perfect place for a stroll in the open; it was the ideal location for military training; and the young men of Rome gathered here to practise each and every sport.

They ran, rode on horseback, drove chariots, wrestled and threw balls, javelins and the discus. The nearby river with its strong current gave the opportunity for an energetic swim. Roman sportsmen crowded the Campus Martius to such an extent that Julius Caesar thought of creating an even larger sports ground on the other side of the river.

Our Roman moves on at about the eighth hour to the Public Baths (**balnea**) for a refreshing wash. There were many of these in Rome and they were all extremely cheap. There were separate facilities in the biggest for men and women; different times could be set aside for the two sexes in the smaller ones.

The bather would start in the changing room (**apodȳtērium**). He would proceed from here to the warm room (**tepidārium**), where he would immerse himself in warm water in preparation for the hot room (**calidārium**). The water was heated by a system underneath the floor called a hypocaust. After a brief bath here, he was oiled with olive oil, which was then scraped off with a strigil (see illustration). Then he walked back through the warm room to the cold room (**frīgidārium**) where he leapt into cold water. He now dried himself with a towel and returned to the changing room.

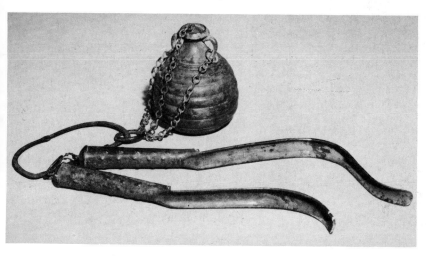

Two strigils and an oil flask

It was all a lively, noisy business, and it was not a good thing to live too near to the baths!

Finally, dinner (**cēna**) was a big affair, starting at about the ninth hour in summer and the tenth in winter, and it was considered short if it lasted only three Roman hours. This is a long time to spend eating! But there was plenty of conversation and often some entertainment.

Our Roman returns home nervously after dinner through the dark and narrow city streets, earnestly hoping that he will not be mugged.

PS (**post scrīptum**) There were twelve hours in a Roman day. Each hour was one-twelfth of the time from sunrise to sunset. Thus hours were longer in summer than in winter and varied between about ¾ and 1¼ modern hours.

Describe a visit either to the Campus Martius or to the baths.

CHAPTER XIX

Quīntus ad rhētorem ībat; trēs hominēs, gladiīs armātī, eum oppugnāvērunt.

Quīntus ē manibus eōrum ēvāsit
domumque fūgit.

tōtam rem patrī nārrāvit; ille fīliō 'haec
urbs nōn tūta est,' inquit; 'parvam spem
dē rēpūblicā habeō.'

G The fifth (and last) declension

In this declension the vowel **e** predominates throughout.

rēs, **reī**, *f.* thing, affair, matter

	singular	*plural*
nom.	rēs	rēs
acc.	rem	rēs
gen.	reī	rērum
dat.	reī	rēbus
abl.	rē	rēbus

rēspūblica
rempūblicam
reīpūblicae
reīpūblicae
rēpūblicā

Note **rēspūblica** public
affairs, politics, the
state; both halves
decline

All nouns of this declension are *feminine*, except for **diēs**, which is
usually *masculine*.

Learn **spēs**, **speī**, *f.* hope.

The mixed conjugation

These verbs have already been explained in Chapter 8. They are verbs ending in **-iō** which go like **audiō** except for their infinitive, which is **-ere** (not **-īre**) and imperative, which is **-e** (not **-i**), e.g.

capiō, **capere** imperatives **cape**, **capite**

You have met the following

capiō, capere, cēpī	I take
accipiō, accipere, accēpī	I receive
faciō, facere, fēcī	I do, make
interficiō, interficere, interfēcī	I kill
iaciō, iacere, iēcī	I throw
coniciō, conicere, coniēcī	I hurl
fugiō, fugere, fūgī	I flee
cupiō, cupere, cupīvī	I desire
rapiō, rapere, rapuī	I seize, snatch
cōnspiciō, cōnspicere, cōnspexī	I catch sight of
īnspiciō, īnspicere, īnspexī	I look at, inspect

Compounds of 'dō'

dō, **dare**, **dedī** (I give) is 1st conjugation.
But all compounds of this verb are 3rd conjugation.

addō, addere, addidī	I add
ēdō, ēdere, ēdidī	I produce, put forth
reddo, reddere, reddidī	I give back, return
condō, condere, condidī	I build, found; I hide

Exercise 19.1

Translate

1 tōta rēspūblica in perīculum vēnit.
2 Orbilius puerīs multa nārrābat dē rēbus Rōmānīs.
3 Quīntus carmen faciēbat; magister īrātus erat tabulamque eius rapuit.
4 Quīntus ad rhētorem ībat sed nōn cupiēbat dē lēgibus cognōscere.
5 mālēbat carmina facere, quod cupiēbat poēta esse.
6 dum Quīntus domum redit, fūr accurrit capsulamque eius rapere temptāvit, sed Quīntus celeriter fūgit.
7 Quīntus tōtam rem patrī nārrāvit.
8 pater cōnsternātus erat; parvam spem dē rēpūblicā habēbat.
9 fuge, Quīnte; fūr tē petit.
10 cape hoc iaculum, Quīnte, et temptā id conicere.

   mālēbat he preferred   **fūr** thief   **iaculum** javelin

IDUS MARTIAE

Idūs Martiae 15 March, the Ides of March

Idibus Martiīs Quīntus, ubi Hēliodōrus discipulōs dīmīsit, domum lentē ībat. illā nocte tempestās dīra fuerat sed iam diēs amoenus erat; aura mītis per viās flābat; arborēs iam flōrēs ēdēbant. omnia nova et pulchra erant.

dīra terrible
amoenus pleasant; aura mītis a gentle breeze
flābat was blowing

Quīntus cōnstituit ad Campum ambulāre. forum trānsiit et mox ad Viam Triumphālem advēnit. sed ubi ad theātrum Pompēiī accessit, magnam turbam hominum vīdit circā ātrium Pompēiī stantem. Quīntus, quī parvus erat, per turbam ad prīmum ordinem sē īnsinuāvit, unde omnia vidēre poterat.

Triumphālem Triumphal
turbam crowd
circā around; ātrium hall
stantem standing
ordinem row; sē
īnsinuāvit wriggled through

iānuae apertae erant. multī senātōrēs aliīque virī īnsignēs ātrium inībant. Quīntus Gāium Iūlium Caesarem vīdit cum magistrātibus ineuntem; togam purpuream gerēbat et in capite corōnam lauream. omnēs senātōrēs surrēxērunt Caesaremque salūtāvērunt. dum assidet, multī senātōrēs eum circumstetērunt.

īnsignēs famous
magistrātibus magistrates
ineuntem going in
purpuream purple
corōnam lauream a crown of laurel
assidet he sat down

deinde ūnus eum aliquid rogābat et togam eius manibus tenēbat. Caesar eum repellere temptāvit. eō ipsō tempore alter senātōrum eum pūgiōne ferit; tertius bracchium vulnerat. Caesar surgere temptāvit, sed coniūrātī eum undique oppugnābant. inter aliōs Caesar Brūtum vīdit, amīcum suum intimum, in sē irruentem;

aliquid something
repellere push away; eō ipsō tempore at that very moment
pūgiōne with a dagger
ferit strikes; bracchium arm
coniūrātī the conspirators
intimum closest
irruentem rushing upon

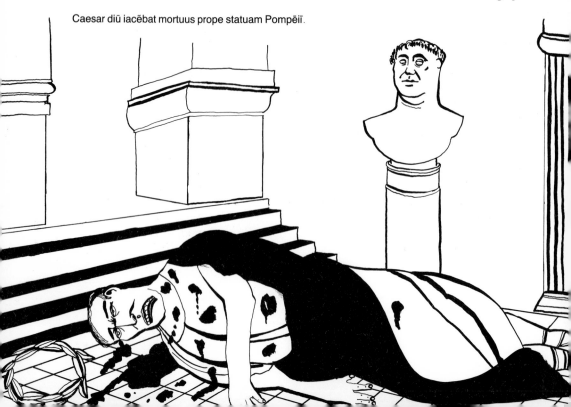

Caesar diū iacēbat mortuus prope statuam Pompēiī.

'et tū, Brūte?' inquit; tum caput togā obvolvit et dēcidit ad terram, tribus et vīgintī vulneribus cōnfossus. diū ibi iacēbat, mortuus, prope statuam Pompēiī.

intereā coniūrātī ex ātriō in āream ērūperant et populō clāmābant: 'mortuus est tyrannus; populum Rōmānum līberāvimus.' sed omnēs tacitī stābant, rē dīrā obstupefactī. Quīntus sē vertit et domum cucurrit, territus.

postrīdiē Quīntus paterque ad Hēliodōrī scholam pervenīre nōn poterant. ubīque manūs hominum eōs prōcēdere prohibēbant, quī clāmābant, rēs rapiēbant, saxa iaciēbant; aliī clāmābant: 'mortuus est tyrannus; tandem līber est populus Rōmānus.' aliī: 'Caesar, amīcus populī, pater patriae, mortuus est; hominēs scelestī eum necāvērunt.' Flaccus timēbat Quīntumque domum redūxit.

quīntō diē post mortem Caesaris, ubi Quīntus ad forum advēnit, ingentem turbam vīdit, quae tōtum forum complēbat. nōn poterat pervenīre ad viam quae ad scholam Hēliodōrī ferēbat. itaque in ultimā parte forī manēbat gradūsque templī ascendit, unde omnia vidēre poterat.

magnam pompam cōnspexit, quae in forum prōcēdēbat. magistrātūs feretrum portābant, in quō iacēbat corpus Caesaris. in medium forum prōcessērunt et feretrum prō rōstrīs dēposuērunt. Marcus Antōnius, amīcus Caesaris, rōstra ascendit et ōrātiōnem ad populum habuit. Caesarem laudāvit, coniūrātōs vehementer accūsāvit, populum ad furōrem excitāvit.

ubi Antōnius ōrātiōnem cōnfēcit rōstrīsque dēscendit, hominēs ubīque clāmābant et furēbant; fustēs saxaque per auram volābant. duo hominēs, quī prope rōstra stābant, gladiīs armātī facēsque manibus tenentēs, ad feretrum accessērunt. feretrum facibus incendērunt. aliī accurrērunt et virgulta in flammās iēcērunt; aliī subsellia rapuērunt et imposuērunt. mox ingēns pyra ārdēbat et corpus Caesaris flammīs cremātum erat. tum manūs hominum ē forō ēvolāvērunt, quī coniūrātōs quaerēbant, certī mortem Caesaris vindicāre.

et tū you too; **obvolvit** he covered
cōnfossus pierced through
statuam statue
āream courtyard
ērūperant had burst out
tyrannus the tyrant
dīrā terrible
obstupefactī struck dumb

pervenīre to get; **manūs** bands

scelestī criminals
necāvērunt have butchered

quae which
complēbat filled
ferēbat led

pompam procession
feretrum the bier; **in quō** on which
rōstrīs platform

habuit delivered
vehementer passionately
furōrem frenzy
excitāvit roused
cōnfēcit finished
furēbant raged
fustēs clubs; **auram** air
volābant were flying
facēs torches
tenentēs holding
virgulta brushwood
subsellia benches
pyra pyre; **ārdēbat** was burning
cremātum burnt
ēvolāvērunt flew out
certī resolved
vindicāre avenge

duo hominēs gladiīs armātī facēsque manibus tenentēs ad feretrum accessērunt.

līberō, līberāre, līberāvī	I free
līber, lībera, līberum	free
accūsō, accūsāre, accūsāvī	I accuse
vulnerō, vulnerāre, vulnerāvī	I wound
vulnus, vulneris, *n.*	wound
prohibeō, prohibēre, prohibuī	I prevent
incendō, incendere, incendī	I set on fire
rapiō, rapere, rapuī	I snatch
patria, patriae, *f.*	native land
toga, togae, *f.*	toga
saxum, saxī, *n.*	rock
soror, sorōris, *f.*	sister
caput, capitis, *n.*	head
corpus, corporis, *n.*	body
alter, altera, alterum	one or the other of two
ubi?	where
ubīque	everywhere
ibi	there
unde?	whence, from where?
unde	whence, from where
undique	from all sides
inde	then, thence
pro + ablative	in front of, on behalf of
trāns + accusative	across

160

Numerals: eleven to twenty

ūndecim	eleven	**septendecim**	seventeen
duodecim	twelve	**duodēvīgintī**	eighteen
tredecim	thirteen	**ūndēvīgintī**	nineteen
quattuordecim	fourteen	**vīgintī**	twenty
quīndecim	fifteen		
sēdecim	sixteen		

The declension of 'hic' this

singular				*plural*		
	m.	*f.*	*n.*	*m.*	*f.*	*n.*
nom.	hic	haec	hoc	hī	hae	haec
acc.	hunc	hanc	hoc	hōs	hās	haec
gen.	huius	huius	huius	hōrum	hārum	hōrum
dat.	huic	huic	huic	hīs	hīs	hīs
abl.	hōc	hāc	hōc	hīs	hīs	hīs

The singular needs careful learning; the plural is like **bonus** except for the neuter nominative and accusative.

Exercise 19.2

Translate

1 vīgintī iuvenēs in hāc scholā sedent Hēliodōrumque intentē audiunt.
2 Quīntus sēdecim annōs nātus erat cum togam virīlem sūmpsit.
3 quis iēcit hoc saxum? paene mē vulnerāvit.   **paene** almost
4 fūr saxum iēcit; huius puerī capsulam rapuit.   **fūr** thief
5 ubi est fūr? prohibē eum effugere.
6 duodecim iuvenēs eum petunt; ecce, iam eum capiunt.
7 iubē fūrem capsulam huic puerō reddere.
8 hic puer capsulam iam recēpit. dēbēmus hunc fūrem ad magistrātūs dūcere.
9 magister Decimum rogat: 'adde quīndecim tribus; quot habēs?' Decimus respondet: 'duodēvīgintī habeō.'   **quot** how much?
10 magister 'iam,' inquit, 'dēme quīnque dē tredecim; quid restat?' Marcus respondet: 'octō.'   **dēme** subtract
restat is left

Exercise 19.3

Translate into Latin

1 Take this garland to that girl.   garland **corōna, -ae,** *f.*
2 What if she doesn't want to accept it?   what if? **quid sī?**
3 Don't be tiresome. Go and give it to her.   tiresome **molestus-a-um**
4 Did she accept the garland? Tell me the whole thing.
5 She snatched it and fled into the house.
6 Poor boy, I have little hope for you, if this girl is so   for **dē** + ablative
   shy.   shy **verēcundus-a-um**

Exercise 19.4

Either translate the following passage or answer the questions below

Quīntus forō discessit domumque festīnāvit, territus.
patrem, quī domī illō diē mānserat, vocāvit et tōtam
rem eī nārrāvit. ille omnia ānxius audīvit; caput dēmīsit   **dēmīsit** lowered
oculōsque manibus operuit. tandem Quīntō respondit: **operuit** covered
'fīlī,' inquit, 'Rōma nōn tūta est. ubīque tumultus,   **tumultus** uproar
ubīque perīcula. cīvēs furunt. quid futūrum est? nūllam   **furunt** are mad; **futūrum**
spem habeō dē rēpūblicā. ego dēbeō domum redīre et   going to happen
mātrem tuam sorōremque cūrāre. tū dēbēs Rōmā
discēdere; tempus est Athēnās nāvigāre et philosophiae   **Athēnās** to Athens
studēre.'   **philosophiae** philosophy

1 Why was Quintus terrified?
2 What did Flaccus do when Quintus told him what he had seen?
3 Why was Flaccus so depressed?
4 What did he decide that (a) he and (b) Quintus should do?
5 The following English words are derived from Latin words in this
  passage: mansion, capital, oculist, debt. Say from what Latin word
  each is derived and explain the connection in meaning between the
  Latin and English words.
6 In what case is each of the following and why: **forō** (1.1); **illō** (1.2);
  eī (1.3); **ille** (1.3); **caput** (1.3)?
7 Give the first person singular of the present of the following verbs:
  discessit (1.1), **mānserat** (1.2); **dēmīsit** (1.3).
8 Translate into Latin:
(a) When Quintus saw Caesar's body burnt (**cremātum**), he fled
    home.
(b) He told his father everything.
(c) His father said, 'We must leave Rome at once.'

THE END OF THE REPUBLIC

A key moment in the long drawn out death of the Roman republic occurred in 60 BC. The three most powerful men of the time, Julius Caesar, Gnaeus Pompey and Marcus Licinius Crassus, joined in an alliance known as the First Triumvirate (a ruling group of three men). They made it clear that nothing would stand in their way and Caesar made sure that nothing did when he became consul in 59 BC. The Triumvirate was supported by the army, the knights and the people, so the senate was unable to oppose it. Nobody paid any attention to Cicero's appeals to save the republic.

Caesar fought his famous and brilliant campaigns over the next decade in Gaul (France, Holland and Belgium) and Britain (which he invaded in two raids in 55 and 54 BC). However, the situation at Rome was less happy for him. The unity between the men of great ambition lasted a surprisingly long time and a meeting of the Triumvirate in 56 BC smoothed over the problems which had arisen. Crassus, however, was killed in Parthia in 53 BC (see the end of Chapter 12), and Pompey became more and more an ally of the Senate. Caesar and Pompey were being driven further apart, and the Senate voted on 1 January 49 BC that Caesar, who was still in Gaul, should lay down his command.

Caesar's response came on 10 January, when he brought his army into Italy. This was really a declaration of civil war since it was treason for a general to enter Italy at the head of an army. Caesar fully realized the great significance of what he was doing. He spent one hour in solitary thought. Then he crossed the river Rubicon, which marked the frontier between Gaul and Italy, and exclaimed, 'iacta ālea est!' ('The die is cast!')

Pompey and most of the Senate withdrew across the Adriatic to Greece. Caesar defeated Pompey's supporters in Spain, then followed him to Greece and in 48 BC won a great victory over him at Pharsalus. Pompey fled on horseback and succeeded in escaping to Egypt, but was stabbed to death as he landed. Ptolemy, the boy king of Egypt, sent his head to Caesar, hoping to win favour with him, but the victor was revolted and distressed by this grisly gift.

Other wars were to follow – including the one in which he made his celebrated boast 'vēnī, vīdī, vīcī' ('I came, I saw, I overcame'). He had a famous love affair with Cleopatra, the beautiful Egyptian queen. He was by now the most powerful man in the Western world. He was appointed dictator at Rome, first in 49 BC and then for life in February 44 BC. Though he refused the title **rēx** (king), he put on the purple robe worn by the Tarquins, and his supreme power struck many as intolerable. A conspiracy to assassinate him led by Marcus Brutus and Caius Cassius succeeded in 44 BC. His mutilated body fell at the foot of the statue of his great opponent Pompey as you have read.

It was now the task of his friend Marcus Antonius and of his great-nephew and heir Octavian to avenge his death.

Antony

Octavian

Write a paragraph describing Julius Caesar's thoughts as he sat by the Rubicon.

CHAPTER XX

Quīntus Hēliodōrum valēre iubet; nam mox Athēnās nāvigābit.

Hēliodōrus Quīntō 'cum Athēnās advēneris,' inquit, 'hanc epistolam amīcō meō trāde; ille tē iuvābit.'

Quīntus eī grātiās agit et 'cum Athēnās advēnerō,' inquit, 'epistolam tibi mittam.'

The future tense

The future tense of verbs of the 1st conjugation (**amō** class) and the 2nd conjugation (**moneō** class) goes as follows

ama-		mone-		from **sum**	
amā-bō	I shall love	**monē-bō**	I shall warn	**erō**	I shall be
amā-bis		**monē-bis**		eris	
amā-bit		**monē-bit**		erit	
amā-bimus		**monē-bimus**		erimus	
amā-bitis		**monē-bitis**		eritis	
amā-bunt		**monē-bunt**		erunt	

The future of verbs of the 3rd conjugation (**regō** class) and the 4th conjugation (**audiō** class) goes as follows

reg-		audi-	
reg-am	I shall rule	**audi-am**	I shall hear
reg-ēs		**audi-ēs**	
reg-et		**audi-et**	
reg-ēmus		**audi-ēmus**	
reg-ētis		**audi-ētis**	
reg-ent		**audi-ent**	

You must learn both sets of endings and remember that each is future.

Exercise 20.1

Translate

rogābimus, docēbit, dīcent, vidēbis, mittam, pugnābit, scrībēmus, dūcēs, quaeram

Translate into Latin

He will sail, they will fear, I shall laugh, we shall lead, I shall praise, you will sit, they will be, you will depart, we shall sit, I shall conquer

NB The future of **eō**, **īre**, **iī** (stem **i-**) is **ībō**, **ībis**, **ībit**, etc.

G **Connecting words**

tamen (but, however), **enim** (for) and **igitur** (therefore, and so) are written as the second word in the sentence.

Exercise 20.2

Translate

1 Quīntus ad scholam Hēliodōrī ībat; nōn tamen eō pervenīre poterat.
2 ubīque enim manūs hominum eum prōcēdere prohibēbant.
3 domum igitur rediit patrīque omnem rem nārrāvit.

QUINTUS ROMA DISCEDIT

postrīdiē Quīntus māne ad scholam Hēliodōrī festīnābat. multī scelestī adhūc per viās errābant; saxa iaciēbant, aedēs incendēbant, rēs rapiēbant. Quīntus multa aedificia vīdit ārdentia. in forō trēs hominēs ferrō armātī eum oppugnāre temptāvērunt sed ē manibus

māne early
scelestī criminals; **adhūc** still
aedēs houses
ārdentia burning

ēvāsit et fūgit.

tandem ad scholam advēnit; iānua clausa erat.
pulsāvit; nēmō tamen aperuit. ad aedēs igitur
Hēliodōrī, quae vīcīnae erant, cucurrit. diū iānuam
pulsābat. tandem Hēliodōrus fenestram aperuit et
prōspexit. Quīntum vīdit; dēscendit et iānuam aperuit.
'intrā celeriter, Quīnte,' inquit et, ubi Quīntus intrāvit,
iānuam iterum clausit.

pulsāvit he knocked
aedēs (*f.pl.*) house
quae which; **vīcīnae** nearby
fenestram window
prōspexit looked out

magnum numerum nāvium prope lītus vīdērunt.

Quīntus eī tōtam rem nārrāvit. Hēliodōrus
respondit: 'pater tuus vērum dīcit; vir prūdēns est. in
urbe enim in summō perīculō sumus. ducēs nec pācem
nec lēgēs cūrant sed suam potestātem augēre cupiunt.
bella cīvīlia prōvideō et proelia tōtum per orbem
redintegrāta; cīvēs cum cīvibus pugnābunt, patrēs cum
fīliīs. numquamne pācem vidēbimus et ōtium? quis
deus, quis homō rempūblicam servāre poterit? ego
quoque parvam spem habeō.'

potestātem power; **augēre** to
increase; **cīvīlia** civil
prōvideō I foresee
orbem world;
redintegrāta renewed
ōtium tranquillity

nōn poterat plūra dīcere; oculī lacrimīs plēnī erant.
breve tempus tacēbat, tum 'ergō tū, Quīnte, Athēnās
ībis et philosophiae studēbis? euge! iuvenis valdē
ingeniōsus es. sī dīligenter studueris, brevī tempore
multa discēs et valdē doctus eris. sed manē; ego
epistolam scrībam ad amīcum quī in Acadēmīā scholās
habet.'

plūra more
ergō and so
euge! excellent!
ingeniōsus talented

Acadēmīā the Academy
scholās habet gives lectures

167

Quīntus igitur in ātriō manēbat; Hēliodōrus in tablīnum exiit et epistolam scrīpsit. mox revēnit et epistolam Quīntō trādidit. 'cum Athēnās advēneris,' inquit, 'hanc epistolam Theomnēstō trāde. ille enim vetus amīcus est, quī mēcum in Acadēmīā studēbat. tē benignē accipiet iuvābitque. tū eum cole et amā. vir doctus est et gravis. deī tē servābunt; sine dubiō enim poēta clārus eris et Mūsīs cārus. valē.' Quīntus eī grātiās ēgit et domum festīnāvit.

ubi domum advēnit, patrem in aulā sedentem invēnit. ille valdē occupātus fuerat. omnia enim vāsa, omnem supellectilem vendiderat. multum argentum comparāverat; dīmidium igitur Quīntō trādidit, dīmidium ipse retinuit. 'age, fīlī,' inquit, 'nōlī cessāre. nam brevī tempore ad portum ībimus nāvemque quaerēmus. nōlō enim in urbe manēre; nōn tūtum est. melius est statim discēdere.'

Quīntus igitur librōs collēgit et vestīmenta; omnia in ūnam magnam sarcinam composuit. parātus erat. pater fīliusque gradūs dēscendērunt et domō discessērunt, ubi iam diū habitāverant.

scelestōrum manūs vītāre cupiēbant; per vīcōs igitur angustōs festīnābant et mox ad viam advēnērunt, quae Ostia dūcēbat. nox iam vēnerat cum Ostia advēnērunt. pater cōnstituit eam noctem in caupōnā manēre. 'sēra hōra est,' inquit; 'hodiē nāvem invenīre nōn poterimus; māne quaerēmus in portū.'

prīmā lūce surrēxērunt et festīnāvērunt ad portum. magnum numerum nāvium prope lītus vīdērunt; paucae magnae erant, cēterae parvae; ex aliīs nautae frūmentum et aliās rēs ferēbant ad horrea; ibi mercātōrēs aderant, quī frūmentum emēbant. ex aliīs servī, catēnīs vinctī, exībant; ubīque clāmōrēs et tumultus.

Flaccus fīliusque praeter lītus ambulābant, nāvem idōneam quaerentēs. tandem parvam nāvem invēnērunt quae illō ipsō diē Puteolōs nāvigātūra erat; inde multae nāvēs ad Graeciam ībant.

magistrum petīvērunt; ille vir aequus erat; eōs benignē accēpit et viāticum modicum rogāvit. Flaccus argentum eī dedit; tum ad Quīntum sē vertit. oculī lacrimīs plēnī erant; haec verba aegrē dīxit: 'valē, cāre fīlī. cum ad Graeciam advēneris, epistolam statim nōbīs mitte. deī tē servābunt; nam puer bonus es.' Quīntus, patris manum tenēns, ūbertim flēbat; 'valē, cāre pater,'

ātriō hall
tablīnum study

benignē in a kindly way
dubiō doubt
valē farewell

aulā courtyard
occupātus busy; fuerat had been; vāsa pots and pans
supellectilem furniture
comparāverat he had got
dīmidium half
ipse himself
cessāre waste time, be slow
nōlō I don't want
melius better
collēgit collected
vestīmenta clothes
sarcinam bundle

vītāre to avoid; vīcōs streets
angustōs narrow
Ostia to Ostia (the port of Rome)
caupōnā an inn
sēra hōra late
māne in the morning

frūmentum corn
horrea granaries
mercātōrēs merchants
catēnīs vinctī bound in chains

praeter along
idōneam suitable
quaerentēs looking for
quae which; illō ipsō diē on that very day; nāvigātūra about to sail; magistrum captain
aequus fair
viāticum modicum a reasonable fare
aegrē with difficulty

tenēns holding
ūbertim abundantly

inquit; 'grātiās maximās tibi agō, quod tam bene mē cūrāvistī et tantum mihi dedistī. hoc prōmittō; cum prīmum ad Graeciam advēnerō, epistolam vōbīs mittam et omnia dīcam dē itinere. et tū, cum Venusiam redieris, cārae mātrī salūtem dā et Horātiae et Argō. sī deī benignī erunt, vōs omnēs mox iterum vidēbō.'

maximās very great
tantum so much

salūtem greetings

A Roman merchant ship

imperō, imperāre, imperāvī + dative	I order
colō, colere, coluī	I cultivate; I revere
cōnscendō, cōnscendere, cōnscendī	I go on board
prōmittō, prōmittere, prōmīsī	I promise
relinquō, relinquere, relīquī	I leave
lacrima, lacrimae, *f.*	tear
mora, morae, *f.*	delay
vīta, vītae, *f.*	life
numerus, numerī, *m.*	number
ferrum, ferrī, *n.*	iron; sword
proelium, proeliī, *n.*	battle
signum, signī, *n.*	signal; standard
verbum, verbī, *n.*	word
sōl, sōlis, *m.*	sun
pāx, pācis, *f.*	peace
portus, portūs, *m.*	harbour
manus, manūs, *f.*	hand; band (of people)

aequus-a-um	level; equal; fair	**numquam**	never
plēnus-a-um + ablative	full (of)	**umquam**	ever
brevis, breve	short	**sī**	if
prūdēns, prūdentis	sensible	**sine** + ablative	without

Exercise 20.3

The following list contains nouns on the left and verbs on the right; in every case you know one of the words. *Say what the other must mean* e.g. **dux**, **ducis**, *m.* leader **dūcere** to lead

cēna, cēnae, *f.*	cēnāre
cūra, cūrae, *f.*	cūrāre
lacrima, lacrimae, *f.*	lacrimāre
pugna, pugnae, *f.*	pugnāre
locus, locī, *m.*	locāre
lūdus, lūdī, *m.*	lūdere
nūntius, nūntiī, *m.*	nūntiāre
arma, armōrum, *n.pl.*	armāre

flōs, flōris, *m.*	flōrēre
lūx, lūcis, *f.*	lūcēre
mīles, mīlitis, *m.*	mīlitāre
laus, laudis, *f.*	laudāre
rēx, rēgis, *m.*	regere
vulnus, vulneris, *n.*	vulnerāre
vōx, vōcis, *f.*	vocāre

Exercise 20.4

Give the meaning of these pairs of words. In every case one of the pair is known to you

clāmō (1)	clāmor, clāmōris, *m.* *
labōrō (1)	labor, labōris, *m.* *
terreō (2)	terror, terrōris, *m.* *
timeō (2)	timor, timōris, *m.* *
canō (3)	carmen, carminis, *n.*
fluō (3)	flūmen, flūminis, *n.*
gaudeō (2)	gaudium, gaudiī, *n.*
imperō (1)	imperium, imperiī, *n.* *
incendō (3)	incendium, incendiī, *n.* *
studeō (2)	studium, studiī, *n.* *
amīcus-a	amīcitia, amīcitiae, *f.*
laetus-a-um	laetitia, laetitiae, *f.*
audāx, audācis	audācia, audāciae, *f.* *
prūdēns, prūdentis	prūdentia, prūdentiae, *f.* *
brevis, breve	brevitās, brevitātis, *f.* *
gravis, grave	gravitās, gravitātis, *f.* *
celer, celeris, celere	celeritās, celeritātis, *f.*
pauper, pauperis	paupertās, paupertātis, *f.* *

Exercise 20.5

Give an English word derived from each of the starred words in the previous exercise and say what it means.

The future perfect tense

This tense is formed by taking the perfect stem (**amāv-**, **monu-**, **rēx-**, **audīv-**) and adding the following endings

-erō	-erimus
-eris	-eritis
-erit	-erint

1		*2*	*3*	*4*
amāv-erō	I shall have loved	**monū-erō**	**rēx-erō**	**audīv-erō**
amāv-eris		etc.	etc.	etc.
amāv-erit				
amāv-erimus				
amāv-eritis				
amāv-erint				

The future perfect tense is seldom used in English but is common in Latin in sentences like this

cum advēneris, tibi omnia dīcam When you come (literally, 'when you will have come'), I shall tell you all.
sī domī mānseris, tūtus eris If you stay at home, you will be safe.

'sum' and 'possum'

The infinitive of **sum** is **esse**, the infinitive of **possum** is **posse**. The perfect of **sum** is **fuī**, the perfect of **possum** is **potuī**.

present	**sum**	I am	**possum**	I am able
future	**erō**	I shall be	**poterō**	I shall be able
imperfect	**eram**	I was	**poteram**	I was able
perfect	**fuī**	I have been	**potuī**	I could have
future perfect	**fuerō**	I shall have been	**potuerō**	I shall have been able
pluperfect	**fueram**	I had been	**potueram**	I had been able

Exercise 20.6

Analyse and translate the following sentences

1 cum Athēnās advēneris, hanc epistolam Theomnēstō
 dā.
2 sī dīligenter studueris, multa discēs.
3 cum ad portum vēnerimus, multās nāvēs vidēbimus.
4 cum magister signum dederit, nautae nāvem solvent.
5 numquam vīdī tantum numerum nāvium; quandō
 ad Graeciam discēdent?
6 sī magister prūdēns fuerit, ad portum sine perīculō
 adveniēmus.
7 nāvem statim cōnscendite, nam sine morā
 nāvigābimus.
8 nōlī lacrimāre, Quīnte; mox domum redībis
 mātremque vidēbis.
9 Quīntus verba patris audīvit sed lacrimās retinēre
 nōn potuit.
10 pater sē vertit; portū discessit viamque ad oppidum
 iniit.

solvere to cast off

Exercise 20.7

Translate into Latin

1 When we arrive at Rome, we shall
 stay in an inn.
2 If you see father in the town, tell him
 to come home at once.
3 When I reach Athens, I shall send you
 a letter without delay.
4 If you do that, I shall not be able to
 help you.
5 When the sailors hear the signal, they
 will obey the captain.

 inn **caupōna, -ae,** *f.*

Exercise 20.8

*What do the following pairs of words
mean?*

deus dea,   equus equa,
dominus domina,   fīlius fīlia,
servus serva

Exercise 20.9

Translate

1 puer domum curret et omnia patrī
 dīcet.
2 urbs nōn tūta est; nāvigābimus igitur
 Athēnās.
3 iuvenis valdē trīstis erit; patriam
 enim relinquet.
4 nec patrem nec mātrem umquam
 posteā vidēbitis.
5 cum Athēnās pervēneris, hanc
 epistolām amīcō meō trāde.
6 ille tē benignē accipiet et iuvābit.
7 mox magister signum nautīs dabit;
 tum nāvis lentē ē portū prōcēdet.
8 cum magister signum dederit, nautae
 nāvem ad apertum mare rēmigābunt.
9 cum domum redieris, mātrī sorōrīque
 meae salūtem dā.
10 si Athēnās tūtī advēnerimus, sine
 morā epistolam vōbīs mittēmus.
 rēmigābunt will row

Exercise 20.10

Translate the first paragraph and answer the questions below on the second

Flaccus sē vertit et sine morā viam ad oppidum iniit. Quīntus eum spectābat abeuntem dōnec e cōnspectū abiit. tum nāvem cōnscendit. magister signum nautīs dedit imperāvitque eīs fūnēs solvere; nāvem ē portū lentē rēmigābant. mox in apertō marī nāvigant; nautae vēla tollunt. nāvis per undās lentē prōcēdēbat; sōl in caelō lūcēbat.

abeuntem going away;
dōnec until; cōnspectū sight
fūnes the cables; solvere to loose
rēmigābant rowed
vēla the sails; tollunt raise

Quīntus in puppī stābat, ad patriam respiciēns; et trīstis erat et laetus. sōlus erat, patriam relinquēbat, sed novus cursus vītae eī patēbat. deī benignī futūra hominēs cēlant. nec patrem nec mātrem nec sorōrem Quīntus umquam posteā vīsūrus erat.

puppī stern; respiciēns looking back at
cursus way; patēbat lay open; futūra the future
hominēs cēlant hide from men
vīsūrus going to see

1 What were the feelings and thoughts of Quintus as he stood in the stern of the ship?
2 'The gods in their kindness hide the future from men.' Why was it kind to hide the future from Quintus?
3 Give an English word derived from each of the following (all in the second paragraph): **patriam**, **sōlus**, **novus**, **vītae**. Write four English sentences to illustrate the meaning of the words.
4 Translate into Latin:
(a) The captain ordered the sailors to cast off the ship.
(b) Soon we had left Italy and were sailing through the open sea.
(c) A storm is coming; don't you hear the wind?

GREECE AND ROME

You will remember that when the Greeks captured and sacked the city of Troy, Aeneas and his men fled from its smouldering ruins. They established themselves in Italy after many struggles and hardships, intermarried with Italians, and founded the Roman race. The Romans established their rule over the whole of Greece in 197 BC. It was a kind of revenge for the defeat which their legendary ancestors had suffered 1,000 years before. But the victors were in fact not at all vindictive. The Roman general declared at the Games at Corinth the following year that all the Greek states were now free and independent. The enthusiastic shouting of the liberated peoples was so loud that the birds flying overhead are said to have fallen to the ground stunned.

The Romans' attitude to the Greeks was strangely mixed in Horace's day. On the one hand, they despised the present weakness of a nation which had driven huge forces of invading Persians from their native soil five centuries before, and more recently had conquered the known world under Alexander the Great. On the other hand, they enormously admired their great art and literature. Educated Romans were bilingual, speaking both Greek and Latin, as Quintus now does. When Quintus sails to Athens to complete his education in Greek oratory and philosophy, he is making a journey that many Romans have travelled before him.

The extraordinary intellectual and creative inventiveness of the Greeks dazzled the Romans. Their discoveries in mathematics (Pythagoras), geometry (Euclid), astronomy (Ptolemy), science (Archimedes) and natural history (Aristotle), their mastery of the art of speaking (Demosthenes), their unrivalled architecture (Pheidias) and sculpture (Praxiteles), their great philosophical tradition (Plato) – all seemed wonderful to the Roman nation. For the greatest works of art of the Romans were impressive but heavy feats of engineering. Their major achievement was not to create but to conquer and rule.

The pont du Gard, a Roman aqueduct

However, the Romans still felt superior, even while they admired. They had their feet firmly planted on the ground compared with the talented but unreliable Greeks. They rightly saw themselves as a practical and realistic race in comparison with their neighbours across the Adriatic.

It was perhaps in literature especially that the superiority of the Greeks lay. The poems of Homer, the tragic plays of Aeschylus, Sophocles and Euripides from the fifth century BC, the historical writings of 'the father of history' Herodotus and of his successor Thucydides, and a whole treasury of lyric poetry – here was a great literary inheritance that gave the Romans everything to study and little to invent.

So while Rome had captured Greece, Greece captivated Rome.
As Horace himself put it, 'Graecia capta ferum victōrem cēpit.'
(Captured Greece captured her wild conqueror.)

The Parthenon, the temple of Athene in Athens

There have always been some people who have admired the Greeks
more than the Romans. From what you have read so far, what is your
view? You will learn more about the Greeks in Part 2.

Look up in an encyclopaedia two of the famous Greeks mentioned in
the third paragraph above and write a paragraph on each of them.

nec patrem nec mātrem nec sorōrem Quīntus umquam posteā vīsūrus erat.

SUMMARY OF GRAMMAR

NOUNS

	1st declension	*2nd declension*		*3rd declension*	
	stems in **-a**	stems -in **-o**		stems in consonants	
	feminine	*masculine*	*neuter*	*masc. & fem.*	*neuter*
singular					
nom.	domin-a	domin-us	bell-um	dux	caput
acc.	domin-am	domin-um	bell-um	duc-em	caput
gen.	domin-ae	domin-ī	bell-ī	duc-is	capit-is
dat.	domin-ae	domin-ō	bell-ō	duc-ī	capit-ī
abl.	domin-ā	domin-ō	bell-ō	duc-e	capit-e
plural					
nom.	domin-ae	domin-ī	bell-a	duc-ēs	capit-a
acc.	domin-ās	domin-ōs	bell-a	duc-ēs	capit-a
gen.	domin-ārum	domin-ōrum	bell-ōrum	duc-um	capit-um
dat.	domin-īs	domin-īs	bell-īs	duc-ibus	capit-ibus
abl.	domin-īs	domin-īs	bell-īs	duc-ibus	capit-ibus

	3rd declension		*4th declension*	*5th declension*
	stems in **-i**		stems in **-u**	stems in **-e**
	masc. & fem.	*neuter*	*masculine*	*feminine*
singular				
nom.	cīvis	mare	grad-us	rēs
acc.	cīv-em	mare	grad-um	rēm
gen.	cīv-is	mar-is	grad-ūs	reī
dat.	cīv-ī	mar-ī	grad-uī	reī
abl.	cīv-e	mar-ī	grad-ū	rē
plural				
nom.	cīv-ēs	mar-ia	grad-ūs	rēs
acc.	cīv-ēs	mar-ia	grad-ūs	rēs
gen.	cīv-ium	mar-ium	grad-uum	rērum
dat.	cīv-ibus	mar-ibus	grad-ibus	rēbus
abl.	cīv-ibus	mar-ibus	grad-ibus	rēbus

Notes

1 The vocative case, used in addressing or calling someone, is the same as the nominative, except in the second declension, where nouns ending **-us** form vocative singular **-e**, e.g. **Quīnte**, and nouns ending **-ius** form vocative singular **-ī**, e.g. **fīlī**.

2 All words of the first declension are feminine except for those which are masculine by meaning, e.g. **agricola** (farmer), **nauta** (sailor), **poēta** (poet).

3 Some second declension masculine nouns have nominative **-er**, e.g. **puer**, **ager**; of these, some keep the **-e** in their stem, e.g. **puerī**, others drop it, e.g. **agrī**.

4 Third declension. The gender of all third declension nouns has to be learnt. Genitive plural is **-um**, except for (a) nouns which have the same number of syllables in nominative and genitive, e.g. **cīvis**, **cīvis** (b) nouns whose stem ends in two or more consonants, e.g. **urbs**, **mōns**; these two classes have genitive plural **-ium**, e.g. **cīvium**, **urbium**, **montium**.

5 All fourth declension nouns are masculine except for **manus** (and two or three other rare words).

6 All fifth declension nouns are feminine, except for **diēs**, which is usually masculine.

ADJECTIVES

Masculine & neuter 2nd declension; feminine 1st declension

singular	m.	f.	n.
nom.	bon-us	bon-a	bon-um
acc.	bon-um	bon-am	bon-um
gen.	bon-ī	bon-ae	bon-ī
dat.	bon-ō	bon-ae	bon-ō
abl.	bon-ō	bon-ā	bon-ō

plural			
nom.	bon-ī	bon-ae	bon-a
acc.	bon-ōs	bon-ās	bon-a
gen.	bon-ōrum	bon-ārum	bon-ōrum
dat.	bon-īs	bon-īs	bon-īs
abl.	bon-īs	bon-īs	bon-īs

Like **bonus, bona, bonum** go **miser, misera, miserum**; **līber, lībera, līberum**; **pulcher, pulchra, pulchrum**; **sacer, sacra, sacrum**.

Third declension

consonant stems			stems in **-i**	
singular	m. & f.	n.	m. & f.	n.
nom.	vetus	vetus	trīstis	trīst-e
acc.	veter-em	vetus	trīst-em	trīst-e
gen.	veter-is	veter-is	trīst-is	trīst-is
dat.	veter-ī	veter-ī	trīst-ī	trīst-ī
abl.	veter-e	veter-e	trīst-ī	trīst-ī

plural				
nom.	veter-ēs	veter-a	trīst-ēs	trīst-ia
acc.	veter-ēs	veter-a	trīst-ēs	trīst-ia
gen.	veter-um	veter-um	trīst-ium	trīst-ium
dat.	veter-ibus	veter-ibus	trīst-ibus	trīst-ibus
abl.	veter-ibus	veter-ibus	trīst-ibus	trīst-ibus

The only other 3rd declension adjective in a consonant stem you have learnt is **pauper**, genitive **pauperis**.

Other types of **-i** stems are **audāx** (neuter **audāx**), genitive **audācis**.
ingēns (neuter **ingēns**), genitive **ingentis**.

ADVERBS

1 From **bonus** type adjectives, adverbs are normally formed by adding **-ē** to the stem, e.g. **laetus** happy, **laet-ē** happily; **miser** miserable, **miserē** miserably. A few add **-ō** instead of **-ē**, e.g. **tūt-us** safe, **tūt-ō** safely.

2 From third declension adjectives, adverbs are normally formed by adding **-ter** to the stem, e.g. **fortis** brave, **forti-ter** bravely; **audāx** bold, **audāc-ter** boldly; **celer** quick, **celeri-ter** quickly. A few third declension adjectives use the neuter singular of the adjective as an adverb, e.g. **facilis** easy, **facile** easily.

NUMERALS

1 ūnus	11 ūndecim
2 duo	12 duodecim
3 trēs	13 tredecim
4 quattuor	14 quattuordecim
5 quīnque	15 quīndecim
6 sex	16 sēdecim
7 septem	17 septendecim
8 octō	18 duodēvīgintī
9 novem	19 ūndēvīgintī
10 decem	20 vīgintī

first	**prīmus**
second	**secundus**
third	**tertius**
fourth	**quārtus**
fifth	**quīntus**
sixth	**sextus**
seventh	**septimus**
eighth	**octāvus**
ninth	**nōnus**
tenth	**decimus**

Declension of **ūnus**, **duo**, **trēs**

masc.	fem.	neuter
ūnus	ūna	ūnum
ūnum	ūnam	ūnum
ūnīus	ūnīus	ūnīus
ūnī	ūnī	ūnī
ūnō	ūnā	ūnō
duo	duae	duo
duo, duōs	duās	duo
duōrum	duārum	duōrum
duōbus	duābus	duōbus
duōbus	duābus	duōbus
trēs	trēs	tria
trēs	trēs	tria
trium	trium	trium
tribus	tribus	tribus
tribus	tribus	tribus

Prīmus, secundus etc. decline like **bonus**:
prīmus, prīma, prīmum.
quattuor . . . vīgintī do not decline.

PRONOUNS

singular

nom.	ego (I)	tū (you)		Possessive adjectives
acc.	mē	tē	sē (himself, herself)	meus-a-um (my)
gen.	meī	tuī	suī	tuus-a-um (your)
dat.	mihi	tibi	sibi	suus-a-um (his own)
abl.	mē	tē	sē	

plural

nom.	nōs (we)	vōs (you)		noster, nostra, nostrum (our)
acc.	nōs	vōs	sē (themselves)	vester, vestra, vestrum (your)
gen.	nostrum	vestrum	suī	suus-a-um (their own)
dat.	nōbīs	vōbīs	sibi	
abl.	nōbīs	vōbīs	sē	All go like **bonus-a-um**, but the vocative of **meus** is **mī**.

singular

	m.	*f.*	*n.*	*m.*	*f.*	*n.*	*m.*	*f.*	*n.*
nom.	hic	haec	hoc (this)	ille	illa	illud (that)	is	ea	id (he, she, it)
acc.	hunc	hanc	hoc	illum	illam	illud	eum	eam	id
gen.	huius	huius	huius	illīus	illīus	illīus	eius	eius	eius
dat.	huic	huic	huic	illī	illī	illī	eī	eī	eī
abl.	hōc	hāc	hōc	illō	illā	illō	eō	eā	eō

plural

	m.	*f.*	*n.*	*m.*	*f.*	*n.*	*m.*	*f.*	*n.*
nom.	hī	hae	haec	illī	illae	illa	eī	eae	ea
acc.	hōs	hās	haec	illōs	illās	illa	eōs	eās	ea
gen.	hōrum	hārum	hōrum	illōrum	illārum	illōrum	eōrum	eārum	eōrum
dat.	hīs	hīs	hīs	illīs	illīs	illīs	eīs	eīs	eīs
abl.	hīs	hīs	hīs	illīs	illīs	illīs	eīs	eīs	eīs

VERBS

Active

		1st conjugation	2nd conjugation	3rd conjugation	4th conjugation	mixed conjugation
		stems in **-a**	stems in **-e**	stems in consonants	stems in **-i**	stems in **-i**

present

singular	1	am-ō	mone-ō	reg-ō	audi-ō	capi-ō
	2	amā-s	monē-s	reg-is	audī-s	capi-s
	3	ama-t	mone-t	reg-it	audi-t	capi-t
plural	1	amā-mus	monē-mus	reg-imus	audī-mus	capi-mus
	2	amā-tis	monē-tis	reg-itis	audī-tis	capi-tis
	3	ama-nt	mone-nt	reg-unt	audi-unt	capi-unt

future

singular	1	amā-bō	monē-bō	reg-am	audi-am	capi-am
	2	amā-bis	monē-bis	reg-ēs	audi-ēs	capi-ēs
	3	amā-bit	monē-bit	reg-et	audi-et	capi-et
plural	1	amā-bimus	monē-bimus	reg-ēmus	audi-ēmus	capi-ēmus
	2	amā-bitis	monē-bitis	reg-ētis	audi-ētis	capi-ētis
	3	amā-bunt	monē-bunt	reg-ent	audi-ent	capi-ent

imperfect

singular	1	amā-bam	monē-bam	regē-bam	audiē-bam	capiē-bam
	2	amā-bās	monē-bās	regē-bās	audiē-bās	capiē-bās
	3	amā-bat	monē-bat	regē-bat	audiē-bat	capiē-bat
plural	1	amā-bāmus	monē-bāmus	regē-bāmus	audiē-bāmus	capiē-bāmus
	2	amā-bātis	monē-bātis	regē-bātis	audiē-bātis	capiē-bātis
	3	amā-bant	monē-bant	regē-bant	audiē-bant	capiē-bant

perfect

singular	1	amāv-ī	monu-ī	rēx-ī	audīv-ī	cēp-ī
	2	amāv-istī	monu-istī	rēx-istī	audīv-istī	cēp-istī
	3	amāv-it	monu-it	rēx-it	audīv-it	cēp-it
plural	1	amāv-imus	monu-imus	rēx-imus	audīv-imus	cēp-imus
	2	amāv-istis	monu-istis	rēx-istis	audīv-istis	cēp-istis
	3	amāv-ērunt	monu-ērunt	rēx-ērunt	audīv-ērunt	cēp-ērunt

	1st conjugation	2nd conjugation	3rd conjugation	4th conjugation	mixed conjugation
	stems in **-a**	stems in **-e**	stems in consonants	stems in **-i**	stems in **-i**

future perfect

		1st conjugation	2nd conjugation	3rd conjugation	4th conjugation	mixed conjugation
singular	1	amāv-erō	monu-erō	rēx-erō	audīv-erō	cēp-erō
	2	amāv-eris	monu-eris	rēx-eris	audīv-eris	cēp-eris
	3	amāv-erit	monu-erit	rēx-erit	audīv-erit	cēp-erit
plural	1	amāv-erimus	monu-erimus	rēx-erimus	audīv-erimus	cēp-erimus
	2	amāv-eritis	monu-eritis	rēx-eritis	audīv-eritis	cēp-eritis
	3	amāv-erint	monu-erint	rēx-erint	audīv-erint	cēp-erint

pluperfect

		1st conjugation	2nd conjugation	3rd conjugation	4th conjugation	mixed conjugation
singular	1	amāv-eram	monu-eram	rēx-eram	audīv-eram	cēp-eram
	2	amāv-erās	monu-erās	rēx-erās	audīv-erās	cēp-erās
	3	amāv-erat	monu-erat	rēx-erat	audīv-erat	cēp-erat
plural	1	amāv-erāmus	monu-erāmus	rēx-erāmus	audīv-erāmus	cēp-erāmus
	2	amāv-erātis	monu-erātis	rēx-erātis	audīv-erātis	cēp-erātis
	3	amāv-erant	monu-erant	rēx-erant	audīv-erant	cēp-erant

Infinitive	amā-re	monē-re	reg-ere	audī-re	cap-ere

Imperative

	1st conjugation	2nd conjugation	3rd conjugation	4th conjugation	mixed conjugation
singular	amā	monē	reg-e	audī	cap-e
plural	amā-te	monē-te	reg-ite	audī-te	cap-ite

Irregular verbs

sum: infinitive **esse**		**possum**: infinitive **posse** (**pot** + **sum**)	**eō**: infinitive **īre** (stem **i-**)
present			
singular	1 sum	possum	eō
	2 es	potes	īs
	3 est	potest	it
plural	1 sumus	possumus	īmus
	2 estis	potestis	ītis
	3 sunt	possunt	eunt
future			
singular	1 erō	pot-erō	ī-bō
	2 eris	pot-eris	ī-bis
	3 erit	pot-erit	ī-bit
plural	1 erimus	pot-erimus	ī-bimus
	2 eritis	pot-eritis	ī-bitis
	3 erunt	pot-erunt	ī-bunt
imperfect			
singular	1 eram	pot-eram	ī-bam
	2 erās	pot-erās	ī-bās
	3 erat	pot-erat	ī-bat
plural	1 erāmus	pot-erāmus	ī-bāmus
	2.erātis	pot-erātis	ī-bātis
	3 erant	pot-erant	ī-bant
perfect stem	fu-	potu-	i-
singular	1 fu-ī	potu-ī	i-ī
	2 fu-istī	potu-istī	īstī
	3 fu-it	potu-it	i-it
plural	1 fu-imus	potu-imus	i-imus
	2 fu-istis	potu-istis	īstis
	3 fu-ērunt	potu-ērunt	i-ērunt
future perfect	fu-erō etc.	potu-erō etc.	i-erō etc.
pluperfect	fu-eram etc.	potu-eram etc.	i-eram etc.
imperatives			
singular	es, estō		ī
plural	este		īte

Principal parts of irregular and third conjugation verbs

1st conjugation

dō, dare, dedī I give
iuvō, iuvāre, iūvī I help
stō, stāre, stetī I stand

2nd conjugation

augeō, augēre, auxī I increase
ārdeō, ārdēre, ārsī I am on fire
fleō, flēre, flēvī I weep
iubeō, iubēre, iussī I order
maneō, manēre, mānsī I remain, stay
moveō, movēre, mōvī I move
persuādeō, persuādēre, persuāsī + dative I
  persuade

respondeō, respondēre, respondī I answer
rīdeō, rīdēre, rīsī I laugh, smile
sedeō, sedēre, sēdī I sit
videō, vidēre, vīdī I see

3rd conjugation, arranged by types

dīcō, dīcere, dīxī I say
dūcō, dūcere, dūxī I lead
gerō, gerere, gessī I do, I carry
intellegō, intellegere, intellēxī I understand
regō, regere, rēxī I rule
scrībō, scrībere, scrīpsī I write
surgō, surgere, surrēxi I rise, get up
vīvō, vīvere, vīxī I live

cēdō, cēdere, cessī I yield, give way
claudō, claudere, clausī I shut
ēvādō, ēvādere, ēvāsī I get away, escape
lūdō, lūdere, lūsī I play
mittō, mittere, mīsī I send

nōscō, nōscere, nōvī I get to know, learn
cognōscō, cognōscere, cognōvī I get to know, learn
petō, petere, petīvī I seek for; I attack
quaerō, quaerere, quaesīvī I look for
colō, colere, coluī I cultivate; I revere
pōnō, pōnere, posuī I place, put
dēserō, dēserere, dēseruī I desert

cadō, cadere, cecidī I fall
currō, currere, cucurrī I run
discō, discere, didicī I learn
crēdō, crēdere, crēdidī + dative I believe
reddō, reddere, reddidī I give back, return
trādō, trādere, trādidī I hand over
vēndō, vēndere, vēndidī I sell
cōnsistō, cōnsistere, cōnstitī I halt
resistō, resistere, restitī + dative I resist

agō, agere, ēgī I do
emō, emere, ēmī I buy
legō, legere, lēgī I read
vincō, vincere, vīcī I conquer

ascendō, ascendere, ascendī I climb
dēscendō, dēscendere, dēscendī I descend

bibō, bibere, bibī I drink
contendō, contendere, contendī I march, hasten, compete
incendō, incendere, incendī I set on fire
ostendō, ostendere, ostendī I show
vertō, vertere, vertī I turn

cōnstituō, cōnstituere, cōnstituī I decide
induō, induere, induī I put on

4th conjugation

aperiō, aperīre, aperuī I open
veniō, venīre, vēnī I come

Mixed conjugation

capiō, capere, cēpī I take
cōnspiciō, cōnspicere, cōnspexī I catch sight of
īnspiciō, īnspicere, īnspexī I look at
cupiō, cupere, cupīvī I want, desire
faciō, facere, fēcī I do; I make
fugiō, fugere, fūgī I flee
iaciō, iacere, iēcī I throw
rapiō, rapere, rapuī I snatch

Compound verbs

Compound verbs normally have the same principal parts as the simple verb, e.g. **veniō, venīre, vēnī; adveniō, advenīre, advēnī**.
NB 1 Note the following changes in the stems of compound verbs:
cadō: incidō etc.
capiō: incipiō, accipiō etc.
faciō: interficiō etc.
iaciō: coniciō etc.
rapiō: corripiō etc.

2 Compounds of **currō: incurrō, incurrere, incurrī** (*not* -cucurrī)
cadō: incidō, incidere, incidī (*not* -cecidī)

PREPOSITIONS

The following take the accusative

ad to	**post** after, behind
ante before	**prope** near
circum around	**super** above
contrā against	**trāns** across
extrā outside	
in into	
inter among, between	
per through	

The following take the ablative

ā/ab from
cum with
dē down from; about
ē/ex out of
in in
prō in front of; on behalf of
sine without
sub under

LATIN–ENGLISH VOCABULARY

ā/ab + ablative from, by
absum, abesse, āfuī I am absent, I am away
accēdō, accēdere, accessī I approach
accendō, accendere, accendī I light
accipiō, accipere, accēpī I accept, receive
accurrō, accurrere, accurrī I run to
accūsō, accūsāre, accūsāvī I accuse
ad + accusative to
addō, addere, addidī I add
adeō, adīre, adiī I go to, approach
adsum, adesse, adfuī I am present
adveniō, advenīre, advēnī I arrive
aedēs, aedium, f.pl. house
aedificium, aedificiī, n. building
aedificō, aedificāre, aedificāvī I build
aegrē reluctantly
aequus-a-um equal, fair
age! come on!
ager, agrī, m. field
agricola, agricolae, m. farmer
agō, agere, ēgī I do; I drive
alius, alia, aliud other
alter, altera, alterum one or the other (of two)
altus-a-um high, deep
ambulō, ambulāre, ambulāvī I walk
amīcus, amīcī, m. friend
amō, amāre, amāvī I love
amor, amōris, m. love
animus, animī, m. mind
annus, annī, m. year
ante + accusative before
ānxius-a-um anxious
apertus-a-um open
aperiō, aperīre, aperuī I open
aqua, aquae, f. water
arbor, arboris, f. tree
ārdeō, ārdēre, ārsī I am on fire
ārdēns, ārdentis burning
argentum, argentī, n. silver, money
arma, armōrum, n.pl. arms
armātus-a-um armed
arō, arāre, arāvī I plough
arātrum, arātrī, n. plough
arrīdeō, arrīdēre, arrīsī I smile at
ascendō, ascendere, ascendī I climb, board
attendō, attendere, attendī I attend
attonitus-a-um astonished
audāx, audācis bold
audeō, audēre I dare
audiō, audīre, audīvī I hear, listen to
augeō, augēre, auxī I increase
aut or
aut ... aut either ... or
auxilium, auxiliī, n. help

bellum, bellī, n. war
bene well
benignus-a-um kind
bibō, bibere, bibī I drink
bonus-a-um good
brevis, breve short

cadō, cadere, cecidī I fall
caedō, caedere, cecīdī I beat; I kill

caelum, caelī, n. sky, heaven
calidus-a-um hot
campus, campī, m. plain
capiō, capere, cēpī I take
canis, canis, c. dog
capsula, capsulae, f. box
caput, capitis, n. head
carmen, carminis, n. song
cārus-a-um dear
casa, casae, f. house
castra, castrōrum, n.pl. camp
caupōna, caupōnae, f. inn
cecidī see cadō
cēdō, cēdere, cessī I yield, give way
celebrō, celebrāre, celebrāvī I celebrate
celer, celeris, celere quick
cēna, cēnae, f. dinner
cēnō, cēnāre, cēnāvī I dine
centuriō, centuriōnis, m. centurion
cessō, cessāre, cessāvī I tarry, idle
cēterī, cēterae, cētera the rest, the others
cibus, cibī, m. food
circum + accusative around
cīvis, cīvis, m. citizen
clāmō, clāmāre, clāmāvī I shout
clāmor, clāmōris, m. shout
clārus-a-um clear; famous
claudō, claudere, clausī I shut
clausus-a-um shut
cognōscō, cognōscere, cognōvī I get to know, learn
collis, collis, m. hill
colō, colere, coluī I cultivate; I revere
comes, comitis, c. companion
cōmis, cōme friendly
commoveō, commovēre, commōvī I move
commōtus-a-um moved, upset
compleō, complēre, complēvī I fill
compōnō, compōnere, composuī I put together, compose
condō, condere, condidī I found
condūcō, condūcere, condūxī I hire
cōnfectus-a-um finished; worn out
cōnficiō, cōnficere, cōnfēcī I finish
coniciō, conicere, coniēcī I throw, hurl
cōnscendō, cōnscendere, cōnscendī I board
cōnsistō, cōnsistere, cōnstitī I halt, stand
cōnspiciō, cōnspicere, cōnspexī I catch sight of
cōnsilium, cōnsiliī, n. plan; advice
cōnstituō, cōnstituere, cōnstituī I decide
cōnsul, cōnsulis, m. consul
contendō, contendere, contendī I march, hasten; I compete
contrā + accusative against
conveniō, convenīre, convēnī I come together
convocō, convocāre, convocāvī I call together
corpus, corporis, n. body
cotīdiē daily, every day
crās tomorrow
crēdō, crēdere, crēdidī + dative I believe
culīna, culīnae, f. kitchen
cum (conjunction) when
cum + ablative with
cupiō, cupere, cupīvī I desire, wish

cūr? why?
cūra, cūrae, *f.* care
cūrō, cūrāre, cūrāvī I care for, look after
cursus, cursūs, *m.* course

dē + ablative about; down from
dēbeō, dēbēre, dēbuī I ought, must
dēcidō, dēcidere, dēcidī I fall down
deinde then, next
dēnique finally
dēscendō, dēscendere, dēscendī I descend
dēserō, dēserere, dēseruī I desert
dēspērō, dēspērāre, dēspērāvī I despair
deus, deī, *m.* god
dīcō, dīcere, dīxī I say, tell
diēs, diēī, *m.* day
difficilis, difficile difficult
diffugiō, diffugere, diffūgī I flee away
dīligenter carefully
dīmittō, dīmittere, dīmīsī I send away, dismiss
discēdō, discēdere, discessī I go away, leave
discipulus, discipulī, *m.* pupil
discō, discere, didicī I learn
diū for a long time
dō, dare, dedī I give
doceō, docēre, docuī I teach
doctus-a-um learned
dominus, dominī, *m.* master, lord
domus, domūs, *f.* home
domī at home
dormiō, dormīre, dormīvī I sleep
dum while
dūcō, dūcere, dūxī I lead
dūrus-a-um hard, tough
dux, ducis, *c.* leader

ē, ex + ablative out of, from
ēbrius-a-um drunk
ecce! look!
edō, ēsse, ēdī I eat
effugiō, effugere, effūgī I escape
ego I
emō, emere, ēmī I buy
enim for
eō, īre, iī I go
eō (adverb) thither, there
epistola, epistolae, *f.* letter
equitō, equitāre, equitāvī I ride
equus, equī, *m.* horse
ēripiō, ēripere, ēripuī I snatch away, rescue
errō, errāre, errāvī I wander; I err, am wrong
et and; **et . . . et** both . . . and
etiam even; also
ēvādō, ēvādere, ēvāsī I escape
excitō, excitāre, excitāvī I wake, rouse
exerceō, exercēre, exercuī I exercise, train
exercitus, exercitūs, *m.* army
exspectō, exspectāre, exspectāvī I wait for
extrā + accusative outside

fābula, fābulae, *f.* story
facilis, facile easy
facile easily
faciō, facere, fēcī I do, I make
familia, familiae, *f.* household, family

fēmina, fēminae, *f.* woman
ferō, ferre, tulī I carry, bear
ferrum, ferrī, *n.* iron; sword
fessus-a-um tired
festīnō, festīnāre, festīnāvī I hurry
fīlia, fīliae, *f.* daughter
fīlius, fīliī, *m.* son
flamma, flammae, *f.* flame
fleō, flēre, flēvī I weep
flōs, flōris, *m.* flower
flūmen, flūminis, *n.* river
fluvius, fluviī, *m.* river
fōns, fontis, *m.* spring
fortis, forte brave
fortiter bravely
forum, forī, *n.* forum
frāter, frātris, *m.* brother
frūstrā in vain
fugiō, fugere, fūgī I flee
gaudeō, gaudēre I rejoice
gaudium, gaudiī, *n.* joy
gerō, gerere, gessī I carry, wear; I do
gladius, gladiī, *m.* sword
glōria, glōriae, *f.* glory
gradus, gradūs, *m.* step
Graecē in Greek
grātiae, grātiārum, *f.pl.* thanks
grātiās agere to give thanks to
gravis, grave heavy; serious

habeō, habēre, habuī I have
habitō, habitāre, habitāvī I live in, inhabit
hasta, hastae, *f.* spear
hic, haec, hoc this
hīc here
hiems, hiemis, *f.* winter
hodiē today
homō, hominis, *c.* human being, man
hōra, hōrae, *f.* hour
hortus, hortī, *m.* garden
hostis, hostis, *c.* enemy
hūc hither, to here

iaceō, iacēre, iacuī I lie
iaciō, iacere, iēcī I throw
iaculum, iaculī, *n.* javelin
iam now, already
iānua, iānuae, *f.* door
ibi there
igitur therefore, and so
ignis, ignis, *m.* fire
ille, illa, illud that; he, she
illūc thither; to there
imāgō, imāginis, *f.* picture
imperium, imperiī, *n.* order; empire
imperō, imperāre, imperāvī + dative I order
in + accusative into, to
in + ablative in
incendō, incendere, incendī I set on fire
incipiō, incipere, incēpī I begin
inde thence; from there
induō, induere, induī I put on
ineō, inīre, iniī I go into, enter
īnfēlīx, īnfēlīcis unlucky, ill-starred
ingēns, ingentis huge

inquit he, she said
īnspiciō, īnspicere, īnspexī I look at
īnsula, īnsulae, *f.* island; block of flats
intellegō, intellegere, intellēxī I understand
intentē intently
inter + accusative among; between
intereā meanwhile
interficiō, interficere, interfēcī I kill
intrō, intrāre, intrāvī I enter
inveniō, invenīre, invēnī I find
īra, īrae, *f.* anger
īrātus-a-um angry
is, ea, id he, she, it; that
itaque and so
iter, itineris, *n.* journey
iterum again
iubeō, iubēre, iussī I order
Iuppiter, Iovis, *m.* Jupiter
iuvenis, iuvenis, *m.* young man
iuvō, iuvāre, iūvī I help

labor, labōris, *m.* work; suffering
labōrō, labōrāre, labōrāvī I work
lacrima, lacrimae, *f.* tear
lacrimō, lacrimāre, lacrimāvī I weep
laetus-a-um happy
lātus-a-um wide
Latīnē in Latin
laudō, laudāre, laudāvī I praise
laus, laudis, *f.* praise
lautus-a-um elegant, smart
lavō, lavāre, lāvī I wash
legiō, legiōnis, *f.* legion
legō, legere, lēgī I read
lentē slowly
lēx, lēgis, *f.* law
liber, librī, *m.* book
līber, lībera, līberum free
līberō, līberāre, līberāvī I free
littera, litterae, *f.* letter
litterae, litterārum, *f.pl.* literature
lītus, lītoris, *n.* shore
loculī, loculōrum, *m.pl.* satchel
locus, locī, *m.* place
longus-a-um long
longē far
lūdō, lūdere, lūsī I play
lūdus, lūdī, *m.* game; school
lūna, lūnae, *f.* moon
lupus, lupī, *m.* wolf
lūx, lūcis, *f.* light

magister, magistrī, *m.* (school) master
magistrātus, magistrātūs, *m.* magistrate
magnificē magnificently
magnus-a-um big, great
malus-a-um bad
male badly
māne early
maneō, manēre, mānsī I remain, stay
manus, manūs, *f.* hand; band, group
mare, maris, *n.* sea
māter, mātris, *f.* mother
medius-a-um middle
memoria, memoriae, *f.* memory
merīdiēs, merīdiēī, *m.* midday
meus, mea, meum my

mīles, mīlitis, *m.* soldier
mīlitō, mīlitāre, mīlitāvī I serve (as a soldier)
miser, misera, miserum wretched, miserable
mittō, mittere, mīsī I send
moneō, monēre, monuī I warn, advise
mōns, montis, *m.* mountain
mora, morae, *f.* delay
mors, mortis, *f.* death
mortuus-a-um dead
moveō, movēre, mōvī I move
mox soon
multus-a-um much; many
mūrus, mūrī, *m.* wall

nam for
nārrō, nārrāre, nārrāvī I tell, relate
nātus-a-um born, old
nauta, nautae, *m.* sailor
nāvigō, nāvigāre, nāvigāvī I sail
nāvis, nāvis, *f.* ship
-ne (indicates question)
nec, neque nor; and not
nec, neque . . . nec, neque neither . . . nor
nēmō no one
nesciō, nescīre, nescīvī I do not know
nihil nothing
nōmen, nōminis, *n.* name
nōmine by name; called
nōn not
nōnne (indicates question)
nōs we
nōscō, nōscere, nōvī I get to know, learn
noster, nostra, nostrum our
novus-a-um new
nox, noctis, *f.* night
nūllus-a-um no
numerus, numerī, *m.* number
numquam never
nunc now
nūntiō, nūntiāre, nūntiāvī I announce
nūntius, nūntiī, *m.* message; messenger

obsideō, obsidēre, obsēdī I besiege
occupātus-a-um busy
oculus, oculī, *m.* eye
ōlim once, at some time
omnis, omne all
oppidum, oppidī, *n.* town
opus, operis, *n.* work
orāculum, orāculī, *n.* oracle
ōrō, ōrāre, ōrāvī I beg
ōrātiō, ōrātiōnis, *f.* speech
ōrātor, ōrātōris, *m.* speaker, orator
ostendō, ostendere, ostendī I show

pānis, pānis, *m.* bread
parātus-a-um ready
parēns, parentis, *c.* parent
pāreō, pārēre, pāruī + dative I obey
parō, parāre, parāvī I prepare
pars, partis, *f.* part
parvus-a-um small
pater, patris, *m.* father
patria, patriae, *f.* fatherland
paucī, paucae, pauca few
paulīsper for a short time
pauper, pauperis poor

pāx, pācis, f. peace
pellō, pellere, pepulī I drive
per + accusative through
pereō, perīre, periī I perish, die
perīculum, perīculī, n. danger
persuādeō, persuādēre, persuāsī + dative I
  persuade
perveniō, pervenīre, pervēnī I reach, get to
pēs, pedis, m. foot
petō, petere, petīvī I seek, chase
pictūra, pictūrae, f. picture
pila, pilae, f. ball
placeō, placēre, placuī + dative I please
plānē clearly
plaudō, plaudere, plausī I clap, applaud
plēnus-a-um full
poēta, poētae, m. poet
pōnō, pōnere, posuī I place, put
populus, populī, m. people
porta, portae, f. gate
portō, portāre, portāvī I carry
portus, portūs, m. port, harbour
possum, posse, potuī I can, am able
post + accusative after; behind
posteā afterwards
posterus-a-um next
postrīdiē the next day
prīnceps, prīncipis, m. chief, prince
prīmus-a-um first
prīmum (adverb) first
prō + ablative in front of; on behalf of
prōcēdō, prōcēdere, prōcessī I advance, go on
procul far
proelium, proeliī, n. battle
prohibeō, prohibēre, prohibuī I prevent
prōmittō, prōmittere, prōmīsī I promise
prope + accusative near
prūdēns, prūdentis sensible
puella, puellae, f. girl
puer, puerī, m. boy; child
pugna, pugnae, f. battle
pugnō, pugnāre, pugnāvī I fight
pulcher, pulchra, pulchrum beautiful
pūniō, pūnīre, pūnīvī I punish
putō, putāre, putāvī I think, suppose

quae who (feminine)
quaerō, quaerere, quaesīvī I look for
quandō? when?
quantus-a-um? how great?
-que and
quī who (masculine)
quiēscō, quiēscere I rest
quis? quid? who? what?
quīdam, quaedam, quoddam a certain
quō? whither? where to?
quod because
quoque also

rapiō, rapere, rapuī I snatch
recitō, recitāre, recitāvī I recite, read aloud
rēctē rightly, correctly
reddō, reddere, reddidī I give back, return
redeō, redīre, rediī I go back, return
rēgīna, rēgīnae, f. queen
regiō, regiōnis, f. region, district
regō, regere, rēxī I rule

relinquō, relinquere, relīquī I leave
rēmigō, rēmigāre, rēmigāvī I row
rēs, reī, f. thing, matter, affair
resistō, resistere, restitī + dative I resist
respondeō, respondēre, respondī I answer
rēspūblica, reīpūblicae, f. state, republic
retineō, retinēre, retinuī I hold back, restrain
rēx, rēgis, m. king
rīdeō, rīdēre, rīsī I laugh, smile
rīpa, rīpae, f. bank
rogō, rogāre, rogāvī I ask, I ask for
ruō, ruere, ruī I rush
rūrsus again

sacer, sacra, sacrum sacred
sacrificium, sacrificiī, n. sacrifice
saepe often
saevus-a-um savage
salūs, salūtis, f. greetings
salūtō, salūtāre, salūtāvī I greet
salvē! greetings!
saxum, saxī, n. rock
schola, scholae, f. lecture; school
scelestus-a-um criminal, wicked
sciō, scīre, scīvī I know
scrībō, scrībere, scrīpsī I write, draw
scrība, scrībae, m. secretary
sed but
sedeō, sedēre, sēdī I sit
sella, sellae, f. chair
semper always
senātor, senātōris, m. senator
senex, senis, m. old man
sērō late
servō, servāre, servāvī I save
servus, servī, m. slave
sevērus-a-um severe
sī if
sīc thus
signum, signī, n. signal; standard
silva, silvae, f. wood
simul at the same time
sine + ablative without
sōl, sōlis, m. sun
sōlus-a-um alone
somnus, somnī, m. sleep
soror, sorōris, f. sister
spectō, spectāre, spectāvī I look at
spērō, spērāre, spērāvī I hope
spēs, speī, f. hope
splendidus-a-um splendid
statim at once
stō, stāre, stetī I stand
strēnuē strenuously
studeō, studēre, studuī + dative I study, am keen on
studium, studiī, n. study, enthusiasm
sub + ablative under
subitō suddenly
subsellium, subselliī, n. bench
sum, esse, fuī I am
summus-a-um highest, greatest
sūmō, sūmere, sūmpsī I take up
super + accusative above
superō, superāre, superāvī I overcome, outdo
surgō, surgere, surrēxī I rise, get up

tabula, tabulae, f. tablet

taceō, tacēre, tacuī I am quiet
tacitus-a-um quiet, silent
tam so
tamen but, however
tandem at length
tantus-a-um so great
tempestās, tempestātis, *f.* storm
templum, templī, *n.* temple
temptō, temptāre, temptāvī I try, attempt
tempus, temporis, *n.* time
teneō, tenēre, tenuī I hold
terra, terrae, *f.* land, earth
terreō, terrēre, terruī I frighten
territus-a-um terrified
timeō, timēre, timuī I fear
timor, timōris, *m.* fear
toga, togae, *f.* toga
tollō, tollere I raise
tōtus-a-um whole
tradō, trādere, trādidī I hand over
trahō, trahere, trāxī I drag
trāns + accusative across
trānseō, trānsīre, trānsiī I cross
trīstis, trīste sad
tū you
turba, turbae, *f.* crowd
tūtus-a-um safe
tum then
tumultus, tumultūs, *m.* riot, uproar

ubi? where
ubi when
ubīque everywhere
ultimus-a-um furthest, last
umquam ever
unda, undae, *f.* wave

unde? whence, where from?
undique from all sides
ūnus-a-um one
urbs, urbis, *f.* city
uxor, uxōris, *f.* wife

valdē very
valē! farewell
valēre iubeō I bid farewell, say goodbye
vēndō, vēndere, vēndidī I sell
veniō, venīre, vēnī I come
ventus, ventī, *m.* wind
verbum, verbī, *n.* word
verēcundus-a-um shy
versus, versūs, *m.* verse
vertō, vertere, vertī I turn
vērus-a-um true
vesper, vesperis, *m.* evening
vetus, veteris old
via, viae, *f.* road, way
vīcīnus-a-um neighbouring; neighbour
victor, victōris, *m.* victor, winner
villa, villae, *f.* country house
vincō, vincere, vīcī I conquer
vīnum, vīnī, *n.* wine
vir, virī, *m.* man, husband
virīlis, virīle manly
vīs-ne? do you want?
vīta, vītae, *f.* life
vīvō, vīvere, vīxī I live
vocō, vocāre, vocāvī I call
vōx, vōcis, *f.* voice
vulnus, vulneris, *n.* wound
vulnerō, vulnerāre, vulnerāvī I wound
vultus, vultūs, *m.* face, expression

ENGLISH–LATIN VOCABULARY

ble, I am **possum, posse, potuī**
ccept, I **accipiō, accipere, accēpī**
advice **cōnsilium, cōnsiliī,** *n.*
afraid, I am **timeō, timēre, timuī**
again **iterum**
all **omnis, omne**
almost **paene**
already **iam**
always **semper**
and **et**
anger **īra, īrae,** *f.*
angry **īrātus-a-um**
answer, I **respondeō, respondēre, respondī**
anxious **ānxius-a-um**
army **exercitus, exercitūs,** *m.*
approach, I **accēdō, accēdere, accessī** (+ **ad**)
arrive, I **adveniō, advenīre, advēnī** (+ **ad**)
ask, I **rogō, rogāre, rogāvī**
at once **statim**

bad **malus-a-um**
bank **rīpa, rīpae,** *f.*
beautiful **pulcher, pulchra, pulchrum**
because **quod**
board, I **cōnscendō, cōnscendere, cōnscendī**
book **liber, librī,** *m.*
boy **puer, puerī,** *m.*
brave **fortis, forte**
bravely **fortiter**
brother **frāter, frātris,** *m.*

call, I **vocō, vocāre, vocāvī**
camp **castra, castrōrum,** *n.pl.*
can, I **possum, posse, potuī**
captain **magister, magistrī,** *m.*
carry, I **gerō, gerere, gessī**
city **urbs, urbis,** *f.*
climb, I **ascendō, ascendere, ascendī**
close, I **claudō, claudere, clausī**
come, I **veniō, venīre, vēnī**
come down, I **dēscendō, dēscendere, dēscendī**
come together, I **conveniō, convenīre, convēnī**
comrade **comes, comitis,** *c.*
course **cursus, cursūs,** *m.*

danger **perīculum, perīculī,** *n.*
daughter **fīlia, fīliae,** *f.*
dawn **prīma lūx, prīmae lūcis**
day **diēs, diēī,** *m.*
decide, I **cōnstituō, cōnstituere, cōnstituī**
delay **mora, morae,** *f.*
despair, I **dēspērō, dēspērāre, dēspērāvī**
dine, I **cēnō, cēnāre, cēnāvī**
dinner **cēna, cēnae,** *f.*
do, I **faciō, facere, fēcī**
dog **canis, canis,** *c.*
don't **nōlī, nōlīte**
door **iānua, iānuae,** *f.*

enter, I **intrō, intrāre, intrāvī**
every day **cotīdiē**
exercise, I (**mē**) **exerceō, exercēre, exercuī**
expression **vultus, vultūs,** *m.*

father **pater, patris,** *m.*
fear, I **timeō, timēre, timuī**
field **ager, agrī,** *m.*
fight, I **pugnō, pugnāre, pugnāvī**
find, I **inveniō, invenīre, invēnī**
first **prīmus-a-um**
flee, I **fugiō, fugere, fūgī**
flower **flōs, flōris,** *m.*
for **nam**
forum **forum, forī,** *n.*
friend **amīcus, amīcī,** *m.*
from **ā, ab**

garden **hortus, hortī,** *m.*
garland **corōna, corōnae,** *f.*
gate **porta, portae,** *f.*
general **dux, ducis,** *m.*
girl **puella, puellae,** *f.*
give, I **dō, dare, dedī**
give back, I **reddō, reddere, reddidī**
go, I **eō, īre, iī**
go away, I **abeō, abīre, abiī**
go back, I **redeō, redīre, rediī**
good **bonus-a-um**
great **magnus-a-um**
greatest **maximus-a-um**
greet, I **salūtō, salūtāre, salūtāvī**
Greek **Graecus-a-um**

hand over, I **trādō, trādere, trādidī**
happy **laetus-a-um**
hard **dīligenter**
have, I **habeō, habēre, habuī**
hear, I **audiō, audīre, audīvī**
help, I **iuvō, iuvāre, iūvī**
here **hīc;** to here **hūc**
hill **collis, collis,** *m.*
him **eum**
hold, I **teneō, tenēre, tenuī**
home **domus, domūs,** *f.*; at home **domī**
hope **spēs, speī,** *f.*
horse **equus, equī,** *m.*
hour **hōra, hōrae,** *f.*
house **casa, casae,** *f.*
hurry **festīnō, festīnāre, festīnāvī**

if **sī**
in **in** + ablative
into **in** + accusative

joy **gaudium, gaudiī,** *n.*

king **rēx, rēgis,** *m.*

land **terra, terrae,** *f.*

late **sērō**
laugh, I **rīdeō, rīdēre, rīsī**
lead, I **dūcō, dūcere, dūxī**
learn **discō, discere, didicī**
leave, I (go away from) **discēdō, discēdere, discessī**
letter **littera, litterae**, *f.*; **epistola, epistolae**, *f.*
listen to, I **audiō, audīre, audīvī**
little **parvus-a-um**
look at, I **spectō, spectāre, spectāvī**
look for, I **quaerō, quaerere, quaesīvī**
loud (voice) **magna (vōx)**

man **vir, virī**, *m.*; = human being **homō, hominis**, *c.*
many **multī, multae, multa**
march, I **contendō, contendere, contendī**
master (of school) **magister, magistrī**, *m.*
   (of slaves) **dominus, dominī**, *m.*
me **mē**
message **nūntius, nūntiī**, *m.*
messenger **nūntius, nūntiī**, *m.*
mother **māter, mātris**, *f.*
must, I **dēbeō, dēbēre, dēbuī**

near **prope** + accusative
never **numquam**
night **nox, noctis**, *f.*
nothing **nihil**
now **iam**

obey, I **pāreō, pārēre, pāruī** + dative
old man **senex, senis**, *m.*
open, I **aperiō, aperīre, aperuī**
open **apertus-a-um**
other **alius, alia, aliud**
others, the **cēterī, cēterae, cētera**
ought, I **dēbeō, dēbēre, dēbuī**
out of **ē, ex** + ablative
overcome, I **superō, superāre, superāvī**

plan **cōnsilium, cōnsiliī**, *n.*
play, I **lūdō, lūdere, lūsī**
poor **pauper, pauperis**
   = unhappy **miser, misera, miserum**
praise, I **laudō, laudāre, laudāvī**
prepare, I **parō, parāre, parāvī**
prince **prīnceps, prīncipis**, *m.*
punish, I **pūniō, pūnīre, pūnīvī**

quickly **celeriter**

reach, I **perveniō, pervenīre, pervēnī** + ad
read, I **legō, legere, lēgī**
ready **parātus-a-um**
ready, I get **mē parō**
receive, I **accipiō, accipere, accēpī**
remain, I **maneō, manēre, mānsī**
reply, I **respondeō, respondēre, respondī**
return, I **redeō, redīre, rediī**
   = give back **reddō, reddere, reddidī**
river **flūmen, flūminis**, *n.*
road **via, viae**, *f.*

run, I **currō, currere, cucurrī**
run to, I **accurrō, accurrere, accurrī**

sad **trīstis, trīste**
safe **tūtus-a-um**
sail, I **nāvigō, nāvigāre, nāvigāvī**
say, I **dīcō, dīcere, dīxī**
school **lūdus, lūdī**, *m.*
sea **mare, maris**, *n.*
see, I **videō, vidēre, vīdī**
send, I **mittō, mittere, mīsī**
serious **gravis, grave**
ship **nāvis, nāvis**, *f.*
shore **lītus, lītoris**, *n.*
show, I **ostendō, ostendere, ostendī**
signal **signum, signī**, *n.*
sit, I **sedeō, sedēre, sēdī**
sleep, I **dormiō, dormīre, dormīvī**
smile, I **rīdeō, rīdēre, rīsī**
snatch, I **rapiō, rapere, rapuī**
so **tam**
so great **tantus-a-um**
son **fīlius, fīliī**, *m.*
soon **mox**
speak, I **dīcō, dīcere, dīxī**
stay, I **maneō, manēre, mānsī**
step **gradus, gradūs**, *m.*
storm **tempestās, tempestātis**, *f.*
study, I **studeō, studēre, studuī** + dative
supper **cēna, cēnae**, *f.*
sword **gladius, gladiī**, *m.*

take, I **capiō, capere, cēpī**
   = lead **dūcō, dūcere, dūxī**
tell, I **dīcō, dīcere, dīxī**
   = order **iubeō, iubēre, iussī**
that **ille, illa, illud**
them **eōs, eās**
thing **rēs, reī**, *f.*
this **hic, haec, hoc**
through **per** + accusative
time **tempus, temporis**, *n.*
tired **fessus-a-um**
to **ad** + accusative
town **oppidum, oppidī**, *n.*
Trojans **Trōiānī**
Troy **Trōia, Trōiae**, *f.*
turn, I (mē) **vertō, vertere, vertī**
understand, I **intellegō, intellegere, intellēxī**
us **nōs**

verse **versus, versūs**, *m.*
voice **vōx, vōcis**, *f.*

wait for, I **exspectō, exspectāre, exspectāvī**
wake, I **excitō, excitāre, excitāvī**
walk, I **ambulō, ambulāre, ambulāvī**
wall **mūrus, mūrī**, *m.*
want, I **cupiō, cupere, cupīvī**
war **bellum, bellī**, *n.*
warn, I **moneō, monēre, monuī**
wash, I **lavō, lavāre, lāvī**

water **aqua, aquae,** *f.*
wave **unda, undae,** *f.*
way **via, viae,** *f.*
well **bene**
what? **quid?**
when **ubi**
where? **ubi?**
where to? **quō?**
while **dum**
who? **quis?**

whole **tōtus-a-um**
why? **cūr?**
wind **ventus, ventī,** *m.*
with **cum** + ablative
without **sine** + ablative
wood **silva, silvae,** *f.*
work, I **labōrō, labōrāre, labōrāvī**
write **scrībō, scrībere, scrīpsī** I write

young man **iuvenis, iuvenis,** *m.*

INDEX OF GRAMMAR